Whitewater
Rescue
Manual

Whitewater

Rescue Manual

New Techniques for Canoeists, Kayakers, and Rafters

Charles Walbridge and Wayne A. Sundmacher Sr., NREMT-A

Ragged Mountain Press
Camden, Maine

Published by Ragged Mountain Press

10 9 8 7 6 5 4

Library of Congress Cataloging-in-Publication Data

Walbridge, Charles C., 1948–
    Whitewater rescue manual : new techniques for canoeists, kayakers,
  and rafters / Charles Walbridge and Wayne A. Sundmacher, Sr.
      p.   cm.
  Includes bibliographical references and index.
  ISBN 0-07-067790-5 (acid-free paper)
    1. White-water canoeing—Safety measures—Handbooks, manuals, etc.
  2. Rafting (Sports)—Safety measures—Handbooks, manuals, etc.
  3. Kayaking—Safety measures—Handbooks, manuals, etc. 4. Search
  and rescue operations—Handbooks, manuals, etc.   I. Sundmacher,
  Wayne A.   II. Title.
  GV788.W35 1995
  797.1'22'0289—dc20   95–18767
                                      CIP

Questions regarding the content of this book should be addressed to:
Ragged Mountain Press
P.O. Box 220
Camden, ME 04843

Questions regarding the ordering of this book should be addressed to:
The McGraw-Hill Companies
Customer Service Department
P.O. Box 547
Blacklick, OH 43004
Retail customers: 1-800-262-4729
Bookstores: 1-800-722-4726

A portion of the profits from the sale of each Ragged Mountain Press book is donated to an environmental cause.

♻ *Whitewater Rescue Manual* is printed on 60-pound Renew Opaque Vellum, an acid-free paper that contains 50 percent recycled waste paper (preconsumer) and 10 percent postconsumer waste paper.

Unless otherwise noted, photos are by Charlie Walbridge.
All illustrations are by Wayne A. Sundmacher Sr.
Printed by Quebecore/Fairfield, Fairfield, PA
Design and Production by Dan Kirchoff
Edited by Jonathan Eaton, Pamela Benner, and Judith Terrill-Breuer

WARNING

This is an instructional book for a potentially dangerous activity. River rescue takes paddlers into harm's way, exposing them to risks well in excess of those normally encountered running rapids. Drowning, falling, cold-water exposure, broken bones, and other potentially life-threatening injuries may result, leading to permanent disability or death.

    Brand-name equipment mentioned or shown in this book is for the purposes of illustration or discussion only and does not constitute the authors' recommendation for use by readers.

    This book assumes that paddlers possess knowledge common to intermediate river runners. It is not intended to replace instruction by qualified teachers, and the authors recommend that readers seek instruction before attempting a rescue. Even after such training, this book cannot substitute for good personal judgment on the water.

    By using this book the reader releases the author, publisher, and distributor from any liability for any injury, including death, that may result from attempting the techniques covered within. It is understood that you paddle and attempt rescues at your own risk.

Contents

Acknowledgments

Our acknowledgments and thanks to the people who reviewed drafts of our book: Dennis Kerrigan for his helpful clarification of first aid concepts; Richard Manning for carefully proofreading the first few chapters; Tim Delaney for providing up-to-date information on rafting safety and other areas; Glen Carlson for showing us new ways to reach entrapment victims; Chuck Brooks, EMT-P, an Ohio flight medic, and to Dr. Joe Braden, a former military chopper pilot, for providing valuable insight into helicopter operations; our editors at Ragged Mountain Press for their care and thoroughness.

And a special thanks to these strong influences: Les Bechdel and Slim Ray for their excellence in writing and teaching; Payson Kennedy for teaching a young Charlie Walbridge the fine points of rope handling and trip management;

Ray Miller of the American Red Cross for bringing rescue bags from navy archives to whitewater sport; Jim French, Pam Dillon, Emily King, and the other staff at Ohio Division of Watercraft for creating the first professional-level river rescue course; Peter D'Onofrio and the EMS training staff of the Ohio Fire Academy; Jim Seggerstrom and Rescue III for pioneering a more aggressive approach to river rescue; Greg Kobol, who took the cover photo and other technical rescue photos. We'd also like to recognize the help of Katie Heisler, Donald Raugh, Dan Hoyt, Ned Hughes, and students in our rescue classes for their help in setting up the photographs.

And a special thanks to our wives, Sandy Walbridge and Jane Sundmacher, for their patience and helpful comments during the writing of this book.

Introduction

In the late 1960s whitewater paddlers were innovators, using self-taught skills and home-made gear. The rivers they ran were easy by today's standards, and boaters seldom encountered anything more serious than a trashed boat or a bruised rear end. Rescue skills were improvised as needed; most people used aluminum canoes without flotation, so everyone got lots of practice recovering boats. More exotic ways of getting into trouble, such as foot entrapments or vertical pins, had yet to be encountered.

The next two decades saw explosive growth and innovation. People took to rivers by the thousands, and the quality of gear and instruction improved rapidly. Paddlers started working on rescue techniques ahead of time rather than improvising when trouble struck. River rescue developed as a separate discipline in the mid-70s, led by the Nantahala Outdoor Center and the Ohio Department of Natural Resources. Many of the skills they taught were drawn from mountaineering. Some techniques worked and are still in use today; others are now considered too slow, complex, or even dangerous.

My own introduction to river rescue came as a professional rafting guide. We didn't set up complex rope systems; we boated or swam to the accident site and applied muscle power directly. This required a rescuer to be as comfortable in the river as on it. Years later I drew on this experience to develop a "whitewater self-defense" course, a one-day program emphasizing swimming and wading skills. Still later, I collaborated with Wayne Sundmacher, a local outfitter with instructor certifications in river rescue, ice rescue, vertical rescue, and first aid. He helped me understand the physics of rope handling, and he selected the best available mechanical systems for presentation in this book.

We jointly taught a rescue course over six years, gradually expanding it to two days. After refining it considerably, we offered it to the American Canoe Association, and it became the basis of their river rescue program. Simultaneously, similar ideas were developed and taught by other groups, notably the Nantahala Outdoor Center and Rescue III. Constant communication allowed each group to benefit from the others' ideas and experience.

Since the easiest rescues are the ones you don't have to make, the initial chapters in this book discuss prevention. We start by covering the precautions and mind-sets needed to keep individuals and groups out of trouble, then move on to a review of paddling equipment from a safety standpoint. Rescue gear is introduced next, followed by a discussion of basic in-water survival skills such as swimming and wading. Because the throw line is the most important rescue tool paddlers carry, we devote an entire chapter to it.

We're then ready to discuss more complex skills that build on this base of knowledge. We show techniques for line-supported river crossings and explore the use of rescue life vests and their built-in, quick-release harnesses. One chapter deals with the life-threatening problems encountered in rescuing unconscious swimmers and entrapment victims, while another covers techniques for running down, recovering, and emptying swamped or runaway boats. A later section discusses recovering pinned canoes, kayaks, and rafts, including setting up hauling systems and the safety precautions needed when using these systems.

Next, the book deals with the aftermath of a rescue, discussing first aid and evacuation from a paddler's perspective. The last chapter describes a few of the more complex, sophisticated, and less used techniques. These include the telfer boat lower, vertical extrication, and low-head dam rescue.

Wayne and I have worked together for six seasons, testing new ideas and learning from each other. For this book, we've chosen skills that work best with equipment normally carried by noncommercial paddling groups. We've assumed that our audience is made up of competent whitewater paddlers, so we haven't covered the basics of water reading and boat handling for the less experienced audience. We split the writing duties in this book according to our expertise, then carefully reviewed and critiqued each other's work. My photos and Wayne's illustrations will help explain the concepts.

Our book is not the last word. River rescue is evolving rapidly, and we've seen tremendous changes in the last few years. More than half of the material in this book was not in general use five years ago. Watch for new ideas yourself, test them, then teach others. That way we'll all go forward together.

Charlie Walbridge
Penllyn, Pennsylvania

Wayne Sundmacher
Mercerville, New Jersey

CHAPTER 1

Keeping Out of Trouble

There are many risks connected with white-water sport, and keeping clear of them is a challenge for paddlers of all abilities. But danger is an integral part of the sport, focusing a paddler's physical and mental abilities, heightening concentration, and intensifying their awareness of the water and its surroundings. While you are scanning a rapid, looking for the subtle signs of rock or current that hold the key to safe passage, the ambiguities and inconsistencies of modern living fade away. To run rivers is to live in the present, realizing ever more fully what it means to be a human being moving across the earth amid powerful natural forces.

River running has evolved tremendously during the past two decades. These changes have simultaneously reduced and increased the risks. Improved gear, technique, and training make it possible to run increasingly difficult rapids safely. Rivers once considered the exclusive domain of elite experts are now being traveled comfortably by large numbers of advanced paddlers. But the limits of the sport have also been extended. The cascades and falls now being attempted by the best paddlers truly defy the imagination. Those running such extreme rapids are superb athletes with unusual skill, fitness, and presence of mind. While experts of previous generations might have thought they were risking their lives, many of today's white-water boaters *know* they are!

Regardless of skill, running rapids that push the limits of one's ability is physically and mentally taxing. Cool concentration is needed to control mind and boat while in the grip of the vast and shifting forces of a powerful rapid. A

Figure 1-1. Running steep, powerful drops takes concentration and commitment, but thanks to better gear and training, waters that were once the limit of navigability are now commonly run.

successful run brings with it a sense of exhilaration and power. As your skills increase, so do the speed and complexity of the rapids you can sanely attempt. To push yourself without miscalculating requires an odd mixture of aggressiveness and restraint. This is true for beginners running rivers for the first time, intermediates attempting to advance their skills, and experts exploring difficult unknown waters.

While the goal is always a safe and uneventful trip, accidents still occur. In any natural setting some hazards are hidden, and unexpected problems arise at any level of difficulty. A random, uncontrolled element of risk is always present, and even the most skilled paddler is not immune from danger. Our main goal is to stay out of trouble so that we don't have to use the gear and skills described in this book. But if trouble strikes miles from any phone or outside help, a group must be able to take care of its own.

Developing Judgment

The most important component of river safety is individual judgment. Because a safe recovery from some situations is unlikely, each paddler must make the right decisions to avoid trouble in the first place. This responsibility makes kayaking and canoeing an intensely personal endeavor. Although it's always fun to cruise rivers that lie well within one's ability, most boaters want to test and extend their personal limits. To be bold yet careful, to push hard while still knowing when to back down, creates real dilemmas. Resolving them requires total honesty about one's physical and mental limits, coupled with a sense of personal accountability seldom found in modern American culture. No one can make these decisions for you, and anyone who wants to be "looked after" had better find another activity!

The motivations for running rivers are not always clear. We do it to travel to interesting places, to experience unique wild settings, to impress our friends and acquaintances, to prove things to ourselves, even to get our picture taken! The ability to match your skills to conditions on the river is developed gradually over years of paddling. It can be nurtured but never rushed. Inexperienced paddlers are often tempted to hurry into difficult rapids with minimal preparation. They think that because everything flushes out at the bottom, all they need is a good roll. This may be acceptable for tough, athletic beginners who are willing to absorb punishment, but for most of us the risks are too great. A person who consistently makes the decisions needed to keep out of trouble is said to have good judgment; those who paddle from one predicament to another should back off and develop their skills on less demanding water.

Accepting Personal Limits

Boaters must always be truthful with themselves as they approach the limits of their skill. A difficult rapid, run by experts, always looks easy. Novices often assume that the main difference between them and an expert paddler is physical courage, but relying on guts alone is an invitation to disaster. High-level river skills require considerable training and practice. It's not enough merely to see a line: You must be able to execute the maneuvers needed to follow this route through the rapids. Smart paddlers advance slowly, in a series of carefully considered steps. The learning process is lots of fun, so there's no need to rush.

It's often hard to be truly candid about your physical and mental ability. People vary not only in skill but also in physical condition and mental toughness. These attributes can vary from day to day. They become stronger over the course of a season and with increasing years of experience. Regular river running improves strength and timing, builds confidence, and sharpens skill. Poor health, low levels of fitness, and infrequent practice erode these abilities. In time, most paddlers develop the self-assurance needed to execute complex maneuvers in violent rapids despite significant physical risks.

Perhaps the hardest adjustments of all are allowances for decline in physical condition caused by inactivity, illness, or injury, as well as the insidious changes of aging. Admitting that one's skills are below par requires honesty and courage, but it can help avoid accidents. Confidence also varies. Paddlers who believe in their abilities will always outperform those who don't. A series of successful runs builds confidence; a bad experience may shatter that self-assurance. People who train novices must try to ensure that their early experiences are positive, to provide a solid base for future efforts.

When considering the chances of success on the river, you must also ascertain the price of failure. The more severe the consequences, the more certain you must be of your ability to run a rapid without mishap. We can encourage beginners to "go for it" after they've been taken to a relatively safe place to make their mistakes. More skilled boaters must make decisions on the spot, picking the places to probe the outer limits of their abilities with great care. Some drops, while difficult to run cleanly, are surprisingly forgiving. Other rapids of modest difficulty must be treated with respect because of serious, often obscure hazards. Here the experience and advice of other paddlers can be helpful.

Making good decisions usually involves weighing the positive and negative aspects of a situation. Unusual problems such as cold water, bad weather, floods, ice, isolation, or fading light must be taken into account. Can the strength of a party, combined with excellent weather conditions, really offset the added dangers of high water? Does a remote location, far from help, mean that you may need to carry a rapid you might otherwise run? Will the combination of a small or weak group, difficult water, and unfamiliar equipment cut the margin of safety too thin? Accidents often result from a series of small miscalculations that lead to disaster when combined. Don't let pressure from friends or disappointment after a long drive lure you or your group into a trap!

Coping with Fear

Fear is a vital component of safety. Beginning paddlers often confuse fearlessness with skill, but only the ignorant and foolish are "never scared." A boater's skill and confidence can lower fear to a manageable level. Everyone reacts differently to stress: Some people thrive on it, while others try to avoid it at all costs. You must do what is right for you, and learning to "listen to your body" is an important skill for any whitewater paddler.

Fear starts out as a low feeling of apprehension as boaters find themselves pressed. These "whitewater butterflies" are a positive sign; they mean that your body is preparing itself for peak performance. But higher levels of anxiety, left unchecked, can stiffen muscles and slow reaction time. This is a signal to stop and reevaluate the situation, weighing your ability to manage the drop against the consequences of a miscue. Consider the actual consequences of a mistake and how you would deal with it. Scouting the rapid, talking with your companions about what the water is doing, or watching someone else's run may reduce fear to a manageable level. If not, a portage should be arranged. If anxiety gives way to terror or panic, maneuvers that usually come easily are impossible to execute. This is a sure sign that you are boating over your head, and continuing the run is not a good idea.

Often a run may be within a paddler's ability except for a few individual drops. Some people start worrying about these rapids long before reaching them—even before putting on the river. This may increase stress so much that the river cannot be enjoyed. Unless the drops in question can't be carried, you should put your fears aside until you arrive on the scene. At that point you can evaluate the rapid, master your fears, or make the decision to carry.

River Classification

The six-point international scale of river difficulty was developed to help paddlers match their ability with a rapid or a river. The full descriptions of the classes, designated I through VI, are part of the American Whitewater Affiliation Safety Code (AWA) listed in Appendix B. These measurements are relative, not absolute. They are subject to widely varying regional interpretations. In areas of the U.S. (Texas, for example) that lack many difficult rivers, rapids are frequently rated higher than the norm. Likewise, boaters in states with an abundance of challenging rivers and an active boating community (such as California) may underrate the difficulty.

In addition, a trend toward down rating rapids has been at work since the scale came into use 30 years ago. Some rapids once rated Class V are now considered Class III! There are significant variations among guidebook authors and even within a single guidebook. Ideally, rapids should be classified for first-timers, taking into account the consequences of a swim, but this is not always done. Our best advice is to use the classification numbers as a general guide, starting out slowly in an unfamiliar area until you gain an appreciation of how rapids are classified locally. Asking experienced boaters to compare an unfamiliar river with a familiar one is always a good idea. Ask about the character of a run, any unusual dangers, and the difficulty of portaging.

River difficulty changes significantly as the water level rises and falls. More water usually makes a river harder by increasing current speed and turbulence. But some drops become easier as obstacles are covered by rising water and dangerous holes "wash out" into big waves. On the other hand, low water, while slower, exposes more obstacles and increases the danger of pinning. Consider weather as an additional variable, too. Warm temperatures and sunny skies boost everyone's confidence, while cold air and water temperatures make any trip more challenging. Short days reduce the time available to complete a run, while longer ones permit more time on the water. Look at the whole picture before committing yourself to a rapid.

Paddling within a Group

Whitewater paddling is usually done as part of a self-sufficient, interdependent group. Each paddler stands ready to help other members of the team if necessary. Except when novices are present, few parties adopt a rigidly defined leadership or command structure. But despite this informality, boaters must remember that the actions of each individual affect the well-being of the entire group. Carelessness puts at risk not only the careless, but also those who have to deal with the consequences. Even successful rescues use up valuable time and energy, and this may cause serious hardship when the weather is bad or time is short. Minor mishaps, such as a series of short swims, may consume a surprising amount of time. The paddler who stays out of trouble helps keep a trip moving steadily, allowing everyone to fully enjoy the river.

Setting Reasonable Goals

Setting reasonable goals is vital for groups as well as individuals. Just as you must be honest with yourself about readiness, a group must be candid about its combined strength. Plans may need to be modified when a team includes less skilled boaters—or even a proven veteran who is having an off day. This is especially true when the length or remoteness of a run forces everyone to rely on each other. Such things as the pace of the trip, the time allowed for scouting, and the safety precautions required should be adapted to the size and strength of the party. Some runs allow extra time to scout rapids, portage, and paddle at a slower pace; others demand fast, efficient paddling to avoid being overtaken by darkness.

People paddling together in the same canoe, kayak, or raft must concentrate on teamwork. All decisions are made jointly; everyone in the boat must agree to a run, giving the weakest member of the team veto power. Experienced boaters taking novices down a run in a team boat must remember that beginners can't fully participate in the decision-making process and may not be able to handle the stress of dangerous rapids. It's best to back off before boating into something too intense for the less skilled members of the team.

Party Size

The size of a group is a vital factor in making plans. Solo paddling, for example, is extremely exposed. A soloist can travel quickly but has absolutely no backup in the event of trouble. A mistake almost always results in lost gear, and a minor injury may be disastrous. To compensate for the added risk, lone paddlers must be extremely cautious. The extra effort and added stress may take the fun out of paddling. A two-boat party is almost as fast and provides limited backup in the event of a mishap. However, it often takes at least two boats to assist a swimming paddler and recover loose gear. Three or four paddlers are much better: The additional muscle comes in handy when rescue is required, while adding few group management hassles.

As a group grows, it moves more slowly and becomes harder to manage. With more than six boats on the water, watching out for everyone becomes troublesome, and keeping the group moving can be a real challenge. Considerable time is lost waiting to see each member of the group past a difficult spot or gathering the party together to count heads. In groups of 10 or more, a single person may slip out of sight for a time without being noticed. People in larger groups should "buddy up" so that their absence is noticed immediately. On small streams with many rapids and limited eddy space, bottlenecks develop. Patience is required to avoid collisions, and some group members may be frustrated by the discipline needed to run safely.

Group Management

Keeping a group together so that help is available if trouble arises is extremely important. When experienced paddlers are leading novices, *lead* and *sweep* boaters are designated. The leader knows the river, is never passed, and stops the group when necessary to portage or scout. The sweep paddler brings up the rear, keeping the entire group in front of her, and is prepared for rescue. If someone is pinned, help arrives first from upstream. Sweep paddlers are more vulnerable because help is slower in reaching them. The rest of the group is "sandwiched" between these two experienced boaters, supplemented by head counts as needed.

In experienced parties, the leadership is shared among the participants. Typically, the positions of the leader (more accurately called *the point*) and the sweep pass casually back and forth. On tougher runs boaters leapfrog one another, sharing the stress of leading. Paddlers assuming front or rear positions must remain aware of the responsibility of the point position and the exposure that comes with bringing up the rear. Within a group, boaters keep an eye on the person behind them. If a boat is not in sight, those ahead should stop and wait; they must not continue into the next rapid until the missing paddler appears. If he fails to arrive after a short wait, they should head upstream to investigate. This eventually brings the entire group to a halt and guarantees that reinforcements will arrive quickly to assist in a rescue.

Spacing between boats is a complex issue. Paddling close together improves communication and support but reduces freedom of movement. Novice groups stay close together, gathering in an eddy at the bottom of each danger spot until everyone has passed through safely. With skilled paddlers, the gaps increase; the entire group doesn't need to wait at the base of a big drop—one or two paddlers can stay to serve as backup. This gives everyone more room to operate, but help may be slower to arrive. Finding the spacing that suits your group may require some discussion and experimentation, but most boaters fall into a comfortable arrangement easily.

Groups often include paddlers of varying skills. If the weaker paddlers in a group are feeling pushed, the best place for them is near the front of the group. This puts potential rescuers both upstream and downstream. Keeping these paddlers in position requires effort. The more confident paddlers are likely to move up front and fight for the lead; the less assured boater is likely to eddy out and watch. Stronger paddlers continue to move ahead and, before you know

Figure 1-2. Good spacing between paddlers enables a trip to run smoothly. These boaters have enough space between them to permit free movement, yet are close enough to assist each other.

it, the people you're trying to protect are stranded at the end of the line! Restraining the hotshots and encouraging the less skilled to keep up is a thankless but essential task.

When to Scout

Smart paddlers don't travel blindly down the river. When the course isn't clear, they stop and scout. Scouting a rapid varies from a quick look at the top of a tricky but straightforward stretch of whitewater to a step-by-step, inch-by-inch examination of a truly dangerous drop. A boater's skill also comes into play; paddlers who read water well and move confidently from eddy to eddy will stay in their boats through sections of river that force less experienced boaters to scout from shore. But this can be carried to unhealthy extremes, particularly on tough, pushy water. The more difficult the river, the more cautious a group should become.

The paddler in the point position should consider the ability of the entire group before continuing, especially when novices are involved. With strong groups, one person may be able to run first to demonstrate a line, or she can scout and describe the route for everyone else. Sometimes a confident paddler may agree to lead a less skilled boater through the drop. These techniques help move a group along, but don't press your luck! None of these "timesavers" are worth the risk of serious trouble. Be sure to speak up if the pace seems too ambitious, and demand to look at a drop first if needed.

A "scout and watch" approach is a potential time-waster on any trip. Here's how it works. Everyone scouts. One person runs. After he or she succeeds, the next person goes. And so on. Watching others run a drop is entertaining and helpful, but it really slows a group down. If time is short, all paddlers should stop, scout, and decide individually whether to run or carry, depending on their skill. Exceptions can be made when there is plenty of time for a slow-moving trip or when encountering rapids so severe that downstream safety backup is required.

Setting Safety

Where danger exists, it is sometimes wise to have one or more paddlers in position to initiate a rescue. Sometimes this means standing on shore with a throw line; in other cases, one or two paddlers waiting downstream in their boats may be enough. Novices need support at the bottom of any drop, while experts may choose to take these time-consuming precautions only in the most extreme circumstances. Some very difficult rapids may require several people, stationed at numerous potential hazards, before anyone should attempt the run.

It's important to consider the number of people you will need for rescue when setting backup. A raft flip typically produces four or more swimmers, and yet these craft often travel

Figure 1-3. If the potential for swimming exists and more rapids lurk downstream, place someone downstream with a throw line for backup. Here, a paddler practicing aggressive swimming in a rescue class is protected by one of his classmates.

alone or accompanied by a single other boat. Many multiple fatalities have been caused by raft flips in difficult water when a group was unable to rescue everyone. This vulnerability can be offset by paddlers on shore equipped with throw lines, or by a sufficient number of accompanying boats.

Setting the Pace

A group's pace depends on many things: the length and difficulty of the run, the weather, and the skill and fitness of the boaters. Strong paddlers move quickly, scout less frequently, and make fewer mistakes that require rescue. They're in good enough shape to paddle hard hour after hour. This level of skill and fitness allows them to tackle longer, demanding runs. Less skilled boaters move slowly, scout often, and are more likely to require rescue. The length and difficulty of the rivers they can safely attempt is correspondingly limited. There are days when even the best paddlers slow their pace to play or simply enjoy the river. But those who are consistently late, slow to get ready, and always in trouble will slow an entire group down. These minor hassles may cause serious problems when time is short.

River Signals

It's often necessary to communicate with members of your group. Shouting is lost in the noise of the rapids, but hand signals can be seen for a considerable distance. The universal hand signals used in the American Whitewater Affiliation Safety Code (see Appendix B) can be used to show paddlers the correct route. A paddle or arm held straight up indicates a run down the center; when angled to one side, it means to run over in that direction. A paddle or arm held horizontally means stop; no clear passage exists. A useful memory tool is to think of a railroad crossing: When the arm is up, passage is safe; when the arm is down, you should stop. A German company makes a paddle with garish green and red blades that are useful in signaling. In an emergency, wave your paddle or arms back and forth over your head to summon help.

Whistles are carried for emergencies only. The international distress signal is three whistle blasts followed by a pause. Occasionally a short "chirp" is used as a "heads up" signal to focus the attention of an individual or group on a dangerous situation that is developing, such as an unseen swimmer or a need to paddle immediately into an eddy. Overuse of whistle signals creates a summer-camp atmosphere that most river runners find annoying and confusing.

Etiquette

Etiquette and manners are important to river runners. Being ready to go and keeping up with a group are important basics. If you have to leave a group for any reason, tell someone first so your party won't have to stop and search for you later. This is true even if you're stopping on shore momentarily to dump your boat, take a photo, or answer the call of nature. Boaters who decide that a trip is "too slow" or "too fast," then quietly leave the group without telling anyone, cause worry, frustration, and lost time for their companions.

Collisions between boats in whitewater are unnerving and may cause serious injuries. In general, downstream traffic has the right of way. Look upstream before leaving an eddy to avoid cutting someone off. Before playing a wave or hole, check upstream for oncoming boaters. This may avoid a nasty surprise later, when you're fully engaged with the river. Those upstream can help reduce risks, too. Don't tailgate: leave plenty of distance between yourself and the boat ahead so that you can paddle freely without running into anyone. Good spacing takes conscious effort. If you begin to close the distance, catch an eddy and wait until an appropriate interval is restored. Anticipate bottlenecks and increase the gap accordingly. Wait for a boater to get completely through a tight spot before following.

On difficult runs, the best routes through a rapid may be extremely tight. People running these drops need space to maneuver, and there's seldom room for more than one boat. Wait for your turn, and be sure there's a spot for another boat before coming in. Crashing into paddlers in small eddies above steep drops is distracting and annoying. If in doubt, stop upstream and wait for an opening. Boaters often must sit patiently for long periods, waiting for a rapid ahead to clear. In large eddies, paddlers should move away from the eddyline to a spot that makes it possible for others to enter. Moving next to the rock at the top of the eddy or hard against the shore are two good options.

The Importance of Rescue

When skill and judgment fail, rescue skills must fill the gap. This is a weak spot for many of

Figure 1-4. On crowded rivers, the greatest danger is a collision with another boater. Constant attention to river etiquette can lower this risk.

today's paddlers, since improved gear and skill have decreased the number of the minor mishaps that old-timers used for training. Today, a skilled paddler with a good roll can go for years without encountering anything more perilous than an occasional swimmer or runaway boat. Although most boaters will never be involved in a life-threatening accident, it's best to be prepared.

Rescue skills, like paddling techniques, take time to develop. Training cannot be done overnight. The more you know, the more likely it is that a good solution to a problem will come to mind. Never assume that an accident can't happen because you're a careful, conservative boater. Accidents on wild rivers often show a random streak of unfairness; a group can be doing everything right and still get into trouble.

Panic can occur when a group believes that an injury or death is imminent and they lack the experience, training, and leadership to make the rescue. In such a situation, uncertainty leads to false starts, a lack of confidence in the strategy being tried, and poor teamwork. Rescue training gives paddlers the knowledge and skill to maintain their confidence, take decisive action, and work together effectively.

River Rescue Guidelines

Rescues are more unpredictable and dangerous than normal river running. Rescuers must help the victim quickly without getting hurt themselves.

Preparing to Intervene

- Prepare for trouble by carrying the right equipment and having the training to use it. While recreational paddlers have no legal responsibility to assist a paddler in trouble, most of us feel a moral obligation to do what we can to help.

- Assess the problem first. Take a moment to examine the entire accident scene. This is especially true when acting alone or with only one other person. Failure to consider the mechanism of injury, the presence of unseen hazards, or the need for backup may lead to trouble. Continue to monitor your progress throughout the rescue.

- Remember that the safety of the rescuer always comes first. You may take calculated risks, but don't add to the problem by getting in trouble yourself. The mnemonic RETHROG (reach, throw, row, go swim) lists available water rescue options in order of increasing danger.

Doin' the Right Thing

Back in the late 1970s, I was a weekend safety boater for a rafting outfitter on West Virginia's Cheat River. It was Memorial Day, and a lot of hard boaters were out. The water was low, so I volunteered to guide in a raft and spare my C-1. My friend Chip Queitzsch was boat-guiding as we entered Coliseum, which before the '85 flood contained a nasty pinning boulder called Trap Rock. His job was to sit in an eddy by the rock and help release any rafts that pinned. We all knew it was there; I'd seen several people caught over the years, but nothing really serious.

Sitting in an upstream eddy, I heard Chip screaming for help. He's a pretty controlled guy and doesn't excite easily. I jumped on shore, grabbed a rescue bag, and sprinted toward his voice. About 30 yards downstream, a fairly large crowd of boaters had gathered. Pushing my way to the front, I saw that a kayaker had wrapped completely around Trap Rock no more than 30 feet from shore. Chip was standing in the downstream eddy, shoulder-deep in the water, holding the guy's head up.

We shouted back and forth. Chip could support the guy, but couldn't do anything else. One man in the crowd asked if he could help. I handed him my throw bag, entered the water, and swam out into the eddy. The kayaker was incoherent with pain. Chip and I talked for a minute, planning our next move. I signaled for the throw line and tied it to the far side grab loop. Then the volunteer and I, working together, slowly peeled the boat off the rock. As we did this, Chip somehow got the guy out of his kayak and into the eddy. By this time several other guides had arrived, and we used another throw line to swing ourselves and the kayaker into shore. I later learned that Chip had jumped out of his C-1 to make the rescue, letting it float downstream. We recovered it in an eddy a half-mile below.

The kayak was trashed and the kayaker was hurting, so he rode out in one of the rafts. His legs were bruised, but nothing was broken. He was able to limp over to his car under his own power, dragging the remains of his boat behind him. He owed his life to Chip's quick thinking and to the fact that others on the scene were ready to help.

Will you be a spectator or a doer when trouble strikes? Many paddlers, like the folks in the crowd, expect others to handle rescues. But preparation is everything. As guides, Chip and I were expected to handle any problem we might encounter. With the right preparation, you can be ready, too.

—CW

Weigh the advantages of a more dangerous technique against the added risk, taking the safest approach that offers a good chance of success.

- Keep a rescue simple. Try uncomplicated solutions before moving on to those that are more complex. Simple techniques are faster to set up, require fewer people and less gear, and present fewer opportunities for mistakes. This increases the chance of success.
- Consider the possibility that someone else may have gotten into trouble at the same time as the victim or in the early stages of a rescue. The second problem may not be noticed until too late.

Starting the Rescue

- Speed can be vital. When the situation is precarious, quick action makes the difference between life and death, and minimizes stress on both victim and rescuer. There's no need for a formal leadership structure when one or two people can provide immediate help. Many rescues are made with very little formal organization.
- However, when time permits, move slowly and carefully. Think things through. Don't take foolish risks to recover gear without first setting backup; a freed craft may continue downstream to become stuck again in a more serious position.
- First, deal with life-threatening problems. Try to keep the predicament from deteriorating. Once the situation is reasonably stable, more time can be taken to develop a final extrication plan.
- Always provide backup. Consider what could go wrong and send people downstream to assist. On heavily used rivers, you'll also need to send someone upstream to direct traffic away from the rescue. These are unglamorous but vital jobs. More than one rescuer has been spared injury by being warned of approaching boats or debris, or saved a

long swim by an alert backup person with a throw bag.
- Consider the mental and physical state of the victim. Be prepared to confront panic, exhaustion, hypothermia, shock, and pain. Establish communication; keep a trapped or injured paddler abreast of plans and give reassurance as needed.
- Always have a backup plan. Don't waste time continuing an ineffective technique when other methods might achieve better results. While setting up the first rescue, start considering an alternative plan should the first approach fail. In more involved scenarios, it may be advisable to begin setting up "Plan B" while "Plan A" is in operation.

Leadership

- Teamwork involves making the best use of the people and gear available. This may be pretty informal. For example, a boater, observing a boat and a boater being successfully recovered, chases down the paddle. Another paddler, seeing a person out on the rocks working on a pinned boat, moves to shore and offers to throw a rope. A knowledge of river rescue, combined with alertness and common sense, allows paddlers to support one another without a formal leadership structure.
- Rescues involving more than two or three people may need a leader. With larger groups and more complex situations, this may be vital. If no leader exists, one should be appointed. Everyone in the group can have input, and there will be disagreements about the best methods to use—but the leader makes the final decision.
- If a group is large enough, the leader should take no direct part in the operation but instead direct the team. This gives the leader a clear view of the entire operation, rather than just a small part.

It helps ensure the best use of available resources and makes it more likely that appropriate safety precautions will be taken. A leader must be a good manager, but it's often a waste of talent to assign this job to the most technically skilled rescuer in the group.

- In organized rescues, freelancing only complicates matters and may jeopardize the safety of other rescuers. Everyone must concentrate on the assigned task. If you come upon a rescue in progress, approach the leader or some other involved person and ask if help is needed before doing anything.
- Prepare to evacuate the injured. In situations where injuries are known to be present, the group should not wait for the final extrication to begin planning first aid and evacuation. It often makes sense to send for help at once.

Managing the Moment

This seems like a lot of information to keep in mind, but the decision-making process in a rescue can be broken into three stages: deciding to intervene, making the rescue, and treating the victim. Each stage includes a period of assessment followed by action. We offer this in the hope that it will help organize your thoughts when confronted with a serious incident.

Deciding to Intervene

First, you must decide to become involved. Is there a problem? Is your help really needed? Do you have the skill and gear needed to help? What are the risks to you and your group? Do you need to take charge, or should you coordinate your activities with others? Except in the most extreme circumstances, ask if help is needed before becoming involved.

Making the Rescue

Next, evaluate the predicament. If someone's life is in danger, stabilize the situation quickly. This provides more time to plan the next move. Next, extricate the victim. In less serious situations, you may be able to skip the stabilization and extricate at once. Complex rescues require a leader and a plan. If the rescue will block a popular river, designate an upstream lookout to warn oncoming river traffic and a downstream safety person for backup. Once everyone is out of danger, recover the gear. If a boat is badly pinned, this may be the most demanding part of the rescue. When enough help is available, some members of the group can assist the paddler while others recover the gear.

Treating the Victim

You must now check the victim for injuries and begin treatment as needed. Often a rescued paddler is unharmed, requiring only a short rest before continuing. Occasionally, treatment is lengthy and involved. When the injuries are serious, you need an evacuation plan. Begin thinking about this after the initial examination, as soon as first aid treatment is underway. If an accident is unusually severe and the personnel are available, you may need to prepare for treatment and plan the evacuation during the rescue. This usually means sending for outside help.

Now that we've looked into managing a group before and during a rescue attempt, the next chapter will focus on selecting safe equipment and choosing effective tools for emergencies.

CHAPTER 2

Equipment Safety Check

Choosing the right paddling gear isn't easy. Each item on the market was developed to meet the various, often conflicting demands of paddlers, and any design has advantages and disadvantages. Let's look at the features that have a significant effect on boater safety.

Whitewater canoe and kayak designs are extremely varied, encompassing a variety of handling characteristics. Exactly what constitutes an "appropriate" design for certain types of rivers is controversial, but a few generalizations can be made.

High-performance hulls offer added speed, maneuverability, and control. They often feature sharp edges at the sides, reduced volume, and extreme rocker. Performance kayaks and canoes are easily influenced by strong currents and paddler miscues and take considerable practice to handle effectively. This is especially true of squirt boats and other extremely low-volume designs.

Beginners usually prefer more basic, user-friendly models with less extreme rocker for improved tracking and full-rounded sides to maximize stability. If these are short, with blunt ends and considerable rocker, they become useful on steep, technical runs. Many previously unrunnable rapids have fallen to a new generation of creek boats.

Other designs fall between these two extremes and adapt to a wide variety of rivers. Common sense dictates that you select a boat suited to your ability and the types of rivers you usually run. Always test unfamiliar designs in moderate water before attempting more serious rapids.

Kayaks and C-1s

The fact that a paddler sits inside a kayak or decked canoe, rather than on it, makes everyone a little nervous. If a decked boat gets wrapped around a rock and collapses, the boater may be trapped inside. Early fiberglass boats were rigid and brittle, breaking apart before posing much of a threat. As materials improved, kayaks became tougher and more flexible, and could bend double without breaking. Sometimes they were designed to break in the cockpit area before folding in order to counteract this danger. Roto-molded plastic kayaks, which are much less rigid than comparable fiberglass hulls, can actually be squashed flat without damage. This increases the risk of entrapment. Lower-volume designs, which have less flotation, are especially prone to collapse.

There are two ways to deal with this. The first is to use pillars, or walls, to support the deck. These are made from Minicell, a lightweight, semirigid closed-cell foam, and are standard equipment on most U.S.-made whitewater boats. Adhesives work well when you're installing walls in fiberglass kayaks, but nothing sticks permanently to roto-molded polyethylene surfaces. In these "plastic" hulls, the foam walls must be held in mechanically by the seat, thigh hooks, or other specialized fasteners. European boatbuilders view foam pillars as a potential entrapment risk. They use a more rigid hull construction, with an arched rather than flat deck design to maximize strength. This makes the hull rigid enough that the walls can be safely omitted. The additional room created by this approach is especially useful to larger people. Unfortunately, a thicker hull may be required to add sufficient rigidity, which can make these boats significantly heavier.

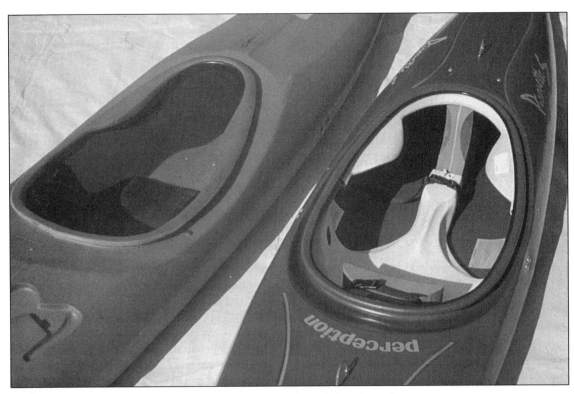

Figure 2-1. An American-made kayak with foam walls to support the deck (right) and a German-made boat constructed without these walls (left).

Neither approach is completely effective. Under the right conditions, the river can easily crush any kayak or canoe hull. The purpose of these features is to slow the process, giving paddlers enough time to get out of their boat.

Rafts

Whitewater rafts have changed considerably in the past decade. Self-bailing floors have made these boats unsinkable and unswampable. High-rockered ends improve maneuverability and, thanks to improved materials and construction methods, the newest models are extremely rigid. Expert rafters fine-tune the pressure of the floor and tubes to optimize handling characteristics for big water or tight, technical rivers. These and other improvements have made it possible to run increasingly difficult water.

Rafts come in various lengths—from 8 to 30 feet—although 12- to 18-foot boats are most commonly seen on rivers. They are powered by paddles, oars, and even motors. Choosing the right boat for a given type of river is beyond the scope of this book, but there are a number of features that can improve your safety.

First, avoid anything that could cause entrapment. Lines running around the perimeter, foot loops, and loose lines have all figured in fatalities over the years. Some rafts use a series of handles on the sides and crosstubes in place of the perimeter line to minimize entanglement risks. Foot cups, rather than loops, keep an ankle from sliding in too far and to the point where it cannot be removed. In self-bailing boats, drain holes should be kept small to minimize entrapment risks.

Since many injuries are caused when rafters are caught between their boat and their gear, stowing the payload requires careful thought. Soft gear bags should be used whenever possible; boxes and hard items like pumps, frames, or spare paddles must be padded and stowed out of the way when not in use. Gear should always be tied snugly, not left at the end of a line that could wrap around an arm or leg at the wrong moment. Spare paddles are best stored flat across the crosstubes or lashed against a rigid raft frame. Don't tie them lengthwise; they'll get bent! Rescue bags are best hung from a D-ring set halfway down the inside of the perimeter tube. Push the rest of the bag into the crack between the floor and the tube and keep it there until needed.

Paddle rafters often use three-compartment rafts. Gear is kept in the center compartment, while boaters sit in the ends. Oar boats are loaded in the opposite manner, with most gear placed in the ends and only a small amount beneath the rower's seat. Passengers now sit on the gear, not in the boat. Give an oarsman plenty of room to move—serious injuries have occurred when the boatman was caught between the gear and an oar. Pad any bolts, edges, corners, or other hardware that could cut or impale someone in a crash. Retractable oars allow a raft to move easily through tight places.

We are seeing an era of vast improvement in inflatable kayaks and canoes. Their outfitting must be designed to enable users to get free quickly. At present the biggest danger of "ducks" is that they make difficult rapids accessible to people with minimal training. Getting in over one's head is the shortest road to trouble.

Flotation

Swamped boats are very hard to control. A canoe or kayak filled with water weighs hundreds or even thousands of pounds. Contoured air bags, shaped to fit each type of boat, displace this water, lightening the load and allowing the boat to float higher in the water. This reduces the chance of pinning or damage. It's not uncommon for a properly bagged boat to run miles of Class V water unattended, only to be recovered unscathed some distance downstream.

Good-quality flotation will seldom burst, but in violent rapids it can be torn loose. Tying in the air bags keeps them in place in really big water. In a kayak or decked canoe, tie the ends of the split bags together in front of the wall. Grommets at the end of the bags are provided

Figure 2-2. Fitted flotation bags displace water and make swamped canoes easier to recover. They must be laced in securely or they will be torn out by the water.

for this, but you'll have to remove the wall. In open canoes, air bags are tied in with accessory cord strung every 6 to 8 inches between the gunwales. The attachment points must be extremely secure; in lieu of fittings, some paddlers drill a series of holes just below the gunwales and thread the line through them. Next, a length of 1-inch webbing is run from one end of the bag to the other, secured by D-rings at the keel line. This keeps the bag from working out from under the lashing. The amount of flotation people use varies, but it's important to leave enough room to bail.

Grab Loops and Painters

Whitewater boats are smooth, sleek craft. It's quite impossible to hold onto one without a grab loop or painter attached to the end. A *grab loop* is a loop of rope or webbing attached to the deck of a kayak just behind each end, or to the bow of a canoe at the tip. A *painter* is a length of line attached to the bow or stern. This line must be secured so that it will not uncoil accidentally, or the boater may get tangled at the wrong time.

Kayaks and C-1s use grab loops almost exclusively, and these are also extremely popular on whitewater open canoes. The loop is commonly made from line a minimum of ¼ inch thick, sized so that it will not admit an average adult hand. Never extend your hand into the loop. People have been caught during a recovery this way and dragged some distance downriver. The grab loop should be anchored at two points at least 4 inches apart. If only one point is used or the two ends are set too close together, the loop can twist around the boater's fingers as the boat rolls, causing broken bones or dislocated joints. Painters are occasionally attached to the stern, then secured with a jam cleat or tucked under a shock cord. This line is easier to find and hold onto than a grab loop and is less likely to cause entanglement. Bow painters interfere with a roll and are not recommended, but some traditional open canoes still use them.

Swimming a raft into an eddy alone is almost impossible. Some rafters secure bags con-

Figure 2-3. Two examples of safe, strong grab loops.

taining very long (50-foot) painters to the bow. After a capsize, a rafter grabs the line, swims into an eddy, finds his footing, and pulls the raft to shore.

The Need for a Fast Exit

Whitewater boats, open or decked, must be set up to permit a fast, unimpeded exit in an emergency. Since people vary greatly in size and build, there is no "perfectly safe" universal configuration for canoe and kayak outfitting. You must personally check out any new or unfamiliar craft for fit on dry land and in calm water to be sure the fittings will not impede a fast exit. Anything that gets in the way should be modified before you run significant whitewater.

Kayak Outfitting

The design of a kayak cockpit has a real effect on a paddler's safety. Kayakers hold themselves into their boats with muscle power, not pressure

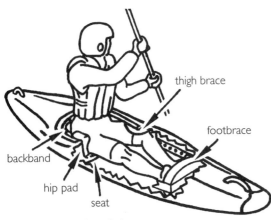

Figure 2-4. Kayak outfitting.

thigh brace

footbrace

backband

hip pad

seat

from their outfitting. Pressing against their footbraces pushes their knees and butt securely into place. The outfitting should be comfortably snug, yet not tight enough to impede a fast exit. There is no advantage in paddling a boat that is

uncomfortably tight. Proper shaping and placement of outfitting components allows you to hold on in the roughest and most violent water.

Kayak designs differ vastly with respect to overall volume and interior roominess. Most designs work best for people within a fairly narrow size and weight range. Low front decks and small seats render some kayaks unpaddleable for anyone above a certain size. Likewise, some very large kayaks may not fit a small paddler correctly, even with well-designed custom outfitting. Sometimes there's a strong temptation to shoehorn yourself into a too-small boat because it's a "hot" design. This is risky unless the outfitting can be modified to accommodate your frame.

Cockpit Size. A large kayak cockpit opening can speed a wet exit, reducing the chances of being trapped inside. This is an advantage in everything from routine launches and landings to serious pins. First developed in Europe, a true

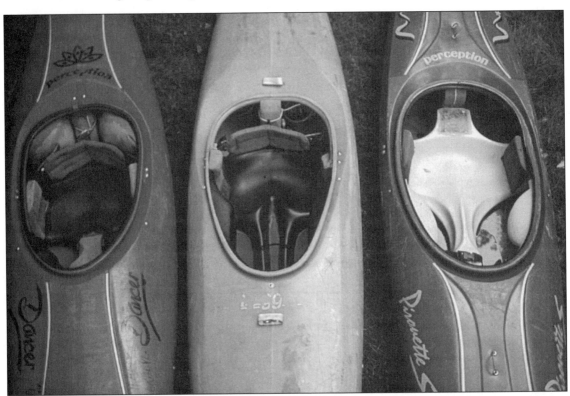

Figure 2-5. The recent trend toward larger cockpit sizes is visible in this photo, which shows a Pirouette S. (right), a Dagger Crossfire (middle), and an old-model Perception Dancer (left).

"keyhole" cockpit permits you to pull your knees clear of the cockpit opening and exit without moving back in your seat. You simply release your thigh braces, pull your legs up under your chin, and fall out. Smaller openings require that you first slide your rear end back over the end of the seat before coming free. But kayak cockpits, like human beings, vary considerably in size. The only way to see if a given opening is "keyhole-sized" for you is to check it personally.

Footbraces. Kayakers press against their footbraces to push themselves solidly into the seat and thigh braces. Adjustability is vital; footbraces should move easily in small increments, yet stay put when set. Strength is important, too. If the footbraces fail, the kayak becomes unmanageable. A kayaker literally stands on the footbraces while running steep ledges and falls. Pop-ups and head-on collisions with obstructions are particularly stressful.

Bar-type footbraces allow a kayaker's foot to become wedged underneath after a collision. This primitive outfitting is seldom seen today; if you encounter such a setup, replace it at once. Pedal-type braces reduce entrapment danger but have some limitations. You can slip off the pedals after a high-speed collision, resulting in a loss of boat control or a serious ankle injury. Bulkhead-style footbraces, consisting of an adjustable plate set across the entire cross section of a kayak, are a better answer for paddlers running steep drops. Your feet can't slip off the sides, and any impact is distributed evenly across the bottom of the foot to reduce the possibility of injury. When padded with foam, bulkheads have a limited shock-absorbing capability. When bulkheads are used with a foam wall, however, you may not be able to take your feet off the pedals, straighten your legs, and rest.

Thigh Braces. Kayakers grip the deck with their legs, so properly positioned thigh braces make a big difference. These are contoured, padded, and placed underneath the deck for comfort and effectiveness. Oversized "thigh hooks" protruding into the open area of a cockpit can impede your exit. Those with excessive hook may catch your knee, resulting in joint and

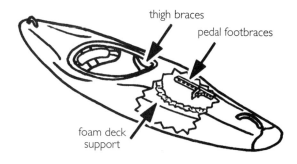

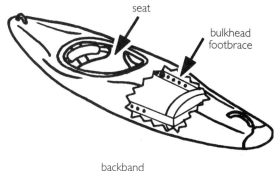

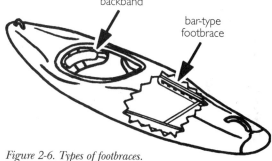

Figure 2-6. Types of footbraces.

ligament injuries. Again, you must find out what's safe for you by careful testing.

Seats. Seats should support the firm, erect posture needed when kayaking. There are many different kayak models available, and no one should have to be uncomfortable. Since paddlers use their bodies to lean and roll their boats, a snug fit at the hips is very helpful. The sides of a seat can be padded out with foam, so don't be concerned if a showroom model is loose. Under no circumstances should the fit be tight enough to interfere with a wet exit.

A backrest improves back support and keeps you from pushing your rear end off the back of your seat. It may consist of a wide, padded backband with adjustable buckles at the side or a contoured foam backrest attached to the rear wall. A few kayak seats are built high enough in the back that no additional support is needed. As discussed earlier, smaller cockpit openings require that you slide backward in your seat to get out. The backband must permit you to do this, so check it out thoroughly on dry land. If your exit is at all restricted, loosen the backrest until you can slide in and out of the cockpit effortlessly.

Canoe Outfitting

Open canoes and fully decked C-1s and C-2s have various fittings to help a paddler hold on to the craft in heavy water. The paddler kneels in the boat, with knees spread slightly wider than shoulder width. Contoured knee pads minimize side-to-side slippage, and his legs are held in place with adjustable thigh straps or some other type of thigh brace. By pressing on the toe blocks, the canoeist forces his legs into the thigh braces, allowing him to grab hold of the boat even when upside down.

Seats. Canoe seating requires special attention. Conventional open canoe seats are designed for flat water and are hung low to improve

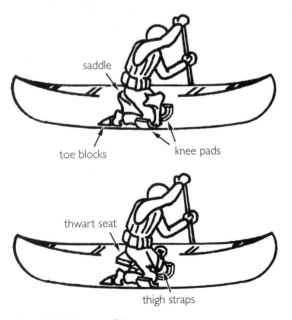

Figure 2-7. Canoe outfitting.

stability. These and the low-hung thwarts preferred by racers can snag a paddler's foot when bailing out, leading to dangerous *lever-lock* entrapments. Pedestal-style seats are much safer because they don't hang over your lower leg and ankle. If you must use a thwart or seat, be certain that there's enough clearance for your lower leg to slide in and out without snagging. This may not be possible in canoes that require a very low seat height (less than 8 inches) to maintain balance and control.

Knee Pads. The spot where your knees meet the hull should be thickly padded for protection and comfort. It's not unusual for a rock to slam into a canoe right under a paddler's knees! Contoured pads create a depression that keeps your knees from moving from side to side.

Thigh Braces. Thigh braces in canoes usually take the form of adjustable nylon straps. These are set to cross your legs diagonally at midthigh, holding your knees securely against the knee pads. Thigh straps are often set across the upper thigh or even at crotch level for added security, but this arrangement is hard to get out of quickly and will not hold down your knees securely during braces and rolls. Toe blocks are a better alternative to increase security without adding entrapment danger. If quick-release buckles are included, they should be set at the top of the straps, near the gunwales, where they are most easily reached.

Toe Blocks. Toe blocks allow canoeists to push their knees forward with their toes, forcing their thighs firmly against the straps. This increases security without the entanglement dangers posed by thigh straps set too high or too tight. Take time to position these fittings correctly. In open boats, set the blocks so your toes curl under them. In decked canoes where space is tight, point your toes, let the top of your feet lie flat against the hull, then position the blocks so that you barely touch them with the tips of your toes. You must always be able to "back out" of your thigh braces without the blocks getting in the way. Toe blocks will often twist your ankle joints into uncomfortable positions; supporting the underside of the foot with properly shaped and positioned foam ankle blocks may offer some relief.

Sprayskirts

A sprayskirt has two contradictory functions. It should fit tightly enough to keep out all but the smallest amount of water, but must release quickly and reliably when a fast exit is required. Most whitewater sprayskirts are fabricated from ⅛-inch neoprene wetsuit material and are sized to fit tightly at the waist. The bottom is elasticized to grab underneath the lip of the cockpit rim, holding it securely.

The method used for fastening a sprayskirt to the cockpit rim has undergone some changes over the years. Older designs use an adjustable

Figure 2-8. Sprayskirts seek a compromise between a watertight fit and a quick, sure release.

¼-inch shock cord, which stretches effortlessly into place and pops off easily in emergencies. The grab loop is added more for backup than actual need. This method is inexpensive and works well enough for novice and even advanced paddlers who find that an occasional unexpected release is a reasonable trade-off for not having to find the grab loop before bailing out.

But the narrow cockpit lips of many roto-molded designs, combined with a growing demand for tighter-fitting sprayskirts, has led to stronger methods of securing a spraycover to a decked boat. Among the options: wide, stretchy bands of gum rubber; specially fabricated "rands"; and ultraheavy shock cords. These methods seldom release prematurely, but they are harder to put on and absolutely, positively will not come off unless you pull on the grab loop first. Although well suited to experts who seldom swim and can't afford to have their sprayskirt "pop" in the midst of a nasty rapid, they're a poor choice for anyone who may lack the presence of mind to locate and pull the grab loop while upside down. Several near-drownings have resulted from failure of a sprayskirt to release when the paddler could not or would not find the loop.

A grab loop must remain on the outside of the sprayskirt to work. Fortunately, most are designed so that it's difficult to put on the skirt any other way. Practice locating and pulling the grab loop underwater before running a river!

Protective Gear

Whitewater rivers are fast, rocky, and cold. Paddlers respond to this challenge by choosing and using appropriate protective gear. Without it, even trained paddlers would be hard-pressed to survive a swim.

Life Vests

Life vests (also called personal flotation devices or PFDs) provide the extra buoyancy paddlers need to stay afloat in whitewater. This enables them to devote their energy to self-protection and rescue. Swimming paddlers must hold onto

Figure 2-9. Extrasport's buoyant "Gold" PFD (left) has about 20-percent more buoyancy than a low-cut "Squirt" (right).

gear, fend off rocks, and try to work their way to shore. They don't need to worry about whether or not they'll float! Many rapids have powerful currents that can pull a person down underwater. What is merely exhausting to someone wearing a life jacket might be fatal to an unprotected swimmer.

Vest-type life preservers combine comfort with protection. They're cut to distribute the foam flotation around a paddler's body without restricting freedom of movement, offering substantial impact protection for the back and shoulders. The amount and placement of flotation vary considerably. Canoeists like full-length models extending just below the waist for added protection. Kayakers prefer waist-length "short" models that don't interfere with their sprayskirts. Some people like the added protection of a padded shoulder; others prefer the slim profile of unpadded designs.

Buoyancy values differ also. The minimum requirement for U.S. Coast Guard approval is 15.5 pounds, enough to float a 160-pound person chin-high in the water. The low-volume "racer" or "squirt" designs stay close to the minimum buoyancy and coverage to maximize freedom of movement, while some full-length, high-flotation models contain almost twice as much flotation. Most fall between these extremes, with 19 pounds being average.

More buoyant life vests float a swimmer higher in the water. In violent, aerated turbulence, a person may spend considerable time beneath the surface. Additional flotation pulls him to the surface more often, translating into more air during a bad swim. But bigger life vests can be annoyingly bulky, compromising freedom of movement. They may also cause a swimmer to be caught and recirculated in some types of holes and interfere with certain squirt boat maneuvers. Lower-flotation models are less bulky but may offer less protection. There is no perfect life vest for all conditions, so pick the one most suited to your type of paddling.

Whatever the design, a good fit is essential. A life vest should fit snugly yet comfortably. If it's too loose, it will slide up over your head. The adjustment buckles provided with most whitewater life vests work well for most people, but young children and pot-bellied adults are hard to fit. These folks and anyone else who wants a life jacket to stay on at all times should consider using crotch straps, which run from the back of the life vest to the front, through the user's crotch. Properly fitted, they're quite effective, but adjusting them so they are comfortable to sit on and won't interfere with a sprayskirt can be difficult. For obvious reasons, men need to be cautious about where they place the straps, especially before jumping into the water from high places.

The fabric and foam in life vests deteriorate over time. Their useful life is a factor of exposure to the sun and abrasive wear, and these in turn are linked to use and climate. As the fabric fades, it loses strength. When small rips and tears appear, you've lost significant strength and buoyancy, and the vest should be replaced.

Helmets

Head injuries, though rare, are almost always serious, and head protection is becoming the norm on all but the easiest whitewater rivers. Rafts and open canoes without thigh braces throw paddlers clear when capsizing; by contrast, kayaks and open canoes with thigh braces hold a capsized paddler upside down, close to the boat, with his or her head exposed. The AWA Safety Code recommends the use of helmets at all times in kayaks and outfitted canoes, and in rafts and other craft when attempting rapids of Class IV or greater difficulty.

Paddlers, unlike rock climbers and motorcycle riders, seldom need high-speed collision protection. Whitewater helmets can therefore be less substantial than those used for other activities. One-half to three-quarters inch of shock-absorbing foam or a solid, workable suspension system provides sufficient impact protection.

The most important feature of any river running helmet is the coverage it gives the head. Blows can come from any angle; the fore-

Figure 2-10. A selection of popular helmets. Check for a snug fit and good coverage at the temple and forehead. The one on the far left is no longer made; it was too lightweight and did not protect the temple and forehead.

head above the eyebrows, the temple, and the back of the head are the most common targets. Many hockey helmets have excellent coverage; most climbing or biking helmets do not. Ear coverage provides protection from impact with the water as well as with rocks. The shell should be light, reasonably rigid, and tough. Drain holes to let water out are a plus, but are not necessary in fitted helmets that have little space inside where water can collect. The chin strap should keep the shell from rotating backward, exposing the forehead. If the helmet does not fit securely, it's probably the wrong size. Face guards for added protection are available on some helmets. While they are popular among Europeans for steep, rocky runs, they haven't become standard equipment in the USA. Most of the people you see wearing them have experienced some type of facial injury.

Cold-Water Protection

Water draws heat from the body 25 times faster than air. Like windchill, the effects of cold water increase when the current is fast. Sudden immersion in snowmelt or spring runoff is extremely debilitating, causing a substantial loss of strength, coordination, and judgment rather quickly. All cold-weather paddlers should select the gear needed for the insulation required to stay warm.

Drysuits and wetsuits both work effectively in cold water. In a wetsuit, air is trapped inside the neoprene material, and the suit fits snugly enough to keep most cold water out. What little water gets inside is quickly warmed by the user's body heat. Drysuits create an actual barrier between the environment and the paddler, eliminating that initial "cold-water shock." Paddling

Figure 2-11. Wetsuits remain popular because they are comfortable over a wide temperature range. Paddlers typically wear pile and a paddle jacket over their arms for maximum upper-body mobility. A drysuit functions as a waterproof coverall, creating a total barrier against cold water. Varying amounts of clothing can be worn underneath to suit paddling conditions.

drysuits are made of a waterproof material with latex seals at the neck, wrists, and ankles. The paddler regulates the inside temperature by adding or removing layers of insulation, such as pile or polypropylene. In milder weather, a waterproof shell top or paddle jacket can be combined with pile clothing or a wetsuit for comfort.

The first goal is to protect the torso, which shelters the "core" of the body. The greatest heat loss occurs in the armpits and crotch. Next, pay special attention to the extremities. The head radiates a surprising amount of heat. If the helmet alone is not warm enough, pile or neoprene liners can be worn inside. Neoprene booties cover the paddler's feet, and if the sole is thick enough they can be used alone. Another alternative is to wear lightweight neoprene socks inside sneakers. In cold weather a boater's hands quickly lose the strength and sensitivity needed for effective paddling. Neoprene gloves or mittens are one answer; mittens are warmer than gloves, but more awkward and harder to find. Pogies (mittens that cover both the hand and the paddle) permit direct hand-to-paddle contact for maximum control with a kayak paddle. In borderline weather, carry hand protection along for possible use later in the day.

Rescue Gear

All paddlers, no matter how skilled, eventually encounter trouble. Everyone should carry sufficient rescue gear to deal with common predicaments. Minimal gear includes the following:

- *A throw line.* Seventy feet of ⅜-inch line is standard, usually carried in a rescue bag. The selection and use of throw lines is discussed in considerable detail in Chapter 4.
- *Carabiners* are aluminum or stainless steel ovals with spring-loaded gates that open and close. Originally designed for mountaineers, they're a quick alternative to knots in river rescues. Some types of 'biners have locking gates. These are more secure, but the mechanism can become choked with sand and jam unexpectedly.

Carabiners are often clipped to the

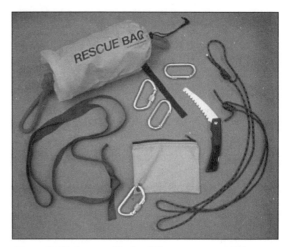

Figure 2-12. A rescue kit should be compact and lightweight. All of the smaller components go into the pouch, which in turn goes into the top of the rescue bag.

waist belt or adjustment straps on a life vest. But if the gates do not lock, a 'biner can accidentally clip into a line during a rescue. Attaching them to the shoulder strap of a life vest creates a new problem: the impact from a rock can drive a 'biner directly into an unprotected body. One safe way to carry 'biners is in a small gear pouch stuffed inside a rescue bag or in a life jacket pocket. Another option is to clip them into the wide knife strap found on many life vests. Attach carabiners with the gate facing in, where it can't snag.

- Two *prusik loops* are needed to set up the hauling systems described in Chapter 6. You'll need about 6 feet of small-diameter nylon cord, roughly 50 to 60 percent of the thickness of the haul line you expect to use. A standard ⅜-inch haul line, for example, requires a prusik loop made from 5.5- to 7.0-mm cord. The ends of the cord are tied to each other with a double fisherman's knot (see Appendix A) to form the loop.

Five-millimeter nylon accessory cord has a breaking strength of 1,200 pounds—less than a third of the 4,500-pound breaking strength of 5.5 Titan, a cord with a nylon sheath and a Spectra core. But nylon is more flexible than Titan, giving it a better grip on the rope and making the knots easier to tie. Titan is expensive and vulnerable to shock loading, so its advantage may be less than the numbers indicate. A triple fisherman's knot (see Appendix A) should be used to tie prusik loops in Titan!

- *Webbing* is inexpensive and strong: the 1-inch tubular material preferred by paddlers has a breaking strength of close to 4,000 pounds. A loop of this material, made by tying the ends together with a water knot (see Appendix A), can be worn around the waist and secured, like a belt, with a carabiner. It is very handy for portaging and works as an anchor when setting up haul systems. A waist loop to fit the average person requires 9 to 10 feet of webbing; it should fit snugly, like a belt, to minimize entanglement dangers. Longer lengths of webbing are also useful in creating anchors.

- *River knives* are always useful, but they become especially important when working with ropes. When a line under tension becomes tangled and endangers someone, cutting the rope is the quickest and most effective response. Paddlers tend to favor either small sheath knives or medium-size pocketknives; these can be secured to a life vest or stowed in a pocket. Single-bladed knives are more practical and easier to use in close quarters than double-bladed models, but both are popular. Sheath effectiveness varies from worthless to bombproof. If you have doubts, attach the knife to your life vest with a short lanyard.

  Attaching a knife to a life vest requires care. Some PFD manufacturers provide an anchor point on the left shoulder; lefties can sometimes get one on the opposite side by special order. Try to find a place where it won't get knocked around when paddling. On full-

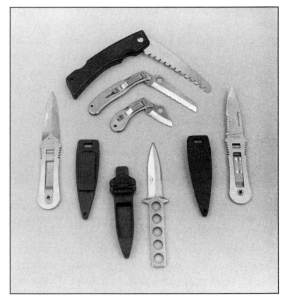

Figure 2-13. A selection of popular river knives.

length life vests, you can attach a sheath knife to the waist tie. Some life vests have pockets where a small pocketknife can be stowed.

Seat belt cutters can be used in place of knives. They're inexpensive, effective, and can cut a wetsuit off an injured person without inflicting injury. They stow easily in a life vest pocket and look much friendlier to nonpaddlers.

- *Saws.* In the last few years, a number of small folding saws have become available. These store easily in a gear pouch and can be used to trim brush, cut small strainers, or as a last resort, cut someone out of a pinned kayak.

- *Whistles* can be worn on your life jacket zipper and used for emergency communication. Some of the newer models are very loud; the Fox 40 will hurt your ears when you blow it!

Other items are optional, to be taken or not according to personal preference. These include:
- *Pulleys* are used with carabiners to reduce the friction in a hauling system, transferring the pull more efficiently to the line.

Also, by increasing the radius of the bend in the rope, pulleys reduce the strain on a line. Full-size pulleys are 2 inches in diameter; these create an almost ideal "bending radius" but are too bulky for compact rescue kits. Some miniature pulleys are simply not strong enough for the forces generated by mechanical advantage; others are made to the same specifications as the larger ones, with breaking strengths of 3,000 to 5,000 pounds.

- *Paddle hooks* attach to the end of a paddle to extend a rescuer's reach. Some models utilize a carabiner, while others are actual hooks. The paddle merely sets the hook in place in the grab loop of a pinned kayak; the actual hauling is done by a rope attached to the hook.

- *Rescue life vests* are life jackets with a built-in quick-release chest harness (Figure 2-15, page 28). This harness is made of nylon webbing with a quick-release buckle in the front, permitting the user to tie herself safely into a rope. This allows effective belaying in and out of the water. If the rope becomes entangled or the water pressure unbearable, the user releases the buckle and floats free. Using a harness takes practice and a working knowledge of river rescue skills. These are discussed in detail in Chapter 5.

- Several items are used in conjunction with a quick-release harness. A *self-tether*, consisting of a short length of elasticized webbing tied to the back D-ring with a carabiner at the other end, permits harness users to clip themselves into a belay without relying on untrained bystanders. An elastic holds it close to the body to minimize entrapment risks. A *cowtail* is a longer length of webbing used to rescue boats. Set up in the same manner, the extra length must be stowed to fit close against the body. A *carabiner loop*, made from webbing with a cam-lock buckle installed backward, provides a quick-release point for a tether or cowtail on the front of the vest, where they are readily accessible.

    Rescue life vests may feature a number of pockets to hold carabiners and other small items. One recent innovation is a large back pocket that holds a small rescue bag. Since these pockets hold water, vests that use them cannot be Coast Guard approved. Pockets present some added snag hazard and may interfere with a kayaker's roll, but this method of stowing a line is innovative and will be watched closely in the coming years.

- *Boat tow systems* are helpful in rescuing whitewater boats on milder stretches of moving water. The several types are

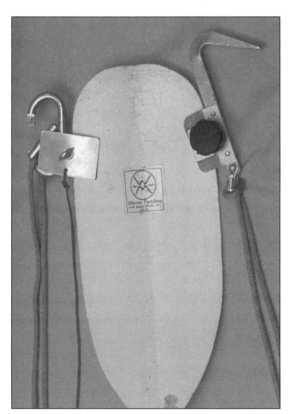

Figure 2-14. Paddle hooks increase a paddler's reach in rescues. The HF version (right) is quite robust; the American Hair Clip (left) works with most carabiners.

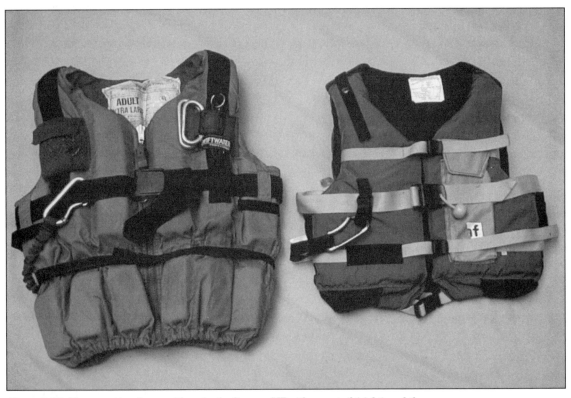

Figure 2-15. Two examples of rescue life vests: the German HF with a cowtail (right) and the Coast Guard–approved Extrasport Ranger (left) with a homemade short tether.

discussed fully in Chapter 7. The American jam-cleat style is cheap and simple, but the pull is directed through the stern grab loop, making ferries and eddy turns a real hassle. European systems mount at the center of the boat, usually in front of or behind the cockpit. This improves boat control, but the mechanisms are more complex and expensive.

Other Gear

Several other pieces of gear can be useful. A spare paddle can save a lot of grief if yours is lost or broken. Kayakers will need a takedown spare. One (or two) extras per party make sense on any isolated stretch of river where walking out would

be troublesome. First aid kits range from small outfits with minimal supplies to the extensive kits carried on expeditions. The components are expensive and water sensitive, so carry the kit in a waterproof bag and store individual components in separate Ziploc bags for additional protection. A compact CPR barrier device protects the rescuer from ingesting a drowning victim's vomit, and can be carried in a sealed container in your life jacket pocket. In cold weather, carry a compact survival kit with matches and fire starter to rewarm hypothermic paddlers. Duct tape has many uses, and a small roll takes up little space. Bring along extra food, patching materials, maps, and other necessities as needed.

CHAPTER 3

Swimming and Wading

Whitewater paddlers don't like to swim. We have unhappy memories of this activity from our days as novices. The emphasis among better canoeists and kayakers is on staying in their boats and rolling back up whenever possible. While some hard-boaters say they have a "100-percent roll" and "never swim," the truth is that getting wet is part of the sport. It's important to be prepared for what you'll encounter after bailing out.

Anyone can learn safe techniques for swimming and wading in fast water. Swimming is the quickest form of self-rescue and a lot of fun on a warm day. Wading allows paddlers to move with confidence in shallow areas. These two skills will boost any boater's confidence and are especially important for those interested in river rescue.

Swimming

Even though river runners wear life vests, they must be competent swimmers. By this we mean not an Olympic-quality performance, just a good working knowledge of several strokes, some stamina, and confidence enough to keep a cool head underwater. Without this foundation, the paddler is likely to be "afraid of the water." For a terrified person, swimming rapids is exhausting, and the capacity for quick thinking is limited. Both the Red Cross and YMCA are excellent sources of swimming instruction. A short course can greatly improve individual swimming ability.

For swimming in rivers, we make a distinction between defensive and aggressive swim-

Figure 3-1. Defensive swimming: legs in front with feet near the surface.

Figure 3-2. Aggressive swimming: stroking for an eddy.

ming. In defensive swimming, you float passively with the current, on your back, with your feet extended in front of you. The idea is to ride with the river, keeping your body parallel to the current while fending off any obstacles. A vest-type life preserver with plenty of flotation and good back coverage is extremely useful here. In aggressive swimming, you roll onto your belly, still feet first, and stroke hard to work across the current into a safe eddy. Most boaters don't switch from a defensive to an aggressive mode quickly enough and miss many opportunities for self-rescue.

Defensive Swimming

Defensive swimming enables you to float in fast water that is too deep to stand in safely but too shallow to swim in effectively. It's also the most reasonable way to confront powerful stretches of big water. Swimming a difficult rapid is extremely tiring even for the very fit. The objective is to ride out the river, conserving energy until an opportunity for self-rescue arises and then "go for it."

Self-protection is a must in shallow, rocky rapids. When floating over thinly padded rocks and ledges, arch your back, pulling up your rear end to avoid bruising your lower back. Your buttocks have plenty of padding, so don't put your hands there! If your body follows the surface of the water closely, you'll greatly reduce your chances of injury. To look forward, don't sit up; this pushes your butt deeper into the water. Instead, tuck your chin against your chest and look ahead. Don't allow the current to force you sideways to the flow; you can be tumbled and badly beaten in the shallows.

Big water can be exhausting to float through. It's very possible to drown in rough rapids while wearing a life vest. Save your strength and make the most of all breathing opportunities. Focus on swimming away from the most dangerous hazards and on getting the air you need. In many large rapids, undercut rocks, pourovers, and debris are most common along the banks. It often makes sense to "ride out" the major drops, conserving strength, then catch an eddy at the bottom.

Waves, Holes, and Ledges

Swimmers tend to go through waves rather than float over them as they would in a boat. Time your breathing to catch air when you can, surfacing only in the troughs. Very large waves (6 to 10 feet) are often easier to breathe in than medium-size waves because the troughs are bigger, and each opportunity for breathing is longer.

When big holes form, water piles up at the base of the steep drop, creating a powerful upstream current. Paddlers floating into these reversals are very likely to flush through.

Figure 3-3. Breathe in the troughs of waves, then hold your breath as you float through them.

Figure 3-4. Swimmers are usually pushed through holes; this swimmer is arching her back to avoid hitting bottom in shallow water.

Swimmers can improve the odds by staying low in the water, then forcing themselves down under the foam on impact, where the main current can wash them through. Be prepared to travel underwater for a surprisingly long time, even in small- to medium-size reversals.

Swimmers may become caught in a hole after surfing it, then bail out. Lacking downstream momentum, they are easily grabbed by the reversal. Here's some advice: First, forget about taking off your life vest; it's not easy to do, and you'll need the buoyancy again downstream. Second, try to relax and conserve energy. Most people who fight the current in holes swim in the wrong direction, only to be ejected later, after losing consciousness. A hole usually carries a person upstream, toward the onrushing water, then pushes him down. If you can swim with the flow, moving upstream toward the current, you may be flushed out.

Figure 3-5. A paddler and boat being recirculated in a large hole. Relaxing and altering one's shape relative to the water improve the chances of escaping.

Diving below the surface takes a lot of stamina and courage; fortunately, this procedure is seldom necessary because the current carries you down without any help. Remember that river holes have an affinity for certain shapes. The best escape strategy is to alter your shape in the water by grabbing or letting go of your boat, or by changing from a spread-eagled to a tight, balled-up posture.

When floating through big ledges and high, rocky chutes, holding your legs straight out may lead to trouble. As you drop over a ledge, your legs may be carried down deep, and a foot may snag under rocks or debris at the base of the drop. To avoid this, bend your legs when entering large holes. In high, steep ledges, tuck into a

Figure 3-6. When you are swimming steep ledges, a feet-first approach can lead to entrapment. Tucking into a ball reduces this risk.

ball. Although this increases the risk of hitting rocks, it reduces the chance of foot entrapment and allows the water to force you to the bottom, then out to safety.

Aggressive Swimming

Aggressive swimming in whitewater takes the form of short, hard bursts to carry you across the river or into an eddy. To cut across the current, use a *body ferry*. Roll onto your belly and swim hard upstream, angling across the onrushing water with your body angling toward your goal. Compared with paddling a canoe or kayak, this is slow, tiring work. Allow plenty of distance and time to make a move. Even if you can't swim to safety, it may be necessary to get from one side of the river to the other to miss nasty rocks, big holes, or strainers. This is vital in rapids of Class IV and above. Since a swimmer rides low in the water, visibility is limited. You'll know which way to go if you scout the rapid before running it.

Swimming in rapids is mostly arm motion. Even in a swimming pool, 80 percent of your power comes from your arms. While a good kick helps in the longer stretches, it's important to keep your legs straight to avoid hitting rocks with your knees and ankles. Stroking with your fingers slightly spread apart increases the surface area of your hand and thus your power to swim—the water encounters more resistance as it accelerates between your fingers.

Getting into Eddies

Entering eddies requires carefully timed effort. Pick a target high in the eddy and aggressively ferry toward it from one side. The easiest way to cross an eddyline is to execute several successive barrel rolls, stroking on your belly, back, and belly in turn. A head-first approach, similar to the line a boat would take, increases the risk of head injury but may be more effective in deep, powerful water. Build up forward speed, cross the eddyline at a 45° angle, and stroke hard to avoid being carried downstream. Never try this without a helmet.

In big water, eddylines are wider and harder to cross. The boils and whirlpools that form along the edges can suck even a life-jacketed paddler underwater. These places are best avoided, but sometimes a swimmer doesn't know about them until it's too late. Remember that whirlpools are transitory; they break up after traveling a short distance downstream. Don't panic! Relax, hold your breath, and wait for your life vest to pull you back to the surface. Boils are impossible to swim across, and it's best to try crossing into an eddy where there are none.

Eventually, you will arrive in relatively calm, shallow water where it's safe to stand. Don't pull your knees underneath you to regain your footing; they will usually slam into unseen rocks. Instead, let your hands find the bottom first, followed by your feet, and then settle your body back onto your haunches and finish in a squat.

Swimming with Gear

In easier water, hanging onto your gear makes sense. It reduces the number of loose floating objects needing rescue. In addition, a boat has lots of buoyancy, provides much-needed support on long swims, and makes you easier to spot. It's especially important to hold on to your gear when boating in small groups, since a paddle or boat can slip away during a rescue. Keeping your boat lined up with the current reduces the chances of a bad pin. Novices learn this in their training classes, and these are good habits to cultivate.

But evasive swimming and self-rescue in hard rapids is almost impossible with a boat and paddle in your hands. At best, it slows you down; at worst, the gear beats you up. The river may throw the boat back at you or smack you with a paddle. Grabbing a wildly bobbing stern in a wave train has been known to result in broken jaws and lost teeth! You could find yourself caught between your boat and a pinning rock, or you could be jammed into a very narrow chute with your gear. All things considered, letting go of equipment in serious drops makes self-rescue easier.

You, the swimmer, must decide what to do. But remember: unless you're on an expedition, you can always buy more gear. If you do hold on to your boat, stay at the upstream end. You don't want to be caught between a rock and your boat by the rushing water. If you find yourself downstream of your craft, get away from it at once! This can happen when your boat hits a rock and stops, allowing the current to push you downstream and under it. Be prepared to release the canoe or kayak quickly; don't let your hands get caught in the grab loop or the painter.

Be ready to improvise as you swim. Keep your eyes open for opportunities and exploit them. Boaters have used a paddle to help swim to safety in very serious water. I've seen people hop into an open boat or on top of an overturned C-1 and paddle it to shore between big Class IV drops. I've also seen kayakers lie on top of their boat, paddling it like a huge boogie board. Learning to do any of these things is a real advantage.

Dealing with Strainers

Strainers are obstacles through which water flows but paddlers can't. Downed trees and debris in the current are dangerous because the current can carry you underwater into an unseen trap. A large percentage of strainer victims are found in a feet-up, head-down position. This suggests that hitting the strainer feet first caused entrapment and that a more aggressive approach is needed.

Strainers are best avoided, but if a collision is inevitable, get on your belly and swim aggressively, head first, toward the strainer. When you make contact, start climbing over the top immediately, before the oncoming water has time to pile up against your body (Figure 3-8, page 36). Grab what you can and fight hard! If you can pull your pelvis clear of the water, you've won. Going under a strainer is much more risky, since you must deal with hazards you can't see in a place where you can't breathe. If this route is inevitable, protect your face with your hands as you go under and keep your body lined up with the current. This improves your chances of coming through without snagging.

One common mistake when switching from a feet-first to a head-first position is to flip through a sitting or standing position rather

Figure 3-7. This strainer drill (above and at right) shows two possible results of drifting into a strainer feet first.

than rolling over. Try not to do this; it will shove your feet down and could force you to push off the bottom and cause entrapment. Another more subtle error is swimming with your head out of the water. Lifting your head forces your legs underwater, increasing drag and slowing your progress. It's better to pick an objective, take a deep breath, then take five to eight strokes without breathing. Remove nose-clips, if you're wearing them, to help you breathe.

Entering the Water

Some rescues require that a paddler enter the current quickly. The safest way is to wade into the water, lean forward when the water becomes deep enough to float, and start stroking. This works best in shallow eddies and on gradually sloping riverbanks, and reduces the chances of unexpected collisions with underwater rocks. It is not effective at the edge of a deep, fast chute where wading is impractical.

Figure 3-8. The best way to attack a strainer: swim into it head first, then vault your body up and over.

Figure 3-9. Strainers often appear without much warning. This one developed overnight on a popular Class V run.

Swiftwater Entries

A *swiftwater entry* is a safe method of entering a powerful current under good control. The water may be quite deep, but you can never be sure. Never, ever risk a broken neck by diving. Instead, execute a precisely controlled belly flop from a low height. This drops you cleanly into the river while protecting you from hitting unseen rocks.

To enter the water, lean out, jump slightly, and fall forward. Arch your back and hold your head back so that your body lands flat. This is not a dive; your head never goes underwater. Cross your forearms in front of your face to protect your head. Your body is protected by a life vest, wetsuit, and helmet. Hit the water stroking hard, keeping your legs straight so that your knees won't hit submerged rocks. Try to angle your leap upstream, into the oncoming current. This keeps you from being washed downstream and makes it easier to start a ferry.

Wading

Good wading technique for fast water is important. it can get swimmers out of the water safely and let rescuers approach and work around an accident site. Opportunities for injury still exist, but the right skills can minimize risk.

River bottoms, banks, and midstream rocks are unbelievably slippery. Total concentration is needed to avoid a fall. Look where you are stepping every second. Don't make the mistake of glancing ahead to your destination as you walk or wade, no matter how important it is to get there quickly. If you look up, you will fall, some-

Figure 3-10. A swiftwater entry is not a dive, but a belly flop into water of unknown depth. For protection, the rescuer holds his head back, and his arms in front of his face.

Saved by a Book!

It was a warm spring day on the Cheat River, with tender green leaves just beginning to show. As you approach High Falls, a rapid cuts a narrow chute on the right side of the river. At the bottom you eddy out, then cut back to center. A short distance below, a huge tree had wedged itself in a choice passage. It was nasty, but easy to avoid.

Our group was in the eddy when we saw an open boater flip upstream. He was coming downstream incredibly fast. As he drifted toward us, we could see he was in trouble. For one moment he looked over and our eyes locked. "SWIM!" I yelled, preparing myself for the worst.

The paddler rolled over on his belly and swam forward like a madman. He hit the tree high on his chest, and with some difficulty struggled over before ducking into an eddy below. His buddies recovered his boat, and my heart rate dropped to a manageable level.

Down below, I complimented him on his swim. I asked him how he'd learned to do that, since we'd just started teaching the skill in our rescue course. He'd never practiced it, he said, but he'd read about it in Bechdel and Ray's *River Rescue*. His mind had reached back and pulled out that idea just in time.

I guess books really can help out after all.

—*CW*

times onto sharp objects, occasionally hard enough to cause injury but always in a way that slows you down. If you need to see farther ahead, stop and look, then continue. Some of the authors' most painful and embarrassing moments have resulted from violating this simple but important rule.

Foot entrapment is a genuine concern when wading. It usually occurs when a swimmer tries to stand up in a fast current and blindly thrusts his foot into the riverbed. If the victim finds his leg caught in a crack between two boulders, there usually isn't enough time to remove it. Unless luck is with him, he'll lose his balance, the current will push him under, and he'll drown.

River rescuers avoid foot entrapment by maintaining balance and control when wading. Each step is taken carefully, without lunging or scrambling. If your foot slips into a crevice and you are not being pushed around by the river, you can usually remove your foot easily. The skills described in this section will enable you to stand up in surprisingly strong current. If you start to lose your footing, don't risk trouble by fighting the current. Just let go, float, then swim to safety.

When you're wading, your feet are your eyes. You may not be able to see where you're stepping, but you can feel where you're placing your feet. Take small steps. Probe ahead carefully. Keep your balance, and don't commit your weight until you're sure of your footing. Place your feet in low places where you're less likely to slip. If you stand on top of a rock, your foot could slide into a crevice or crack. An ensuing loss of balance could spell trouble.

If one technique isn't working, try another one that improves your balance and control. It often helps to turn sideways to the current. This reduces the surface area that the water is pushing against, making it easier to stay upright. In more forceful current, it becomes difficult to stay upright while feeling around with your foot. Reaching down with your hand adds an additional point of contact with the bottom and makes it easier to maintain your position. Sometimes it makes sense to drop to your hands and knees and crawl; it looks silly, but it works.

Wading with a Paddle

Using a paddle for support affords three-point stability and allows paddlers to wade into deeper water with confidence. While a pike pole, stout stick, or tree branch will work, paddle blades are better because they stick to the bottom extremely well when used correctly. Start by facing upstream, with legs slightly wider than shoulder width. Reach out, turn the paddle blade parallel to the current, and plunge it into the water. Just before the blade hits bottom, turn it sideways to the current. The force of the onrushing water will pin it to the bottom.

To work your way across the river, shuffle your legs from side to side. When you're sure of your balance, take your weight off the paddle and again twist it so that the blade is parallel to the current. The paddle can now be lifted and moved easily to the next desired position. Keep two points in solid contact with the riverbed at all times. With practice, you can move swiftly and effectively in waist-deep water.

Figure 3-11. Solo wading with a paddle for support.

Team Wading Skills

A group working together as a team can wade into water far deeper and faster than a single person can. Team members not only support one another but, by standing together, also create eddies that give their mates some protection from the onrushing current. The following techniques for two, three, four, and six people work extremely well. They're easy to teach, and they lend themselves to rescues and evacuations involving inexperienced people. By communicating closely, a group can move through fast current with surprising speed.

- *Double crossings* start with two people facing each other. One person faces into the current, while the other faces away from it. Spreading their feet to shoulder width, the two waders grab each other's life vests at the shoulders. One person moves at a time; the upstream person goes first, then the downstream person steps into an eddy created by her partner. If one person slips, the other can usually offer support while she regains her footing.

  Placing the larger person upstream creates a bigger eddy for the downstream partner. The second person is not getting a free ride but is providing balance and support. The downstream position is a good place for a stranded victim who is being helped ashore. She can't see what's downstream, and this helps her focus on your instructions.

- *In-line crossings* require three people and a paddle or pole. The strongest person takes a position upstream; the weakest person is at the middle. They lock arms, grab the shaft, and line up parallel to the current. As they walk into faster water, each uses the pole for support.

Figure 3-12. Doubles wading. Note the kayaker exiting the eddy created by the waders.

The two downstream members of the team are somewhat protected from the current; the weakest person is supported on both sides. This is the best procedure for helping injured or shaken individuals across a stretch of swift, shallow water.

- *Circle crossings* look like a football huddle with three, four, or five people. Everyone faces into the circle and grabs the waders on either side by the shoulders of their life vests. The upstream person becomes the anchor; the rest pivot around him. When a person is rotated to a position level with the anchor, he achieves stability and the group now pivots around him. If one or two people slip, they can regain their balance with the assistance of the group. If the entire group begins to slide or float downstream, each person should abandon the procedure and swim to safety.

Figure 3-13. Line wading. With arms linked, two stronger paddlers can support a weak or injured person in the center.

Figure 3-14. Four paddlers circle wading in the backwash of a hole.

Figure 3-15. Pyramid wading in a fast current. Note the substantial pillow in front and the eddy behind.

- *Pyramid crossings* require six or more participants. This technique is very effective, allowing a group to cross fast-moving, chest-deep water. A surprisingly strong eddy is created downstream of the team, which can be useful in rescues discussed in later chapters.

    Pick the tallest, strongest, or heaviest individual for the "point" of the pyramid. That person faces upstream as though he were wading alone, using a paddle for support. Two others stand behind the point, each grabbing the point person's life vest at the shoulders. Three more people stand behind the second row, holding on to the life vests of those in front. This creates a V-shaped group with the apex pointing upstream.

    This method works in chest-deep water if the current is not too swift. The "V" must point directly into the current; if the group turns sideways, the water will push the group over. The person in the center of the third row should stay directly behind the leader to keep the team aligned. As with the four-member team, if someone slips, the others are there for support. But if the group as a whole begins to lose ground or stability, each member should relax, float free, and swim to shore.

These self-rescue skills will help you feel safer around whitewater rivers, whether in your boat, swimming, or working at an accident site. The next step is to learn the rope-handling skills needed to assist others.

CHAPTER 4

Throw Ropes: Selection and Use

Rescue becomes increasingly hazardous as you move closer to a paddler in trouble. One way to extend your reach without closing the gap is to use a rope. A skilled person can toss a line across a wide expanse of rough water, reaching a victim quickly while standing safely on shore. A rope can also be used to support a trapped person, retrieve a pinned craft, or prepare downstream safety backup for others working upstream.

Rope Selection

Ropes are made from many different materials and come in numerous diameters and constructions. Understanding the pros and cons of various lines will help you select the most suitable ropes for your needs.

Materials

Buoyancy is the most important characteristic of any water rescue rope. A line that floats on the surface is easier to manage and reduces the chance of underwater entanglement. Polypropylene, the first choice of paddlers, floats. Nylon, the fiber most favored by climbers, sinks. While many people are familiar with monofilament polypropylene, a rather stiff and abrasive fiber, the multifilament type used in river rescue line is soft and supple enough to be indistinguishable from nylon.

Polypropylene and nylon differ in other ways. Nylon is twice as strong, making it ideal for rock climbing and vertical rescue. Polypropylene has a relatively low melting point, losing 50 percent of its strength at only 150°F.

This is a serious shortcoming for climbers because lowering, raising, or rappelling all use friction to slow the descent. The National Fire Protection Association standards for lowering a single person over a drop are a breaking strength of 4,500 pounds and a melting point of 400°F. Polypropylene ropes fail these tests but work fine for catching swimmers and recovering boats.

Solid-braid polypropylene marine line is the most common and least expensive type of rope used by paddlers. A length of ⅜-inch polypropylene line tests at about 1,500 to 2,000 pounds. By contrast, ¼-inch polypropylene line has an 800-pound breaking strength—not nearly enough for river use. Heavy-duty ½-inch line is often used by rescue squads because of its increased strength (4,500 pounds), but it's far too bulky for the average boater to carry.

Kernmantle construction, consisting of a braided sheath around a solid fibrous core, is used to construct a stronger rescue rope. Because the sheath absorbs most of the abrasive wear and leaves the core intact, kernmantle ropes last longer. These ropes are generally made with superior quality control and cost two to three times more than a general-purpose line.

Rope strength can be increased by adding other, stronger fibers—a polypropylene core and a nylon sheath, for example. This combination does not float as well as a solid-braid polypropylene, but it offers improved strength and heat resistance at a moderate cost. The breaking strength for a 10-mm nylon/poly line, which is just a bit larger than ⅜ inch, is 3,600 pounds. The nylon sheath, with a melting point of 480°F, helps protect the polypropylene core from heat. This is a good choice for paddlers who are looking for a stronger, more durable product.

Spectra, another rope material, is a high-strength, low-stretch, lightweight fiber that floats. Pure Spectra is extremely strong and expensive: A ¼-inch solid Spectra cord used by rock climbers tests at 4,500 pounds and costs eight times more than a ¼-inch poly. But it is not as buoyant as polypropylene and is far too slippery to hold a knot. For this reason, Spectra water rescue lines are usually made with a polypropylene sheath; a ¼-inch kernmantle rescue line with a polypro sheath and a Spectra core has a breaking strength of 2,000 pounds; a similarly built ⅜-inch line tests out at around 4,500 pounds.

Static versus Dynamic Ropes

A *static rope* supporting a 200-pound weight stretches only 2 to 4 percent, while a *dynamic rope* elongates almost 8 percent. While a Spectra/polypropylene or nylon static rope will stretch only 15 percent before breaking, polypropylene—a dynamic rope—can lengthen by 40 percent or more! Dynamic ropes have some shock-absorbing ability, which may reduce the shock load on both victim and rescuer when recovering swimmers. But since the stretch must be taken out of the line before the pull is fully transferred to the boat, this elasticity can make it difficult to remove a pinned craft. When a dynamic line breaks, a frightening "kickback" results, similar to the snap of a giant elastic band. Static ropes stretch and kick back less, making them better suited to mechanical hauling systems. Spectra lines, however, are more easily damaged by sudden, intense shock loads, such as a fall from a height. This reduces its strength advantage over polypropylene.

Thickness and Length

Throw lines vary in length from 50 to over 75-plus feet. Seventy feet is optimal; it's the longest length of rope that can be thrown by most people. The ideal thickness is ⅜ inch; ½ inch is too bulky, and ¼ inch is hard to hold on to. A breaking strength of about 1,500 pounds (680 kilograms) is the generally accepted minimum for river rescue ropes in the U.S. Lines less than 60 feet long are used in swimming areas or around pleasure boats but lack the reach needed for whitewater. Rafters sometimes use shorter lengths in waist-belt systems to recover swimmers who have fallen out of their boat. This does the job without putting a lot of line in the water. A coiled rope can also be thrown by itself, a skill we discuss later in this chapter.

Rope Care

Anyone who has spent much time with rock climbers knows the care they give their ropes. Paddlers do well to adopt some general guidelines from their example. Store ropes out of direct sunlight and away from extreme heat. Avoid abrasives and chemicals, particularly grease and gasoline. Don't step on the line; this grinds in dirt particles that can sever individual fibers. Inspect ropes for damage such as lumps, depressions, or dirty spots. To wash a rope, place it in a mesh bag and put it in a washing machine. Use clear water or specially formulated rope cleaners. Ropes should be dried before long-term storage and are often retired after three years' use.

Rescue Bags

Rescue bags were developed by the U.S. Navy in World War II for use with lifeboats. Paddlers rediscovered them in the mid-1970s. In a rescue bag, one end of a rope is tied into the bottom of a nylon sack, and the rest is stuffed inside. The rope seldom tangles, remaining ready for immediate use even after months of storage.

You get what you pay for in a rescue bag. The rope is the most expensive component, and a good-quality line is not cheap! First and foremost, check to see that the bag contains the type and length of rope you need. The bag itself must be carefully put together, especially at the seams. A quick-release clip is a plus. Beware of tightly packed rescue bags; plenty of extra room inside makes it easier to restuff in the field. Rescue bags with warning labels that limit their use to recovering swimmers cannot be trusted for boat recovery. Always buy the best quality you can afford.

Over the past decade a number of compact rescue bags have been produced. Some use short lengths of cheap rope and are almost worthless; others are too lightweight to be thrown well. But a small rescue bag with quality line can be worn for quick access. The Parrot Bag, worn on the shoulder of a life vest, is popular with western raft guides. Waist-belt models are beginning to show potential for many boaters. Sometimes kayakers clip a very small bag into a waist belt, underneath the sprayskirt. Normally, a full-size bag is also carried.

Throwing a Rescue Bag

Rescue bags are most commonly thrown underhand (see photos on page 46). Timing, rather than muscle, is required to achieve distance and accuracy. Grab the top of the bag with your throwing hand and withdraw the end of the rope with the other. Concentrate on a smooth, easy arm swing, and never take your eyes off the target. Release the bag as your throwing hand crosses your line of sight. You can learn this skill quickly with just a few practice throws.

Other techniques require more practice. Overhand throws (see photo on page 47) are very powerful and are especially useful when you're sitting in a boat, standing in deep vegetation or waist-deep water, or for short, close-in situations. Sidearm delivery is a compromise technique that adds power but may compromise accuracy. It's most often used when rocks or shrubbery get in the way of an underhand or overhand throw. In every case, smoothness and timing are what count. Practice to achieve good distance and accuracy.

Holding the Rope. The river can pull on a rope with frightful force. Always be prepared to let go of a rope quickly. Never wrap it around your arm. Rope burns or even broken bones may result. Most rescue bags have a small grab loop at the bottom. It's okay to grab the loop with one or two fingers, but don't wear it around your wrist, as this could cause injury. Often you'll need to haul a rope hand over hand. Instead of holding the rope "naturally" with your thumbs away from you, try the *fireman's grip:* grab the rope with your thumbs facing inward. This creates a camming action that prevents the rope from slipping, enabling you to pull harder. To pull for a long time without exhausting yourself, hang on the rope from your shoulders, with arms straight rather than flexed.

Restuffing the Bag. No special coiling or

Figure 4-1. An underhand rescue bag throw.

packing is needed to restuff a rescue bag. Simply push the rope back inside the way it came out, foot by foot. If you are right-handed, hold the bag in your left hand, letting the rope run through your fingers. Your right hand moves up and down inside the bag, pulling the rope into place; the left hand keeps it from sliding backward between pulls. The over-the-shoulder, four-finger *Carlson method* is especially effective with compact rescue bags. Grab the top of the bag between the second and third fingers of each hand, letting the rope pass over your shoulder. The forefinger and thumb of each hand pull the rope into the bag with surprising efficiency. It looks silly but works quite well, especially with smaller bags.

Making a Second Throw. A fast second throw can be useful if you miss the first time. Recover the line by stepping on one end before pulling the rest of the line in, hand over hand, creating a "spaghetti pile" at your feet. When the

Figure 4-2. Setting up for an overhand throw in waist-deep water where an underhand throw wouldn't work.

Figure 4-3. The fireman's grip allows paddlers to pull a rope harder, without slipping.

Figure 4-4. The right way to pull long and hard. Conserving energy for the long pull, the person in front hangs from straight arms, leaning into the person in the rear, who is in turn leaning into a hip belay.

Tragedy on the Clearwater

In 1982 I was with a group of eastern paddlers on a two-week vacation in Idaho. Working our way north, we ended up in the Golden Canyon of the south fork of the Clearwater. We'd heard the run was tough, but our group was experienced and the river ran beside a road, giving us the opportunity to look it over.

At the put-in, we broke up into two parties of three. Chuck was a last-minute starter; he'd been swimming a lot and had lost a boat the previous week. But he wanted to go, and we figured that he was experienced enough to know his limits. Besides, we'd be scouting the drops, and if he got into trouble, we'd just put him out on the road to wait.

Coming to the first major drop, it was clear that we'd committed a classic error: We'd underestimated the scale and drop of the river. We got out to scout. The drop consisted of several steep offset chutes with bad holes in between. I wanted no part of it. In fact, the river looked so nasty below that I wasn't sure I wanted to get back in at all. I was scouting the drop when somebody yelled that Chuck was out of his boat. And he was. Fortunately, I'd brought my rescue bag along, and he squirted out right in front of me, no more than 20 feet away. I was laughing as I tossed the rope.

The toss was right-on. The bag landed in Chuck's hands. I was getting into a belay stance as the rope extended to its full length. Chuck was carried into the next drop and swung into the backwash of a hole. The pull almost cut me in half. I was holding on . . . holding on . . . getting slammed around and wondering why it was taking so long for Chuck to swing to shore. The low angle of the rope to the current, combined with the eddy behind the reversal, kept him from coming in. One of the guys asked, "What can I do?" I didn't know. Nothing like this had ever happened to me before. Finally, we decided that he should grab the rope ahead of me and work his way down the bank, hand over hand, until he could pull Chuck in. It was a good idea, but we ran out of time.

Nowadays rope throwers know enough to meter their line for short throws, and to "vector" the line when someone gets hung up. Swimmers know how to grab the rope, not the bag, then roll onto their back so they can breathe. Chuck didn't. I don't know how Chuck held on as long as he did before he lost consciousness. He was carried some distance downstream and pinned under a tree. CPR was just a formality—Chuck was dead.

Read this chapter so you won't make the same mistakes.

—CW

bag arrives, full of water, throw it. The weight of the water-filled bag pulls most of the rope behind it.

This technique requires flat, even ground. Don't use it if there are sticks or crevices underfoot that could snag the line. Mesh bags won't hold water. Another alternative is to coil the rope using the bare-line technique described next. Hold the bag in your throwing hand or it will knock the coils around and tangle the rope.

Throwing a Coiled Rope

Lifeguards and sailors were adept at tossing a heaving line centuries before rescue bags were developed. Modern braided ropes make it easier, but practice is still required. River guides often prefer coiled lines because recovery time between tosses is reduced and the amount of rope thrown is more easily controlled.

A heaving line should be ⅜ inch in diameter,

Figure 4-5. *The spaghetti pile method of retrieving a line (top) pulls the rope into a loose pile. Note the foot stepping on the end of the line. The water-filled rescue bag, when thrown (bottom), pulls the rest of the line behind it.*

about 70 feet long, and free of knots or loops that could snag between boulders. The use of a "monkey's fist"—a large, bulky knot at one end of the line—is not recommended. It will sink and snag on rocks and debris.

Here's how to make the throw: First, toss the heaving line into the river, allowing it to extend full length in the current. This removes twists and kinks that can tangle the rope and spoil your throw. Then, follow the steps in Figure 4-6.

A heaving line can be recovered quickly. A trained river guide can pull in a rope and throw it a second time within five seconds! This technique can be used to get a fast "second throw" with a throw bag. By coiling the rope into your

Figure 4-6. *(1) Coil half the line on the bottom three fingers of your throwing hand. Lay the coils evenly and neatly next to each other. You may need to twist the rope slightly between your thumb and forefinger to make the coils lie flat; a 70-foot rope should have 10 to 12 coils.*

(2) Coil the rest of the rope over your first finger. Secure the loose end of the rope by stepping on it or by grasping it with two fingers of your nonthrowing hand.

(3) Split the coils, placing roughly half of the coils in your nonthrowing hand. To make this easier, place 4 or 5 coils in your throwing hand, close two fingers around them, then place the remaining the coils on top of them.

throwing hand, it's possible to throw the loops at any time—as they accumulate—cutting setup time even further.

Coiled ropes also let you "meter" the rope so that no extra line is thrown. This minimizes entanglement danger and keeps the victim on a short line for better control. For example, half of 70 feet is 35 feet; if a swimmer is about 10 yards, or 30 feet, away, you need only throw the coils in one hand. Sometimes, if a victim is very close, you'll want to throw only two or three coils, roughly 5 feet each. You can even rescue two floating paddlers close at hand by throwing one set of coils at the first person, the other set at the second, while holding the rope at the center. Maintaining footing and control can be tricky, so only very experienced people should try this!

Recovering a Swimmer

When you throw a line to a swimmer, three things are important: First, you must throw accurately so the swimmer can grab hold. Second, you must be positioned properly to haul a person quickly and safely into shore. Lastly, you must be able to handle the pull on the line.

Think ahead when setting up a throw line. Paddlers who get into trouble when running a drop must leave their boat and reach the surface of the water before they can grab a rope. Position yourself somewhat downstream of where you expect trouble. Try to anticipate what will happen after the rope hits its target. A per-

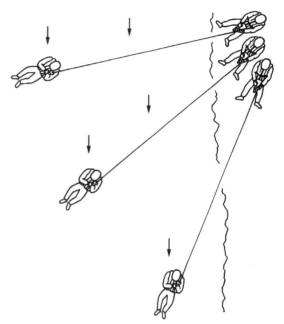

Figure 4-7. A swimmer holding onto a throw line will be swung downstream and into shore by the current.

(4) Throw the coils, pointing the hand that holds the excess rope at the target. When the thrown loops have paid out, the loops in the other hand will be pulled free. Throw as you would a rescue bag: underhand, firm, and smooth. A fast, jerky throw causes the coils to tangle, and the throw will fall short.

(5) The line is on its way.

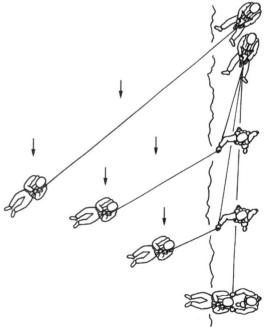

Figure 4-8. Vectoring a throw line (see pages 54–55). A second person assists the line handler by grabbing the line and working, hand over hand, down its length.

son on the end of a line in fast current will swing downstream toward shore in a broad arc. Make certain that this path leads to safety without dragging the victim through nasty rocks, strainers, or holes.

There are differing views about where a thrower should aim. We've heard compelling arguments for deliberately aiming both upstream and downstream of the intended target. Since few of us throw with pinpoint accuracy, the best advice is to aim directly at the person you're trying to help. Try to lay the line across the torso of the floating victim. It's a good attention-getter, and it encourages him to grab the rope as high up as possible. It's a good practice to yell *Rope!* as you throw, but the sound may not carry across the river. Because the swimmer is moving downstream, you'll have to "lead" a bit when you throw. Practice will help you get the feel of it.

When coaching a swimmer or someone on a rescue team, always give positive advice. The phrase *Don't stand up!* could be heard as *Stand up!* over the roar of the river. A command such as *Feet up!* is less likely to be misinterpreted. When using hand signals, always point where you want a swimmer to go rather than toward an obstacle.

As a swimmer, you should know how to catch a throw line. Grab the rope, not the bag. This keeps the distance between you and the thrower as short as possible and makes the rescue easier. If you're holding onto a line in current, you can expect to be pulled underwater as it tightens. Counter this by rolling over onto your back and holding the rope near your shoulder; your body will now plane on the surface so you can breathe.

Don't wrap the rope around your hands or arms. If the pull is harder than expected, you may not be able to let go. Rope burns and even

Figure 4-9. The best way to hold onto a rescue line in current—on your back, with the line passing over one shoulder.

broken bones may result. If your hands are too cold to hold onto the line, tuck the rope under your opposite armpit and press down. This adds friction and reduces the pull on your hands. If you do slide down a rope, the bag at the end acts as a stopper.

Belaying the Line

Pulling in a swimmer puts a lot of stress on the rescuer who is holding the line. Just hanging onto the rope isn't enough: As the pull increases, the rescuer is faced with the unpleasant choice of letting go or being pulled into the water. Since a firm hold is as important as an accurate throw, paddlers have adapted the belaying skills used by mountaineers to enable people of average strength to handle a hard pull. And when setting up to make a throw, check the footing! Slick rocks and steep, unstable shorelines may make standing up a challenge!

A Standing Belay. To *belay*, pass the end of the line behind your back so it rests across your hips. Hold the line on the side opposite the pull in your "belaying hand." For a better hold, increase the friction on the rope by moving the belaying hand deeper between your legs. Use your other hand to keep the line in position across the top of your pelvis. Letting a throw line ride too high can lead to back strain or kidney injury; if it rides too low, it may drop across your legs and pull you over. Brace your feet firmly against the ground, taking full advantage of any footholds.

Belayers must assume this position quickly after a throw. Some prefer to pass the rope behind them before throwing the line; others use the delay between the throw and the arrival of the pull to set up. The pull often comes suddenly, so be careful that the line is positioned correctly.

A Sitting Belay. Here, the belayer sits down with the line running across her hips, bracing

Figure 4-11. A sitting belay. Note how the feet brace off the rock projection.

Figure 4-10. A standing belay with buddy backup. The second person pulls down, not backward, for best results.

her feet against any outcropping or irregularities in the ground. She sits up straight, holding the rope in place while making sure that her body always faces into the pull. Again, the line must not slide high on the back or slip low and underneath her butt.

Belaying on a Bight. When a belay must be set in the middle of a line, don't simply loop the rope around your back. If the pull becomes unmanageable, it's almost impossible to duck under the line. Instead, take a loop (or *bight*) of rope in your hand and pass it behind your back. To release the belay quickly, let go of the loop.

Using Friction Bends. If the pull becomes unbearable, some of the force can be diverted by bending the line around a tree or over the edge of a rock. The resulting friction transfers much of the pull to the object and increases the strength of a belay tremendously. You must be able to release the rope quickly, so don't wrap it or tie it off.

A Buddy Belay. If a belayer is losing control of the line, a second person can assist with a buddy belay. The belayer's buddy provides support by holding on to the shoulders of his life jacket, pulling *down* to offset the tendency of the rope to haul the belayer off his feet. Pulling backward can cause severe back strain or topple the belayer. Holding a line handler around the waist is less effective; the torso can still be pulled forward, causing the belayer to lose his balance.

If the belayer loses his balance, his buddy must be ready. From a standing position, the buddy places one foot between and slightly behind the belayer's feet. If they fall, she can lower him to the ground, easing him into a sitting position if needed. A backup belayer must never let go until the pull is over. The belayer could be sent flying, head over heels and spinning.

Transferring a Belay. It may be necessary for a belayer to pass a line under mild tension to another person. Have the reliever move in front of the sitting belayer, setting up between his legs. The reliever now pulls on the line, gradually reducing the tension. As the pull is reduced, the belayer moves backward, allowing the

Figure 4-12. Belaying on a bight. This method allows someone to secure a line at midlength without risking entanglement.

reliever to ease into the belayer's footholds. Once the reliever is stable, the original belayer slips over the line, passing it forward.

Underwater Belay Stances. Belays in swiftwater don't have to be set up on dry land. Often rocks and ledges with an inch or two of water flowing over them afford excellent footing. If you can't see what's underwater, feel around with your feet and hands. If the water is cold, you don't want to leave someone in this position for too long.

Vectoring the Line

When using a throw line, the angle of the rope to the current decreases as the swimmer

Figure 4-13. Friction bends enable the belayer to transfer most of the pull to a tree, a rock, or other secure object.

approaches and is swung onto shore (Figure 4-7, page 51). This reduces the forces pushing him toward the rescuer, and he may "hang up" on an eddyline or in a hole. The current is now pulling both victim and belayer downstream; the longer the rope, the more likely this is to happen. The added stress may force either the victim or the belayer to lose his grip, in which case the swimmer is pulled underwater and must eventually let go.

To prevent this, a second person can "vector in" a swimmer by grabbing the line near the thrower/belayer and working his way down the rope hand over hand (see Figure 4-8, page 51). This quickly increases the angle of the rope to the current to provide the push needed to pro-

Figure 4-14. Transferring a belay. The reliever sits in front of the belayer (top), assumes the stance, and takes the rope. The belayer then slides the rope under him (bottom), lifts his legs over the rope, and then backs out of the way.

pel a victim to shore. It considerably reduces the strain on the belayer and puts someone near the swimmer, who may need assistance.

If no assistance is available, you can accomplish the same thing by moving down the riverbank, pulling in the line as you go. Or you can move backward, away from the riverbank. Both increase the angle of the rope to the current. Unfortunately, riverside obstructions often limit the practicality of these tactics.

These rope-handling skills are the foundation of other, more advanced rescue techniques that are discussed in later chapters.

CHAPTER 5

Swimming and Line-Based Rescues

T his chapter draws on swimming, wading, and line rescue skills to create techniques that combine these skills. Lines make it possible to cross fast-moving water without a boat, and rescue life vests make possible a number of backup and access techniques.

Line Crossings

A line stretched across a section of swiftwater can be used instead of a paddle to assist waders. Lines can be set in places where the water is too fast for wading and too shallow or congested for a boat.

Stretch a line across the current with belays or anchors at each end. Angle the line downstream, toward your destination, to get a helpful push from the current. The line should not be under tension. If the pull is concentrated at the middle of a tight line, the pressure on the belayer(s) is many times greater than when slack is introduced. Ideally, the "vee" created where the wader holds the rope should be 90°.

Rescuers can wade surprisingly deep, swift sections of river using a line for support. Starting on the downstream side, lean back into the rope. This pushes your feet into the river bottom. Be cautious about foot placement; feel ahead first, then move ahead carefully. If one foot gets caught, use the line to maintain your balance and work free. If you lose your footing, hold onto the rope, let your feet hang, and work hand over hand over to one side. You can use your arms alone to cross current, but this works best over short distances because it is so strenuous.

Another line-crossing technique works better for paddlers with limited upper body

Figure 5-1. Using a line to support aggressive wading in rapids. Note the buddy belay on shore.

strength. Starting on the upstream side of a cross-stream line, hold the line against your upper thighs. The force of the current pushes you against the rope, helping to maintain position. If the water is deeper than crotch level, however, it tends to fold a wader around the line. Be ready to duck under and swim out if necessary.

Zip Lines

A *zip line* facilitates a controlled crossing of water that is too deep or fast for wading. A line is angled across the current, with the direction of travel downstream. A swimmer clips into the line using a webbing loop and carabiner and holds on, letting the river do the work.

The zip line should be set at an angle of 45° to the current. Since the current doesn't always run parallel to the bank, look at the water, not the shore, when setting the angle. The upstream end of the line must be securely anchored. (For information on anchors, see Chapter 6.) Next, pull the line extremely tight, then tie it off to a

Think Fast, Move Faster

In the spring of 1969, my buddy Jim and I had been kayaking Class II and were looking for more excitement. We called our contact at the Penn State Outing Club and got invited on a trip down Loyalsock Creek. This Class III run in north central Pennsylvania is known for its frigid climate and icy water. In addition to our two kayaks, we had four tandem and solo Grumman canoes in our group. Putting in a few minutes behind us was a nationally known group of C-1 racers I'd seen at Penn State's pool sessions.

All went according to plan until we reached S-Turn rapid. I flipped and immediately executed my first river roll in hurtfully cold water. I was whooping and hollering until I was suddenly confronted with a huge pourover. As I went over, I saw that the pourover was created by a pinned Grumman open canoe. One of the Penn State paddlers was caught in the mess. He was struggling for breath and was obviously in desperate trouble.

I eddied out but had no idea what to do. Several other guys were looking at the pin from shore. Suddenly, like the cavalry in a grade B western, three C-boaters paddled around the bend. They paddled into an eddy in a tight cluster. John Sweet grabbed a rope that Rick Rigg lowered from upstream and waded out to the site, followed by Tom Irwin. Sweet shoved his Norse paddle between the boat and the rock and rested it momentarily against his shoulder as Tom held the trapped paddler's head above water. Sweet spoke quietly to Tom, "I'm going to move the boat, and when I say so, I want you to move fast and get him out." He then threw his weight into the paddle, and Tom pulled the victim free. The whole maneuver took less than a minute.

Tom and John, using Rick's rope, pulled the trapped paddler to shore. He was so cold he could hardly walk. They bundled him into the bottom of a canoe and sent Jim and me for help. We got to the road and flagged a car, who took the victim and his rescuers to Forksville, 5 miles downstream. A local person opened up his house to us; someone ran a lukewarm bath while others removed the victim's clothes. We made hot, sugared tea. The victim said he'd been holding onto the back of his boat just as he'd been taught. The boat hit the rock, the current pushed him underneath, and the opening closed. An hour later he was still shivering but was able to get into dry clothes and ride home.

I decided then that if I was going to be a paddler, I'd better learn to make rescues.

—*CW*

Figure 5-2. Here a paddler uses a webbing sling to cross on a zip line.

downstream anchor. If the rope sags as a person crosses, the angle of the rope to the current is gradually eliminated and the person making the crossing tends to stall out in the center. A hauling system is used for tensioning a zip line. (Instructions for setting up hauling systems are found in Chapter 6.)

Once the line is in place, attach a carabiner to a 4- to 6-foot webbing or prusik loop (see the water knot and double fisherman's knot in Appendix A), then clip the loop into the zip line. Face downstream with the rope behind you, lie on your back, and hold the loop on the side opposite the direction you want to travel. This sets your body at an angle to the current, creating a ferry that facilitates the crossing. You can hold the webbing over one shoulder, like a rescue line, or you can stick your elbow or armpit into the loop.

The pressure on a person during a long crossing in fast water can be rather intense. You must be able to let go quickly if the pull becomes unbearable or the crossing stalls out. Downstream backup is advisable in a zip-line crossing. Check to be certain that there is nothing on your life vest that will interfere with the release of the loop; chest-mounted knives and carabiners can be particularly troublesome.

Rescue Life Vests

A paddler's PFD with a built-in, quick-release chest harness is a relatively new innovation,

allowing a rescuer to release himself quickly from a belay line when problems arise. Originally developed in Germany, rescue life vests have gained wide acceptance throughout the paddling world. At twice the cost of a conventional life vest, they're quite expensive. Many recreational paddlers don't really need one; but guides, instructors, and paddlers who attempt extreme whitewater will find them useful.

Ropes work differently on rivers than on land. In mountaineering, it is a common practice to tie a person into a rope for safety. In moving water, this is extremely dangerous. If a person tied into a rope enters the river, the current will pull the line tight. No matter how high or low the line is attached, the water will drag him beneath the surface and hold him there indefinitely. This mechanism is similar to the forces that create a pillow on a midstream rock. As the force of the current builds, water flows over the tethered paddler's head to create a pourover that pushes him down. A person caught in this way is helpless and can easily drown.

The quick-release harness consists of a strap of 2-inch webbing held in place by loops sewn into the PFD itself. A quick-release buckle in the front lets the user out of the harness quickly. When the jacket is put on, the harness is snugly fastened. The method for threading the webbing through the buckle varies depending on the jacket, but in general the webbing passes first through a friction bar, then through a plastic cam-lock buckle. Sometimes the buckle has a ball attached with nylon cord to make the release easier to find. The friction bar takes much of the strain off the buckle, allowing it to work more smoothly. The webbing on a jacket direct from the factory can be too long. For a cleaner release, cut it to a length that exactly fits your needs.

The quick-release harness is used primarily as a belay device to protect rescuers in and out of the water. It's especially useful where footing is poor. This harness is not designed for vertical rescues that involve climbing and lowering. A climber's "sit" harness and chest harness should be used instead.

International paddlesport organizations have set the minimum breaking strength for the components of the "swiftwater rescue chain" at 500 kilograms, or 1,100 pounds. European rescue vests adhere to this standard, as do some— but not all—American vests. If a manufacturer describes a vest as "not intended for strong swimmer rescues," that's a sure sign that it does not meet these requirements.

Some rescue vests have a metal ring in back for attaching a belay rope; others don't. If not, you can clip directly into the webbing with a carabiner. It's important that anyone working with a harness-equipped rescuer know how to attach the rope correctly. Attaching the rope to a webbing loop on the life vest instead of the harness, for example, overrides the quick-release feature. A *self-tether*, made from a short length of elasticized webbing, reaches from the back of the harness to the front of the life vest. A carabiner attached to the front end allows vest users to clip into a safety line themselves.

Many rescue vests feature a quick-release loop on the front of the vest, using a reversed cam-lock buckle. Anything clipped there, such as a tether or cowtail, can be pulled free quickly. If such a loop isn't installed in a jacket, clip the tether directly into the harness webbing itself in front. If the tether becomes snagged, free it by releasing the harness buckle.

Using rescue PFDs effectively requires practice to test and expand the limits of your skills. At a minimum, paddlers should practice swimming in current, with a line attached to the PFD, and releasing the harness when it's under tension. Some potential uses are described below.

Backup Belays on Land

Whether along a riverbank or on a midstream boulder, the places a rescuer must go can be slippery and treacherous. You can hold on to a safety rope, but this occupies your hands and reduces your ability to do the job. Using a rescue PFD, a belayer can stay where the footing is good while the rescuer, securely tied in, can move safely in troublesome terrain with both hands free. Belay techniques are the same as those described in Chapter 4.

Caution: At some point, "belaying" becomes "lowering." If the ground supports most of a rescuer's weight, the rope merely prevents slipping. This is an appropriate use of these jackets. If the *rope* supports most of the rescuer's weight, this is a vertical rescue and a conventional climber's "sit" harness should be used.

Self-Belays

Often the best place to set up a throw line offers poor footing. Using a self-tether, you can clip directly into a secure anchor, such as a length of rope tied around a tree. This way, you can't be dragged into the water, no matter how strong the pull. The quick-release harness lets you disconnect quickly if you need to move beyond the range of the tether.

Backup Belays for Swimmers

It's often easier to swim to an accident site than to approach it by boat. But if you miss your goal and get washed downstream, valuable time and energy will be wasted getting back to shore and returning upstream. A rescue life vest allows a swimmer to be put "on belay"; if she is washed downstream, she can be swung into shore quickly. As with a throw bag, the belayer positions herself so that the tethered swimmer can be swung safely into an eddy. The area downstream should be checked for dangerous rapids, entrapment risks, or other hazards to a tethered swimmer if he or she is released. Be especially wary of anything that could snag the line.

Whether a swimmer wades into the current or uses a swiftwater entry, the line handler must let out enough line to permit freedom of movement but not enough to risk entanglement. He must try to estimate the distance to his objective, placing enough coils in one hand to cover this span. Swimmers may need to modify their strokes to avoid catching a trailing line. A buddy belay or self-belay can also be used to prevent the belayer from being dragged into the water when the pull comes. Full awareness of all these things comes with practice.

Backup Wading

A rescue life vest can also be used to back up waders on long or difficult crossings. If they lose their footing, they can be swung into shore. Plan ahead so you can pull the swimmer into a safe spot.

Active Lowers

A rescuer using a quick-release harness can be lowered downstream to the spot where help is needed. This technique is called an *active lower*. A straight active lower will carry him directly downstream of his belay point. The belayer lets the rope out slowly; the swimmer can reduce the pressure on himself and his belayer substantially by walking on the riverbed. With the support of a belayer's rope, foot entrapment is possible but unlikely.

In strong currents, the pressure on a person being lowered becomes intense. As the current increases, a pillow of water builds up behind the rescuer's head. If the pressure continues to build, the water flows over the head, creating a pourover. An air pocket is formed, but breathing is often difficult due to pressure from the harness. Most people will release long before being pulled far enough underwater to lose the air pocket. Since most harness users (and their belayers) cannot withstand the pressures of even a moderately difficult drop, active lowers should be confined to relatively mild current.

The person being lowered can control the speed of the descent using prearranged hand signals. She should ease into the current, testing its strength. Pulling someone back upstream usually requires more power than the belayer(s) can generate. Instead, the rescuer should swing into a downstream eddy.

If the rescuer appears to be in trouble and the harness doesn't release, the belayer has two

Figure 5-3. A buildup of water behind a tethered swimmer in swift current. Note the air pocket in front of the swimmer's face.

options: He can let go of the rope or cut it. A rope trailing behind a swimmer can become snagged, so either option is a last resort. Cutting the line shortens it and removes knots and other snaggables from the end, but often renders gear useless for the rest of the trip.

A Straight Lower with a Tag Line

Often the objective is not in line with the current, but off to one side. In this case, a *straight lower with a tag line* is called for. A tag line is attached to pull the rescuer to one side or the other. This line does not support the tethered swimmer's weight but merely redirects the lower. It can be set up beforehand or clipped onto a lowering line during a rescue.

A V-Lower

Often there is no convenient lowering point directly upstream of an accident site. The *V-lower* uses two belayers, one on each side of the river,

to lower the rescuer anywhere along its width. Each belayer needs a line long enough to reach 1½ times across the gap between them. The two lines are clipped together with carabiners, and the tethered swimmer clips in at the center using a rescue PFD. He then enters the water and swims out until caught by the rope.

Here are a few reminders. Try to keep the angle between the two lines at 120° or less to reduce the pull on the belayers. Lowering a swimmer is relatively easy; hand signals are used to communicate between the river and shore. The swimmer can be moved to almost any point below. Pulling someone back upstream is quite difficult. Instead, one belayer holds on while the other lets out rope as needed to swing the swimmer into an eddy.

Now that we have the tools to work safely around an accident site, let's move on to the concepts and equipment needed to recover pinned boats.

Figure 5-4. A V-Lower in use. This setup—using one line across the river and a second control line—is less effective than the two-line system.

CHAPTER 6

Recovering Pinned Boats

Pinned boats are much less common now that flotation bags are in wide use, but pinning still happens. Releasing a pin is always challenging. The forces involved are enormous. Even the strongest and best made river craft can be torn apart by a powerful current, and people have been badly injured during recoveries. A successful retrieval requires that rescuers evaluate the situation carefully, making the most of available equipment and personnel while minimizing the possibility of injury.

Types of Pins

Whitewater paddlers will encounter several types of pins. In a *center pin*, the trapped boat is balanced at right angles to the current across an obstacle located near the center of the hull. With an *end-to-end pin*, the hull is caught at both ends and held in place by the current. *Vertical pins* occur when the bow or stern lodges against an obstruction at the bottom of a steep drop. The other end of the hull catches on the bottom or side of the drop, and the boat is held fast. In each of these situations, the force of the current holds the pinned canoe, kayak, or raft firmly in place. Usually, it's necessary to pull the craft upstream in order to dislodge it; however, unless force is applied intelligently, the river will not let go.

Releasing a Center Pin

Center pins are the most common pin (see Figures 6-1 and 6-2). Here, the forces of the current on each end of the boat are roughly, but not exactly, equal. What balances them, keeping the boat pinned, is the friction of the hull

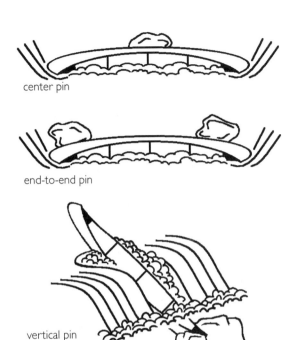

center pin

end-to-end pin

vertical pin

Figure 6-1. Types of pins.

against the rock. If the current is powerful, the hull will be partly or fully wrapped around the obstruction, further increasing the friction.

Pulling against the full force of the current almost never works. To release a center pin, determine which end of the boat is under the least pressure. Sometimes one end is partly out of the water and the other end is buried. In other cases, the current on one side of an obstruction is clearly more powerful than on the other.

Muscle power working on one end can unbalance the pin significantly easier than fighting the full force of the current. Try to lift one end out of the water first; this usually requires less effort than pulling or pushing upstream. If that doesn't work, pull or push one end against the current until the boat pivots free. One way to think about the strategy of unbalancing a center pin is to picture two children playing on a see-saw. If one child is larger and heavier, he has to sit closer to the pivot point to balance out the board. It's easier to lift the lighter child to unbalance the see-saw, allowing the heavier child's weight to

Figure 6-2. A straightforward center pinning of a commercial raft on West Virginia's Cheat River.

pull the other end down. Because of the time required to bring a rope into play, it makes sense to try to "strongarm" the boat loose before attaching a haul line.

Releasing an End-to-End Pin

When a canoe or kayak is caught horizontally against two obstructions (Figure 6-1, page 65), the hull can't pivot free unless one end of the boat is released. This is often a less serious type of pin; but if the current is powerful enough, the boat will be "tacoed," or folded at the center and pushed through the opening. This type of release is hard on a boat! Many end-to-end pins are set at an angle to the current; since this lets some water run off to one side, these are the easiest to work loose. Those caught at right angles to the current are hardest to release, and considerable brute force may be required.

Lifting one end over an obstacle is considerably easier than attempting to pull the boat upstream. Examine both ends to see which one is under less pressure, taking into account which obstacle is lower and thus requires less lift. If the boat lies at a significant angle to the current, it's usually easier to move the upstream end; pulling on the downstream end pushes the boat farther out into the current and creates more resistance.

Rafts are frequently caught in end-to-end pins. In mild conditions, the "rescue" involves little more than moving gear and passengers away from the end that's caught and letting the current push the lightened part of the raft over the obstruction. In more severe examples, members of the crew can attach ropes to the bow or stern and pull one end up and back. Often a raft can be folded through the opening by letting small amounts of air out of the side tubes. In extreme circumstances, a hauling system (discussed later in this chapter) can be set up to run from the bow to the stern or from the affected end to the raft frame. With enough ingenuity, it's possible to fold the boat in half!

Releasing a Vertical Pin

A vertically pinned boat (see Figure 6-1) presents significant safety problems. These pins are often unstable and may involve a trapped victim.

If someone is trapped, immediate action must be taken to stabilize the boat. Vertical pins are a balancing act, much the same as standing on one's head against a wall. Fluctuations in current or a gradual failure in the structural integrity of the boat can cause it to shift or break. Once the boat shifts, the resulting pin is almost always harder to dislodge. For now, we will consider only the mechanics of boat extrication, leaving discussions of entrapment for a later chapter.

Usually, you remove a vertically pinned boat by pulling it back upstream, freeing the bow. This sounds easy enough, but in practice, attaching a rope to the boat requires creativity and a lot of in-water physical activity. If this doesn't work, the stern can be pushed or pulled downstream, flipping the boat end over end. Haul lines are inevitably used in either approach.

Approaching a Pinned Boat

Since all pinned boats are actually strainers, they must be treated with the same respect as a downed tree or log jam. Pins in mild current are surprisingly dangerous because the water accelerates as it passes through the gap between the river bottom and a pinned boat. A few years ago, a student in one of our rescue courses was pulled partway under a pinned boat after approaching from upstream. Her paddling pants were torn and sucked under the canoe like a sea anchor, and she required considerable help to get free.

An approach from downstream, where there's almost always an eddy to aim for, usually makes the most sense. If you're concerned that the boat might work loose, approach it from the side and attach a safety line. An unstable boat may work itself loose, or it may be dislodged with surprisingly little effort.

As you approach, remember that pinned boats are often unstable. Broached boats shift about; they may vibrate in the current, work free on their own, or even break in half. Current surges may cause rocking or bending, which may release the pin without warning. At other times the craft will simply wrap more tightly around the obstruction. Becoming trapped between a pinned boat and a rock can result in serious injury, so follow these simple rules: First, maintain contact with the boat so you won't be

Close Doesn't Count

"Initiation" is the first hard drop on West Virginia's Upper Gauley. Although pretty straightforward, the right side conceals a subtle trap. Paddlers often want to sneak the drop, pulling to the right to avoid a large, suspicious-looking wave at the top. On the right, the river slides over sloping rocks, then drops through a space between two giant boulders. This chasm is about 3 feet wide and 30 feet long. Toward the end of the crack the gap narrows, and a rock about twice the size of a basketball is wedged inside. Boaters who find themselves in the wrong place do a wild back pop-up, then pin, stern-first and vertical, in the crack. Over the years there had been many narrow escapes, but no injuries.

In the fall of '82, a group from a college outdoor club was on the river. Bob, the trip leader, had recently been appointed head of the program. He took the right-hand route and found himself pinned, backward and vertical, the bow pointing straight up.

He was pinned in a spot that was difficult to reach. Henry was the first member of his group to get to a house-size rock on the right. From there he braved the treacherous footing to get near enough to talk. They agreed that Henry would give Bob one end of his throw line and retreat to a dry place where he could belay it. Bob would try to use the line to pull himself out. This seemed to work at first, but at the last minute the boat shifted, dropping deeper into the crack and pulling Bob down with it. He was half in the boat, half out, and in desperate trouble.

By this time Dave, another trip member, had made it onto the rock and agreed to serve as a belayer. Henry grabbed the rope with one hand and waded out. The water was sheeting over Bob's head, forming an air pocket. He could talk, but he couldn't move. Dave grabbed Bob's life jacket with his free hand and pulled with all his might, but Bob wouldn't budge. After Dave became exhausted, he traded places with Henry. Now the boat shifted again, and Bob disappeared into the crack. His life vest snagged on a rock flake and was pulled off his body. It was later recovered undamaged.

A few minutes later Walker and Tomko arrived and mounted the rock. Walker, who had been stationed in Germany, had a European rescue harness—the precursor of today's rescue life vests. He clipped in and, belayed by Tomko, waded into the crack. He attached a second rope to the kayak grab loop. Henry and Dave pulled, and the kayak twisted and sank. They had no choice but to cut it loose. Walker re-entered the crack and probed underwater, but there was no sign of Bob. The water was turned off, and a few hours later Bob's body was found downstream.

Henry and Dave risked their lives to help their friend, but the footing was poor, and holding onto a rope as they worked hurt their effectiveness. Walker and Tomko are an impressive rescue team, and the harness is a great tool. It could have made a difference had they arrived earlier. What if Dave and Henry had been wearing rescue life vests? This equipment was just being developed and could have increased their effectiveness and have been enough to save Bob.

—CW

surprised by a sudden movement. Second, always have a preplanned escape route in case the boat moves toward you. And lastly, be wary of sticking your hands, arms, or legs into gaps between the boat and the rock.

Reacting to a boat that shifts unexpectedly may mean climbing higher on the rock that has it pinned, moving into the eddy behind the obstruction, or simply swimming away from it. Decide on your safest course of action before a problem arises: a rock with slippery sides may be difficult to climb onto and the eddy behind an obstruction may not be large or shallow enough to provide a safe haven. Swimming, of course, presents problems of its own.

Most people don't consider swimming an escape method, but it is. On entering the current, you'll be pushed downstream at roughly the same rate as a free-floating boat. Swimming aggressively across the current will quickly move you out of the path of the boat. If the boat should catch up with you, push off with your legs and keep on stroking. Try to stay to one side of the derelict's route through a rapid. The worst place to be is downstream, between a swamped boat and potential pinning spots. But, upstream and in line with the boat is a poor second choice, because the boat may repin and create a dangerous strainer.

After deciding on an escape route, it's imperative to know when to leave. Keeping contact with a pinned boat is vitally important. This may mean eye contact, or a hand or thigh resting against the hull. It's also important to have a fixed point of reference, such as contact with the rock or river bottom, to warn you of any movement. Try to develop a constant awareness of the pinned boat—an awareness keen enough to cut through the mechanics of whatever you're doing and to register danger.

Armstrong Releases

When unpinning boats, always try the simplest and least complex methods first. Sheer muscle power, properly applied, is usually enough. This may require the efforts of one paddler or sev-

eral paddlers working together. Avoid lifting in positions that can lead to back injury. When lifting, keep your back straight and lift using your legs rather than bending over and using your arms. Sitting with your back against the obstruction and pushing out with your legs, which contain the strongest muscles in your body, is very effective.

Working against the full force of current is ineffective and exhausting. Try instead to make the current your ally. Lift one end of a pinned boat, for example, before pulling or pushing one end upstream. Pushing down on the top edge of a pinned boat can sometimes roll it free, releasing water trapped inside so that the hull is lighter and easier to move. When working with open canoes, try not to pull on the gunwales in a way that flattens the midsection of the craft. This will break or bend the gunwale, allowing the boat to fold.

If a boat cannot be recovered quickly, try to develop a complete picture of how it is being held in place before continuing. Rocks or debris hidden beneath the hull, for example, may prevent the boat from rotating or pivoting in the desired direction. Feel around under the boat, in front of the boat, then push and pull on the hull to see which way it will most easily move.

Attaching Haul Lines

Sometimes a *haul line* must be used to apply the additional force needed to release a pin. This creates potential safety hazards for rescuers and others who may be out on the water. Ropes should be used only when absolutely necessary, and rescuers must see that proper precautions are taken.

Let's go over a few of these steps. A haul line under tension is like a rigid steel cable; a rope stretched across a river is a clear hazard to navigation. Upstream river traffic must be warned, redirected, or stopped to prevent others from blundering into it. This is vital on heavily used streams, though much less of an issue in remote areas. Whenever enough people are available, downstream safety backup is a good idea, especially when the consequences of a swim are more serious than an unpleasant dip in cold water.

Once you determine in which direction a boat will move once released, a control line should be attached to the upstream end. This keeps a freed boat from floating downstream and pinning again. If the haul line is already attached there, a second control line won't be necessary.

Ropes can be attached to the extreme ends of whitewater kayaks and canoes using a grab loop or painter. With rafts and open canoes, other points may be used. While thwarts, grab loops, or D-rings are convenient, they may not be able to withstand the forces involved in an extraction. With rigid-hulled boats, wrapping the rope around the entire boat two or three times transfers most of the force of the pull to the hull. This reduces the actual load at the attachment points and minimizes the damage that may occur during a rescue. Multiple-point load-distributing anchor systems are used when the strength of the attachment points are in doubt. These are described later in this chapter.

Wrapping for Rotation

Rescuers pulling on a pinned boat should harness the strength of the current. A canoe or raft can be wrapped with a haul line so that it rotates as force is applied, reducing the effort required. To understand why this works, imagine what happens to the hull from the moment of contact to the moment it finally becomes pinned. Although the craft is initially upright, the force of the water will catch the upstream side, pushing the upstream tube, gunwale, or edge down. Then the boat rolls flat against an obstacle and wraps.

Trying to pull the lower gunwale back up to the surface means working against the current. But if you encourage the rolling motion of the boat by pushing the top edge upstream, three things happen. First, the top side of the boat, now partially exposed, moves more easily against the current because less water is pushing against it. Second, the rolling motion dumps water out of the boat, reducing its weight. Lastly, any air

caught inside the craft during the roll helps to keep it on the surface.

Here's how to wrap for rotation. First wrap the rope over the upper gunwale and down the hull on the downstream side. Flip the line under the end of the boat so it now passes upstream under the lower gunwale. The rope should now run from where you will be pulling over the top gunwale, downstream and down the hull, upstream and under the boat, and finally be secured to a thwart. Open canoes respond best to this technique. A raft can be turned widthwise by attaching a rope to the downstream tube and pulling it over. Releasing some air from the thwarts allows the lower tube to work upward and may unbalance the pin. Decked canoes and kayaks dump little water when rolled because of their small cockpits, and are hard to get a grip on because of their smooth shape.

The Steve Thomas Rope Trick

Sometimes rock or debris in contact with the hull prevents the rope from sliding into position under the craft. And not infrequently the end of the boat is inaccessible. In these situations, you must wrap the rope under and upstream around the hull. The rope must be wrapped in the correct direction, which presents a problem because the current passing under the boat runs the "wrong" way.

Steve Thomas, of Hopewell, Virginia, popularized a useful technique many years ago that solves this problem. The Steve Thomas Rope Trick seems complex but is fairly easy if you remember a few pointers:

- Start with the free end of the rope instead of the bag end. You can do this by throwing a rope from the boat to shore.
- Now, take the free end of the rope and push it under the boat from the upstream side. This starts the wrap around the pinned craft, but in the wrong direction.
- Next, make a loop around the boat by tying the free end to the line extending from

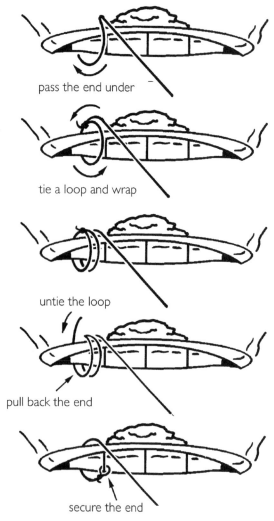

pass the end under

tie a loop and wrap

untie the loop

pull back the end

secure the end

Figure 6-3. The Steve Thomas Rope Trick. As the line is pulled, the boat rotates, dumping water.

shore. You can now pull the end of the rope around the boat in whichever direction you choose.

- The point at which the rope is connected to a canoe is important. You'll need to be as near to one end as conditions allow. When the rope is attached near one end, only that end is pulled upstream. If the line is connected too close to the obstruction, the pinned boat can't pivot and you must pull the entire hull upstream.

- Most people have a problem remembering which direction to pull the loop around the boat. A memory trick from our rescue classes seems to help. Remember that "paddlers always need MORE ROPE!" If you rotate the loop around the boat in one direction, you end up with one piece of rope running through your hands. Rotating the loop in the other direction puts two pieces of rope in your hands. "Paddlers always need MORE ROPE," so pull in the direction that gives you the two pieces of rope. If enough rope is available, make three or four wraps by continuing to rotate the loop around the boat.

- Once the wraps have been made, untie the loop. You now have the free end of the rope on the downstream side of the boat, and a bend of rope in your hand on the other. At this point you need to drop either the bend or the end, so once again remember: "Paddlers always need MORE ROPE!" Keep the bend because that gives you two segments of rope rather than one. Drop the free end and pull it under the boat and upstream by pulling on the bight.

- Attach the rope end to the upper end of a thwart and then slide it underwater to the lower end. Take out the slack in the loops around the canoe, and carefully dress the wraps around the boat so that the lines do not cross.

If enough wraps have been made (usually three or four), the friction of the rope across the hull absorbs most of the pull. Very little stress is actually placed on the attachment point. This can be demonstrated (in practice only) by leaving the end untied. Have someone pull on the rope. If the rope slips at all, it takes only two fingers' pressure to hold the end in place.

The Angle of Pull

Once the line has been secured to the hull, find the best spot from which to haul on the rope.

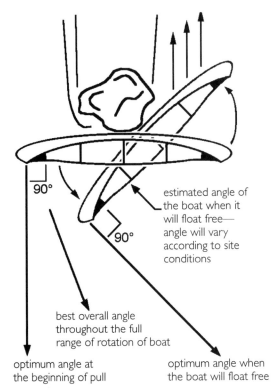

90°

90°

estimated angle of
the boat when it
will float free—
angle will vary
according to site
conditions

best overall angle
throughout the full
range of rotation of boat

optimum angle at
the beginning of pull

optimum angle when
the boat will float free

Figure 6-4. The optimum angle of pull changes as the boat is pulled free; this illustration shows how to estimate the most efficient location from which to pull. Lacking convenient rocks and shoreline, most rescues require settling for a 45° angle to the current.

In most cases where mechanical advantage is unable to dislodge a pinned boat, the real culprit is an ineffective angle of pull. Pulling at a right angle to the length of the craft is optimal. Unfortunately, river rocks and shorelines seldom cooperate, and as the boat pivots, the angle changes. The solution is to estimate what position the boat will be in when it finally comes loose, then choose an angle of pull that will be at a right angle to the boat midway through the extraction. In a center pin, this usually means pulling diagonally across the river at a 45° angle, modified as needed to suit the terrain.

Anchor Points

Once the decision has been made to set up a mechanical advantage hauling system, reliable anchors must be located. Along the East Coast and in the Pacific Northwest, large trees are available, but even in these lush climates, they don't always grow exactly where they're needed. Finding other anchors depends on the rigger's ability to locate rocks, bushes, and surface irregularities capable of supporting the load. In areas with little plant growth or an unfavorable geology, one anchor may not support the full load by itself. A good rigger knows many different types of anchors and can set up multiple points if needed.

The simplest and strongest method of securing one end of a rope is the *tensionless wrap*, also called a *no-knot*. One end of the rope is wrapped several times around a tree, post, or other similar object. To develop enough friction to support the load, a minimum of three wraps is required. As the circumference of the anchor decreases, more wraps are needed. Take care to ensure that the wraps are properly dressed so they do not cross. The free end of the rope can be thrown over or loosely attached to the line under tension. Leave enough slack to allow the line to change its angle freely.

Figure 6-5. A tensionless wrap, also called a no-knot. In a real rescue, the free end must be fastened loosely with a knot or carabiner.

The no-knot has a number of advantages. The load is distributed evenly in the first few wraps, eliminating the reduction in breaking strength created by other knots. Since the free end of the rope remains slack, the system can still be released under full load. Lastly, it is easy to visually monitor a no-knot: if the length of the free end of the rope begins to shorten, the knot is slipping.

When tying into trees or shrubs, attach the rope as low as possible to minimize pressure on the roots. A 100-pound load on an anchor attached to a tree 1 foot from the ground exerts 100 foot-pounds of leverage on the roots (100 lb. x 1 ft. = 100 ft./lb.). If the same anchor point is set 10 feet from the ground, the force is multiplied to 1,000 foot-pounds (100 lb. x 10 ft. = 1,000 ft./lb.). Tree roots are as much a part of an anchor system as the webbing and carabiners, and it's not unheard of for a hauling system to move large rocks or topple sizable trees! This applies to any object used as an anchor: always minimize the stress to the anchor wherever practical.

Abrasion protection for a rope is simple but easily forgotten. Sharp-edged, rough rock or even rough tree bark can rapidly damage rope or webbing. Canvas rope pads are excellent protection, but an old shirt or knapsack is often enough. Although most problems occur at the anchor end, check for sharp edges on the pinned boat as well.

Choosing Webbing for Anchors

Why do people choose webbing for anchors? Because flat tubular webbing is stronger than rope, even if the actual breaking strength is identical. Here's why: When a rope is bent around a small object, the inside radius of the bend has a shorter circumference than the outside radius. The outer half of the rope stretches, carrying most of the load, while the inner half bunches up and contributes almost nothing. To avoid a significant loss of strength, anything that a rope is wrapped around must be at least four times the rope's diameter.

Webbing is much thinner than rope. Ordi-

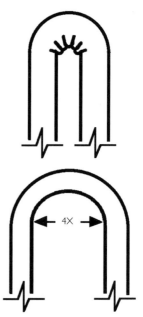

Figure 6-6. Crimping at the center of a tight bend allows most of the pull to be transferred to the outer half of the rope. A bend at least four times the width of the rope prevents this. Pulleys are an effective way to do this.

nary 1-inch tubular webbing holds about 4,000 pounds, withstands abrasion well, and costs very little. When wrapped around a small object like a carabiner, there's much less difference between its inside and outside lengths on a bend. Using the same 4-to-1 rule for bends, a piece of ⅛-inch-thick webbing can be wrapped around an object with a diameter as small as ½ inch without losing strength. By comparison, a ⅜-inch rope would require an object about 1½ inches in diameter.

Attaching Slings

A *webbing loop* is made by tying both ends of the webbing together with a water knot (see Appendix A). It's then wrapped around a tree or another object by fastening the ends together with a carabiner. If equipment is short or a webbing loop will not reach, wrap a single length of line around the object and tie the two ends together.

Webbing that is looped around an object

Figure 6-7. The wrong and right ways to set anchors: In the photo above, the top anchor system is too short, which stresses the webbing excessively. The bottom system shows an anchor of the proper length. In the photo below, a girth hitch (bottom) keeps the anchor from sliding down the trunk but concentrates stress on the tight bend in the webbing. An "inside and outside loop" (top) holds the webbing in place without concentrating stress.

will be pulled into a teardrop shape when a load is applied. The angle at the apex of the loop determines the ultimate load on the anchor; this should be kept less than 90° to minimize rope stress. As the angle approaches 180°, a powerful vector pull is created. This will multiply the force and snap the webbing when a strong pull is applied. When setting the loop, place the water knot so that it does not come in contact with the carabiner even if the angle of pull changes. If the carabiner rides against a knot, stress concentrates at that point and may cause the webbing to break.

A *girth hitch* has been used in the past to attach a web loop around a tree or a shrub. First, the webbing is tied into a loop using a water knot. Next, the loop is wrapped around the object, and one end is passed through the bight formed by the other end.

While a girth hitch will secure an anchor at a desired position, it has a few significant drawbacks. First, on large-diameter objects, the angle where the one end of the loop passes through the other multiplies the stresses on webbing. This mechanical advantage, known as "pulling at a vector," is discussed later. Second, when the direction of pull changes, you not only create a "webbing-against-webbing" sawing action but you also concentrate the stresses where the loop bends back on itself. Either of these stresses may lead to a failure of the anchor.

An *inside loop* keeps a webbing anchor from sliding down a tree trunk without the disadvantages of a girth hitch. A length of webbing is wrapped around the anchor point twice, then the ends are joined using a water knot. The rope is clipped into the longer outside loop with a carabiner, while the inside loop is pulled snugly around the tree. The inside loop holds the anchor at the desired height, even if there is no load on the system. The carabiner slides freely on the webbing, distributing the load smoothly regardless of changes in the angle of pull.

Each of these methods depends upon being able to wrap a rope or webbing around an object. That's fine if a tree, post, large rock, or vehicle frame is available. If such objects are not available, other types of anchors must be used.

Rocks as Anchors

Rock projections, cracks, and openings between rocks make excellent anchor points. Climbers routinely use these features to set protection, and opportunities abound on whitewater rivers for finding potential anchors that are closer and more convenient than trees and shrubs. Locating these anchors is an art that gets easier with practice. After a bit of training, most boaters can locate bomb-proof spots quickly.

Horns

If you're lucky, you'll be able to hook a loop of webbing over a point of rock to anchor your system. The size of these "horns" is limited only by the strength of the rock and the size of the loop. In hard rock like granite, you can depend on surprisingly small protrusions; in softer material, you may have to make a large loop from rope and throw it over a huge boulder. Check the anchor by pulling back hard on the webbing. Any undercut faces should be opposite the direction of pull. Be sure that the anchor will work if the direction of pull changes.

Wraps

You can loop webbing around the junction of two large boulders. This often requires removing debris from between the rocks, but this can usually be done rather quickly. Wraps can also be used around trees and branches wedged among the rocks. As with all anchors, there's no rule that an anchor has to be high and dry. Look under the water as well as above it.

Cracks and Chocks

You can use cracks between rocks as anchors by passing a loop of webbing through a crack and wrapping it with a girth hitch around a *chock* (a rock that is too large to be pulled back through the crack). The chock is set so that pulling wedges it tighter and tighter into the crack. Avoid using soft or brittle stones as chocks for

Figure 6-8. Types of anchors: (1) A rock used as a chock.

(2) A horn.

(3) Webbing wrapped around the spot where two rocks join.

(4) A knot used as a chock in a narrow crack.

obvious reasons; most rocks work fine. Commercially manufactured chocks, or nuts, are made in many sizes and shapes for rock climbers; they're useful but not really necessary. A large knot in rope or webbing works as a chock in very narrow cracks. Check the placement carefully to be sure that changing angles of pull will not dislodge the chock.

Always test any anchor before using it by pulling back and jerking on it with all your might.

Multi-Point Anchors

Whether you're unpinning a canoe on a desert river where a few half-dead bushes are your only anchors or pulling on a badly pinned raft when you're pretty sure that a single D-ring won't hold, the time will come when a single anchor point is clearly not strong enough. When avail-

able anchors are questionable, several of them combined may make a safe, bomb-proof attachment. The trick is to set up multi-point anchors so that the load is evenly distributed over all the points, even if the direction of pull changes. If one anchor fails, the haul line will remain attached.

Two-Point Anchors

Let's start with a *two-point load-distributing system.* Two anchors can be tied into the end of a rope to share the load when pulled at the correct angle. But when the direction of pull changes, as it will when you're unpinning a boat, one anchor will go slack while the other carries the load. If a web sling is attached to two anchors and the haul line is connected to the webbing with a carabiner so that the 'biner can slide back and forth, this allows both anchors to support the load. This creates a so-called *self-equalizing system.* But thanks to friction, no setup is 100 percent effective. A more accurate term is *load-distributing*, which doesn't imply that each point carries an exactly equal share of the load.

This system distributes the load between two points, but there's another problem that must be solved. If one point fails, will the remaining anchor hold the load? The system described above will not. The carabiner that attaches the rope to the web sling is outside the loop and will slip off the end if one anchor fails. To overcome this, we must clip the carabiner *into* the web sling rather than around it. Twisting the web loop into a figure eight connects each anchor point to one loop on each side. Clipping the carabiner across the center of the eight (Figure 6-9) puts it inside the loop. If one point fails, the slack is taken up and the load is transferred to the other anchor.

Think about how far the system will slip if

form a figure 8

clip carabiner
through both loops

connect carabiner to rope

Figure 6-9. A two-point load-distributing anchor.

one of the anchors fails. The farther it can travel before the slack is taken up, the greater the shock load. The principle of *shock loading* can be demonstrated by holding a 1-pound can of vegetables 1 inch above a bare foot and dropping it. The discomfort is minimal. But if the same can is dropped from 5 feet, the effect is quite painful. In the same way, shock loading multiplies the stress when anchors fail. To reduce these effects, keep a load-distributing system as small as possible without affecting its ability to accommodate a changing direction of pull. This is best accomplished by using anchor points in close proximity.

We must also consider the angle formed where the haul line attaches to the sling. An optimum angle is well below 90° (Figure 6-10, page 78). At 45°, the load at each point of a two-point system is reduced to slightly more than half the full load. As the angle increases above 90°, stress increases. At 120°, both anchor points are effectively supporting the full amount of the load, defeating the purpose of a two-point anchor!

Three-Point Anchors

Several methods may be used to build a load-distributing multi-point anchor system. While there is no preferred method, try to minimize friction in any setup. The more force that is required to adjust to a change of direction, the more unevenly the load is shared. Individual anchors should be close together so that the angle at the apex, or collection point, of the system is under 90°. Care must also be taken to design a system that will maintain its integrity if one anchor fails.

One type of multi-point system uses a double-eyed figure-eight knot tied with one small and one very large loop (see Appendix A). The large loop is clipped into carabiners at each anchor point, then the sections of the loop that fall between anchors are drawn back and fastened to the small loop with two additional 'biners (Figure 6-11, page 79). This method works best with a long length of rope or webbing.

Another method employs a large web loop. This is first connected to all the anchor points

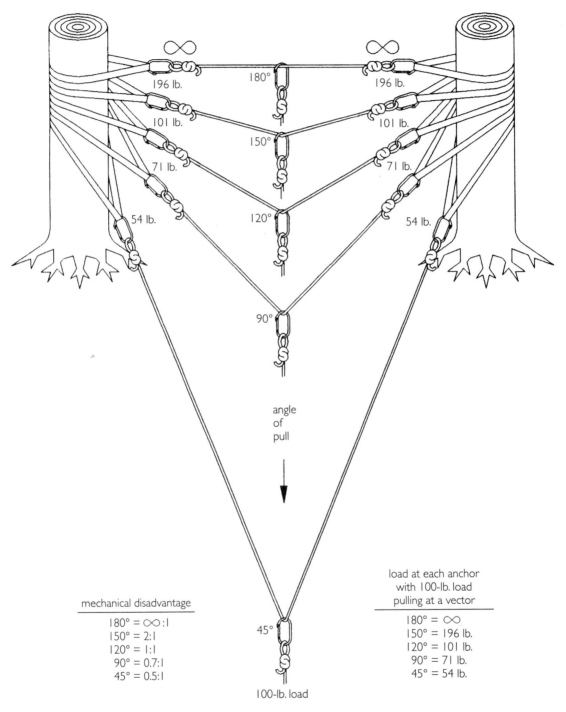

180°

196 lb.   180°   196 lb.

101 lb.   150°   101 lb.

71 lb.   71 lb.

54 lb.   120°   54 lb.

90°

angle
of
pull

mechanical disadvantage		load at each anchor with 100-lb. load pulling at a vector
180° = ∞ :1	45°	180° = ∞
150° = 2:1		150° = 196 lb.
120° = 1:1		120° = 101 lb.
90° = 0.7:1		90° = 71 lb.
45° = 0.5:1		45° = 54 lb.

100-lb. load

Figure 6-10. The leverage created by a vector pull is greatest when a line stretched between two points is under tension. To reduce the strain on the rope and anchors, increase the slack in the line until the bend in the rope is 90° or less.

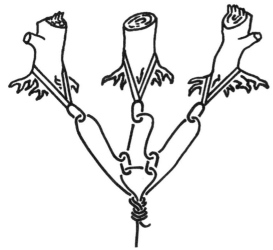

Figure 6-11. Here a double-eyed figure 8 with unequal loops is used to build a three-point load-distributing anchor system.

(Figure 6-12). Another carabiner clips into the large loop and the rope to hold the entire system together; no matter which anchor may fail, the rope stays attached to the anchor that remains intact. Then the sections of webbing between each anchor point are drawn back to the loop at the end of the rope and connected, using a separate carabiner for each.

The final failure protection supplied by the carabiner clipped from the rope directly into the large web loop can also be provided by twisting a loop in one of the segments of webbing between the anchors as you draw them back and clip them to the loop in the end of the rope. This eliminates the need for one carabiner but also introduces additional friction into the system.

Mechanical Advantage Systems

When you can't generate enough force through muscle power alone, mechanical advantage systems become necessary. This can be as simple as a canoe livery employee prying a boat off a rock with a length of pipe, or as complex as a technical rope system employing pulleys and camming devices. Whatever system you choose, always move from low- to high-tech methods.

Systems can and do fail, and more complex systems present more opportunities for mistakes. A good understanding of the forces at work and the strengths of the individual pieces of any hauling system will help you avoid these pitfalls.

The tools used for rope systems include rope, webbing, pulleys, carabiners, and prusik loops. Each component will be subjected to forces far greater than the load you will require them to move. All of the equipment should be of "rescue quality" and maintained as such. The International Canoe Federation (ICF) standard, used in Europe, specifies that all components must have a minimum breaking strength of 500 kilograms (1,100 pounds). Whatever your stan-

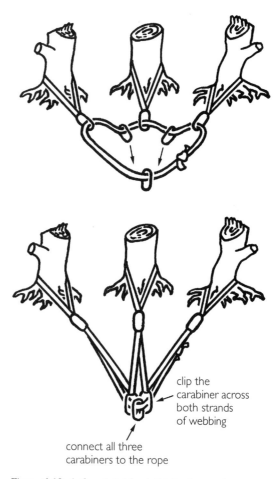

clip the carabiner across both strands of webbing

connect all three carabiners to the rope

Figure 6-12. A three-point load-distributing anchor.

dard, each setup is only as strong as its weakest component.

When selecting rope, the stretch of the line is as important as its strength. Dynamic ropes typically stretch as much as 45 percent at failure, while a static rope stretches 20 percent or less. The elasticity must be taken up in a mechanical rope system before the load can be moved, increasing the length of the pull enormously. As the rope stretches, it also stores significant amounts of energy. When a 70-foot rope is stretched an additional 20 to 30 percent of its original length and suddenly breaks, the rope and anything connected to it is sent flying toward both ends with considerable force.

The Vector Pull

A *vector pull* (a perpendicular pull on the center of a tensioned line) is the simplest form of mechanical advantage. The force developed is quite impressive, but the length of the pull is extremely limited.

In setting up a vector pull, the most common mistake is failing to anchor both ends of the line securely. Any hauling system will move that end of the line offering the least resistance. Imagine a line with one end attached to a boat and the other end belayed by members of your group. If their effort is not enough to move the boat, their belay offers the least resistance, and the vector pull will unseat the belayers. If the line is tied to a large tree instead, the boat will move before the tree does.

The amount of leverage depends on the angle of the line being pulled. In the beginning, the line is straight, with a 180° angle between the two ends. At 180°, the mechanical advantage of a vector pull is almost infinite; no matter how tight a rope or cable is pulled, it can always be flexed by pulling perpendicular to it in the center.

But this mechanical advantage quickly drops (Figure 6-10, page 78). If you stretch a 50-foot line between two points and apply a vector pull at its center, the average mechanical advantage is 114.5:1 over the first 2⅝ inches of perpendicular pull. Between 2⅝ and 5¼ inches of pull, the average mechanical advantage is 38.2:1;

between 5¼ and 7⅞ inches, it drops to 22.9:1. Because the actual movement at the end of the line is much less than the perpendicular pull, it won't move an object more than a small distance. But this extra pull may be what's needed to release a pinned craft. If your group has pulled on a rope all they can, tie the loose end of the rope off. Then use the vector pull as a last-ditch effort to free the boat before setting up a hauling system.

Hauling Systems

The hauling systems used to unpin boats are direct descendants of those used for raising and lowering in mountain rescue. They allow paddlers to use a few lightweight, compact tools to construct a rig with a significant mechanical advantage, making it possible to apply far more force to a pinned boat than could be generated by muscle power alone.

The C-Rig

The least complicated hauling system is the simple 2:1 or *C-rig*. To construct it, attach one end of a line to an anchor point, passing it through a carabiner or pulley attached to (and moving with) the load, and then bring it back to a point roughly in line with the anchor point. The *traveling pulley* is vital to the system. Pulling on the free end shortens the line on both sides of the pulley, creating a 2:1 mechanical advantage. When the line is pulled 2 feet, the pinned boat moves 1 foot.

If a stationary carabiner or pulley is mounted at the anchor point and the pull comes from the pinned boat, there is no mechanical advantage. A fixed pulley creates only a change of direction and does not assist in moving the load.

While a C-rig is simple and easy to remember, it requires enough line to extend from an anchor point to a pinned boat and back again. This is not practical in most river situations.

The Z-Rig

The most widely used hauling system today is the 3:1 *Z-rig* (often called a *Z-drag*). The Z-rig is

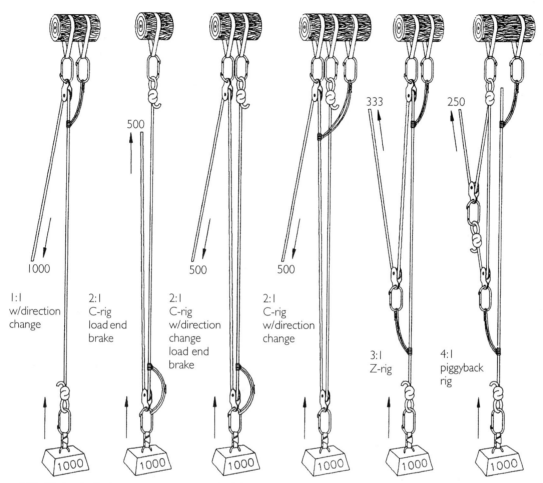

500

1000

1000

500

500

333

250

1:1	2:1	2:1	2:1		
w/direction	C-rig	C-rig	C-rig	3:1	4:1
change	load end	w/direction	w/direction	Z-rig	piggyback
	brake	change	change		rig
		load end			
		brake			

1000 1000 1000 1000 1000 1000

Figure 6-13. Mechanical advantage systems. Note the difference between the change of direction, which confers no mechanical advantage, and the 2:1 C-rig, which does. Pulleys reduce friction and make these systems run smoother, but these setups run almost as well if the rope passes through carabiners.

easy to set up if you start by laying the line out on the ground in the shape of a "Z." Add a carabiner at each of the two bends of the "Z." By connecting the anchor to the closest 'biner, a fixed pulley is established. This creates the change of direction needed to run the line back out to the other point of the "Z." Next, use a *prusik knot* (see Appendix A) to connect a prusik loop to the section of line running from the fixed pulley to the load. Connect the remaining carabiner to the prusik loop to establish the traveling pulley.

When you pull the free end of the line, you shorten the line segment between the load and the fixed pulley, between the fixed pulley and the traveling pulley, and between the traveling pulley and you. Thus, if the free end of the line is pulled 3 feet, that pull is divided equally among the three line segments; the main line moves 1 foot, yielding a 3:1 mechanical advantage.

A *brake prusik* is attached to the haul line between the fixed pulley and the traveling pulley and fastened to an anchor. This gives the Z-rig a ratcheting effect, holding the load while the system is reset. As you pull in the line, the traveling pulley moves closer to the anchor point. When you can pull it in no farther, back off and let the brake prusik take the load. Now the prusik connected to the traveling pulley can be pushed into position again, and the process is repeated.

The Piggyback Rig

The 4:1 *piggyback rig* incorporates positive features from both the 2:1 and the 3:1 in a versatile, easy-to-use system. It has two main advantages: It provides 25 percent more mechanical advantage than a Z-rig, and it sets up with a second line, separate from the main haul line. This is helpful if you have just enough rope to reach the shore but not enough to set up a Z-rig. In complex rescues in which multiple lines may need to be tensioned, a piggyback rig can be removed from the first line and reconnected to a pull on a second one.

Constructing a 4:1 piggyback rig is straight-forward. First, attach a prusik to the haul line as far as possible from the anchor point, and attach a carabiner or pulley. This creates the traveling pulley. Using a rope with a figure-eight loop at one end, run the line through the traveling pulley and leave the loop end next to it. Now, run the other end of the line back to the anchor point, tie a loop in the line using a figure eight on a bight (see Appendix A), and fasten it. Next, connect another carabiner or pulley to the loop hanging out of the traveling pulley. Take the free end of the line from the knot that forms the anchor loop and run it through the second pulley. You have just created two 2:1 C-rig systems, one pulling on the free end of the other.

As with a Z-rig, a brake prusik can be set on the haul line behind the traveling prusik, or the haul line can simply be tied off.

Figure 6-14. Setting up a piggyback rig on a throw rope that barely reaches shore. Note the use of a weighted rescue bag to deflect the rope in case of a kickback. As pressure is applied, those pulling can crouch behind the rock being used as an anchor.

The Limits of Hauling Systems

As with a 4:1 piggyback rig, you can combine various systems, one added to another, to increase the mechanical advantage. But you'll seldom require more than a 4:1 system to recover boats because you reach a point of diminishing returns quickly. Usually, you get the best results by changing the point of attachment or angle of pull, not by increasing the mechanical advantage. The limitations of more complex systems are listed below.

First, more complex systems require many resources. To move a load 4 feet, a 2:1 system requires a pull of 8 feet, a 3:1 system requires a pull of 12 feet, and a 4:1 system requires a pull of 16 feet. More pulleys, prusiks, and other tools are also required. This can quickly deplete the inventory of a typical paddling group.

Second, prusik knots have limited holding capacity. Tests done on dry ½-inch nylon static line show that a prusik knot slips between 900 and 1,200 pounds. With the reduced gripping surface offered by ⅜-inch line, a prusik knot's hold on a throw rope will be weaker. This slippage provides a built-in safety check: when a prusik knot slips, you are nearing the working limits of the lines and should try another method before something breaks.

Lastly, although reducing friction is not critical in most canoe and kayak rescues, its importance increases with system complexity. There are several ways to minimize friction and thereby increase the pull. Hauling systems should be set up so they do not twist, and places where ropes rub together should be reworked to reduce friction. This fine-tuning also becomes more difficult as system complexity increases. Most paddlers use carabiners to create the "pulleys" needed in hauling systems. Attaching rescue-quality pulleys with machined bushings or bearings to the carabiners and running the rope through them reduces friction significantly.

Safety Precautions

When more than two people are pulling on the line, they must prepare for the possibility of kickback before the rope breaks. The first technique for protecting yourself is easy. If you're pulling from behind your anchor, you may be able to duck behind it. Second, don't look down the line to the pinned boat; have someone off to one side check your progress.

A weight hung on the line can absorb considerable energy and redirect the kickback. The heavier the weight, the more force it can handle. Rescue bags, dry bags, or canteens all work well. To properly weight a haul line, consider first where the line is most likely to break. Ropes that have not been well cared for may separate anywhere, but in most cases the weakest points are the knots and the points where the rope is connected to the boat. The weight must be placed more than half the distance between the rescue team and the suspected weakest point, but this may not be possible if the pinned boat is some distance away. Do the best you can. Suspend the item from a prusik loop so it can be pushed back out with a paddle as the rope is pulled in.

We don't recommend using a life vest as a weight. In stressful situations, rescuers often forget that they have loaned out their PFDs. They may then slip, get pulled into the water by throw ropes, or jump into the water on their own, not remembering that their PFD is hanging on a line. Taking off a life vest at a rescue site is foolish. Furthermore, everyone should wear a helmet and PFD when hauling on a line; they offer protection from flying debris and prevent bumps and bruises from falls.

The last technique is to change the direction of the haul line so that the team is out of the way. Should the rope fail, rope and gear will be fired toward the pulley and anchor, not at the hauling team. If a Z-rig is pulled out of shape, however, it won't work well. For maximum efficiency, the change of direction must be set up exactly in line with the hauling system. Often it's difficult to position an anchor so that the rope can be redirected without pulling the system out of line. The best way to do this is to set a second anchor off to one side, then run a line through it with a carabiner at one end. Adjust the second

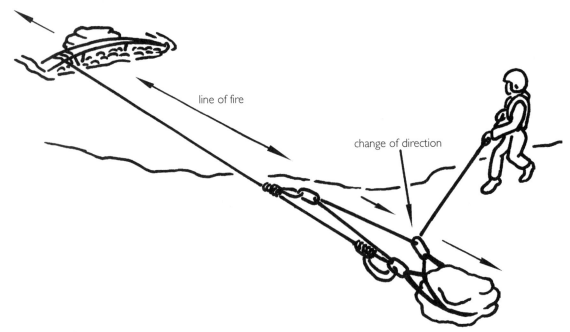

line of fire

change of direction

Figure 6-15. Redirecting the pull on a line takes the rescuers out of the line of fire.

anchor so the 'biner is held in line with the mechanical system.

Unpinning a boat requires that you understand the effects of current, the mechanics of rigging, and the rudiments of safety. Exotic rope systems are seldom necessary. By attacking a problem logically, moving from a simple to a more complex approach, you can reduce time, effort, and risk. As with paddling skills, practice improves performance.

CHAPTER 7

Retrieving Runaway Boats

Recovering a runaway kayak, canoe, or raft is a routine problem for river runners. A quick rescue keeps a group moving downriver with little wasted time and effort; a poorly executed one is painfully slow, and often results in lost or damaged gear. Sometimes a loose boat seems to conspire with the river to make a recovery unusually frustrating and dangerous, but most of the time rescuers simply aren't working together effectively. Here are a few ways to speed the process and reduce the risks.

Picking Up Swimmers

The simplest way for a kayaker to assist a swimmer in fast water is to have the swimmer grab hold of the stern grab loop. The paddler can then support and tow the swimmer to shore. Be cautious when making your approach. Don't paddle directly alongside; a panicky swimmer can grab your paddle, gunwale, or cockpit rim and flip you in an instant. Talk with the swimmer, or at least make eye contact. People who are actively swimming or holding onto their gear are usually safe to help; those who are unresponsive or screaming hysterically should be approached with caution. While you'll get more pulling power if the victim grabs the stern, it's sometimes easier in mild rapids to have the swimmer hold the bow so you can keep an eye on him.

Once a swimmer has grabbed hold, the best tactic is to float the rapids until a large eddy appears, then paddle inside. Avoid boating through shallow areas that could batter the swimmer. When paddling a high-volume boat,

Figure 7-1. A swimmer can often be picked up on the back of a kayak. In this photo he is climbing onto the back deck to reduce the possibility of hitting rocks. (Jane C. Sundmacher photo.)

you can encourage swimmers to grab onto the back of your cockpit rim or your broach loop and pull their torso onto the back deck. This gets them out of icy water and reduces the chance of injury in rocky drops. However, it does make your boat tippier and harder to handle. Squirt boats lack the volume needed in the stern to be much help. If you have a boat with a high-volume bow and a small stern, consider carrying the victim on the front end.

Novice paddlers are often told to hold onto their boat and gear. In easy water this works just fine, but in a fast current the load may be too much for a single rescuer. When several people are available, an alternate strategy is more effective. Go after the swimmer first; the gear can be replaced if needed. The first person arriving should announce, "I've got the swimmer!" to the group. The second and perhaps the third person then call out, "I've got the boat!" and take

charge of working it to shore. The last person might pick up the swimmer's paddle.

Unless injured, swimmers should not be content to hold on to the grab loop and float passively. Instead, they should use their legs and free arm to help pull themselves to safety. This is much easier if other paddlers are managing the gear.

Swimmers are usually better off floating a bad drop alone. In big waves, rocky rapids, or large holes, the added weight makes it harder for a rescuer to stay upright and maneuver. The victim can be pummeled by the stern as it goes up and down in big waves, or pinched between the boat and river rocks. Some people will take a horrible beating rather than let go. The paddler, not the swimmer, is the best judge of whether or not it makes sense to continue with someone holding on. If a rescuer asks you to let go, you should comply. The rescuer can then follow nearby, giving instructions and words of encouragement, picking up the swimmer again at the first opportunity.

Rafts are great for helping swimmers, but their sheer bulk poses a danger to those in the water. You can run over someone in your eagerness to help, trapping them under the raft. If possible, swimmers should be pulled in from the upstream side or along the sides. When you must haul a swimmer in over the downstream end, move quickly to avoid sandwiching the person in between the rubber and a rock. Remember that clothing and life vests can be pulled off. It's much safer to grab the body under the arms or through the crotch.

Snowplow Boat Recovery

Ramming into a runaway canoe or kayak and pushing it to shore is the most popular boat rescue technique. A *snowplow rescue* is simple in theory but harder to execute in practice. Some paddlers don't really understand how it works, while others have trouble working effectively with other boaters.

In a snowplow rescue, the loose boat is first aligned roughly parallel to the current, allowing it to slip through narrow passages without damage. Next, the upstream end is pointed in the direction it needs to go. This sets up a ferry angle, which pushes the boat smoothly into shore. If the angle isn't right, all the muscle strength and sweat in the world do no good. The current grabs the boat and always pushes it in the direction the upstream end is pointed. Then recovery must begin again.

Here are a few hints for snowplow rescues:
- People are a higher priority than boats and gear. Swimmers should be helped first.
- First, line up the boat with the current. This reduces the potential for pinning and lets the boat slip through succeeding drops smoothly, with less chance of damage.
- Establish an objective before blindly pushing the boat around. Look for an eddy large enough to shove the boat into. If there's no suitable landing site, recovery attempts are futile. Drift along with the

boat, wait for an opening, and begin the rescue when the opportunity arises.
- Anticipate or lead your target. Pushing a boat full of water is a lot of work; you'll need to start your drive for the eddy early and hit it high.
- Don't get tunnel vision! Sometimes boaters foolishly try to make a difficult save on one side of the river when a large eddy lies directly behind them.
- Push on the upstream end of the boat from the side opposite the eddy you're trying to reach. This points the upstream end toward the objective, setting the ferry angle. Too often, rescuers mistakenly push on the downstream end and wind up with a ferry angle set in the wrong direction.
- Rescuers have a tendency to slide downstream along the hull as they push a boat toward shore. This pivots the upstream end out into the current. Don't let this happen! Instead, back off, return to the upstream end, and concentrate on maintaining the correct ferry angle.

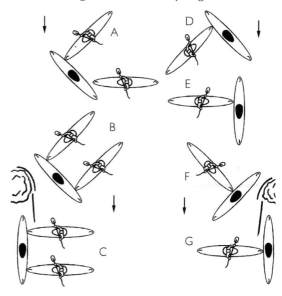

Figure 7-2. Snowplow rescue sequences for two assisting paddlers (A–C) and for one assisting paddler (D–G). The upstream end is angled in the direction you want the boat to go.

- If you can drive your bow under the boat and into the cockpit or between the thwarts, you can hook it and maintain good control as you drive for shore. Make sure you don't get tangled up with any gear that's tied into the boat.
- A second person can reestablish the orientation to the current, or supply more power if the angle is right. Don't slam into the downstream end of the boat and knock it out of alignment! Instead, push on the upstream end. Care must be taken not to apply too much power, as this may cause the boat to spin out.
- Be sure to stay out of the way when a rescue is going well. There's nothing more frustrating than being disrupted by well-meaning helpers. Sometimes people get between a rescuer and her objective and push in the opposite direction. Leave the area if asked. Paddlers who are not in position to work on the boat can assist swimmers or recover paddles and other loose gear.
- Paddlers waiting in their boat to provide backup at the bottom of a drop need to find the best place to sit. Decide which side offers the best spot for landing people and gear, then sit in an eddy on the opposite side. This is the correct side from which to start a snowplow, and the extra push from an upstream ferry on the approach can be very helpful.

Boat Tow Systems

Boat tow systems are more efficient than snowplows because they capture runaway boats on a line, leaving both hands free for efficient paddling. There are three different systems: a simple *hand-held webbing loop*, various *boat-mounted systems* attached to the deck of a kayak or C-1, and *harness systems* that use a tether attached to a quick-release harness on a waist belt or a rescue life vest. Remember that an empty boat is always easier to tow than a swamped one. If you can perform a fast boat-over-boat dump, you'll reach

your objective more quickly, with less chance of snagging or pinning the towed craft.

Webbing Loops

A loop of webbing is often worn around a paddler's waist with the ends secured by a carabiner. The webbing can serve as a simple but effective tow system. The boater removes the waistband and clips into the grab loop of a runaway boat. Kayakers normally place the loop over a shoulder or an arm; canoeists usually prefer to hold it in their lower hand. Holding the line on the same side as the towed craft allows you to let go quickly in case of trouble. Positioning the loop on the opposite side is more secure but increases the risk of entanglement. Your choice.

Field-Expedient Tow Systems

Field-expedient tow systems can be fabricated from a length of rope or webbing. This may be as simple as fastening one end of a rope to a runaway boat, then tying the other end to the center thwart of your canoe with a *slippery clove hitch*. A

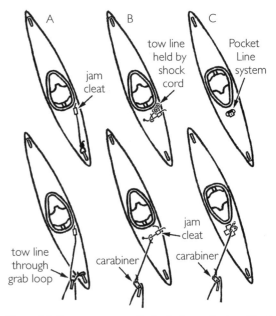

Figure 7-3. Boat tow systems: In A, the line to the towed boat passes through the stern grab loop, making boat handling more difficult. In B and C, the line pulls on the center of the boat, freeing the ends and improving maneuverability.

similar system for a kayak or a raft might use a length of webbing with a loop and carabiner on one end. This can be tied to the broach in front of the cockpit or to a D-ring with a *slippery cow hitch*. These quick-release knots are shown in Appendix A. Practice before you use them in the field.

Deck-Mounted Systems

A *jam cleat* is a fitting used by sailors that pinches into a rope, holding it securely. In some towing systems, you attach the rope directly to the deck of a kayak or C-1 with a jam cleat (Figure 7-3A). The most popular version uses a length of ¼-inch line and a carabiner. The rope goes from the jam cleat, through the stern grab loop, to a point near the cockpit (often the broach loop), where it's secured with a carabiner. The boater unhooks the carabiner and clips it into the run-away boat. The jam cleat holds the line securely during the recovery, but you can release it at a moment's notice by pulling up on the end.

The main disadvantage of this setup is that the pull from the line comes through the stern grab loop, making it difficult to set a ferry angle. It is better to stretch a second line across the back of the cockpit and attach a tow line to it. Attach one end of the second line to the boat and secure the other with a jam cleat (Figure 7-3B). Prepare the tether line with carabiners at both ends. Attach one 'biner to the first rope, and secure the second to the boat in a handy spot. Stow any excess line carefully under a shock cord, keeping it ready for immediate use.

German paddlers have developed several sophisticated deck-mounted devices. One version, the *HF Pocket Line* (Figure 7-3C), can be mounted in front or back of the cockpit opening. The "pocket" includes a length of line, a carabiner, and a quick-release buckle. When deployed, the pull comes from the center of the boat, not the end, which allows better control during the rescue. The unit is attached to the boat with a plastic bolt that will shear off in a serious mishap.

Most users mount the Pocket Line on the rear deck near the cockpit, but some prefer to mount it on the front deck. The line is set so

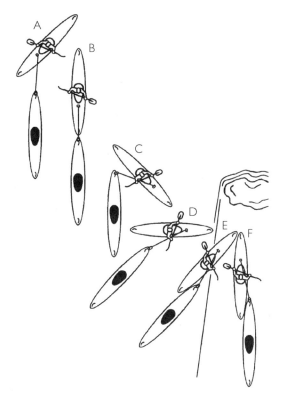

Figure 7-4. The front-mounted Pocket Line. Note how the stern of the rescue boat captures the tethered craft and pushes it into the eddy.

that a tethered boat will clear the bow but not the stern. One advantage of this system is visibility. After making the initial contact and clipping in, a rescuer back-paddles so the tethered boat floats to the front where he can watch it. The second benefit is ease of use. The system is accessible, and the quick-release is easy to find. When the rescuer decides to head for land, the tethered craft is caught by the stern and pushed into the eddy, ending up between the towing boat and the shore. With other systems, a tethered boat may wind up outside an eddy near the eddyline, where the bow can float out and get snagged by the current.

Harness Systems

Tow systems can also be worn as part of a life vest or waist-belt system. The pull comes from the center of the boat for improved control with less

Figure 7-5. Rocky Mountain Outdoor Center developed the bat-tail boat tow system. Made from 1-inch webbing and a cam-lock buckle, this clever, inexpensive unit is popular with its instructors.

effort. On life vests, the boat tether is attached to the quick-release system. Waist belts may serve only as a tow system or double as a throw line. There is significant added risk in being personally attached to a loose craft. Sometimes the pull on the harness is not enough to make it release but more than sufficient to capsize or tangle a boater! The tether must stow securely when not in use; there's nothing more disconcerting than finding a tow system undone and trailing halfway down a big rapid. The quick-release should be easy to locate and absolutely foolproof.

Making Tethered-Boat Rescues

No matter what tow system you choose, take a very conservative approach to tethered-boat rescues. Clipping into a loose boat in difficult whitewater is risky. Steep drops, big waves and holes, and tight boulder gardens are a lot trickier when towing another craft. A towed boat can get caught in holes and surf waves or get pinned on rocks. If these things happen during towing, the

rescuer will be pulled violently backward and will probably capsize. If you and the tethered boat are floating downstream at the same rate of speed, the quick-release may not work. So don't take chances. Use a tow system only in quick water, unobstructed rapids, or clean run-outs below big drops. Practice beforehand and become completely familiar with the unit before using it under difficult circumstances.

Capturing Loose Paddles

Kayak and canoe paddles are extremely awkward for rescuers to manage. Often the best solution is to pick them up and throw them on shore for later recovery. People with big hands can sometimes paddle easy water holding two paddles together. *Paddle carabiners* can be installed on a tow system. These allow boaters to clip into a paddle shaft with their tow system; the paddle will bounce around less if the tow system is pulled tight. If your carabiner is too small to go around a shaft, wrap the line around the shaft and clip back into the rope to form a loop.

To minimize confusion in other rescues, paddle 'biners should be full strength and capable of other uses. Weak "paddles-only" carabiners must not be used with rescue PFDs for belaying or lowering. Remember that paddles are much lighter than boats, and the pull of the current usually will not be enough to activate a quick-release harness. It's best to tow paddles in mild water only.

Recovering Runaway Rafts

Flipped rafts are unsinkable, bulky, and awkward to handle. They're too much for a kayak or canoe to manage except in the mildest water, although a second rescuer in a raft may be able to attach a line and tow it to shore. Rescuers can also climb on top of runaway rafts and paddle them to shore. Swimmers are often able to climb on top of a flipped raft, using the openings found in many self-bailing floors as handholds. On high-rockered boats, it may be easier to climb up the ends than over the center. A fast-moving kayaker or canoeist can paddle up to a flipped raft, hop on, pull her boat on top, and paddle the raft to shore. With a large runaway boat or a swamped raft of conventional design, several people and an assist from an on-shore throw line may be required.

Old-style rafts that lack a self-bailing floor often become swamped and uncontrollable. If they were upside down, you wouldn't have to bail! To regain control, bail you must. Fortunately, a swamped raft can plow through almost anything; but if it's pinned, a wrap can be very dangerous! Occasionally, you'll see a length of webbing stretched tightly across the bottom of a "bucket boat." This is supposed to make it easier to climb on top but it creates a significant entanglement hazard.

Flip Lines

Flip lines are short (10 to 15 feet) lengths of line used to turn capsized rafts upright. They are sometimes stored in small stuff bags with a drawstring closure, then attached to the raft's D-rings on one side. Unfortunately, these bags are often peeled off the raft by river rocks. Most river guides and expert rafters make a flip line from webbing and wear it snugly around their waist. The full length of a flip line varies according to the size of the raft and the height and weight of the rescuer; exact specifications are best found through experimentation.

First, a rescuer climbs on top of the raft and deploys the flip line on the downstream tube. Next, he or she moves to the upstream tube, tightens the line, and leans back. This flips the boat upright, putting the rescuer in the water. This technique works best when the pull is timed to take advantage of the upward "push" from a large wave.

Used correctly, flip lines can bring swimmers back into the boat. They should grab hold on the side opposite a flip-line–equipped rescuer to be pulled into the raft as it is righted. On larger boats, teams of two rescuers with flip lines can pull two to four passengers aboard! Crews running difficult rivers on a regular basis should practice this skill so they can get their group out of the water quickly.

Figure 7-6. Using a flip line on a small raft. Climb onto the bottom of the flipped boat, stand up, and lean back into the line. As you pull the raft upright, a second person can be lifted into the raft.

Boat-Over-Boat Rescues

Canoe-over-canoe rescues have been used for years to recover from capsizes in open water. They can save a lot of time and effort in whitewater, too. You can also perform kayak-over-kayak, canoe-over-kayak, and kayak-over-canoe rescues. You can dump either a canoe or a kayak over a self-bailing raft. This skill works well in large eddies, fast-moving flat water, and even unobstructed Class I to III rapids. Here's how it works:

 1. The rescuer approaches a swamped boat at a 90° angle to its length. The two hulls must remain perpendicular during the rescue; this technique doesn't work if the

Figure 7-7. A canoe-over-canoe rescue: (1) The swamped canoe is approached at right angles to the rescuer.

(2) The canoe is turned sideways, and . . .

craft are parallel to each other.

2. The rescuer lifts the bow of the other boat onto his front deck. This takes some physical strength, but a few tricks will make it easier. An open canoe floating "bottom up" traps air underneath. This may create a vacuum, making the bow almost impossible to lift. Try to "break the seal" by turning the canoe sideways in the water. Now raise one end slowly, allowing the water inside to run out as you lift. To make the lift easier, try pushing down on the bow, then picking it up on the rebound. The person whose boat is being rescued can push down on the far end, which lifts the end you're trying to hoist.

3. The rescuer pulls the swamped boat over his own, bottom up, hand-over-hand, keeping the two boats perpendicular. Open canoes empty out about one-third of the way; they can then be turned

(3) . . . lifted onto the gunwales. The boat is easily dumped and returned to the water.

upright and lowered back into the water. Pull a decked boat over to its balance point, then rock it from side to side to empty it. In a canoe, the water ends up inside, so you'll have to bail. Don't worry about capsizing; the ends of the other boat will act as outriggers. When you're finished, just roll the boat upright and set it afloat.

4. Finally, to help someone back into his boat, hold or brace the side nearest you firmly while he climbs in on the opposite side. With canoes, you can hold the two gunwales together, but watch your hands so you don't get pinched! The swimmer reaches across the canoe to the far gunwales, kicking hard to pull himself aboard. As his rear end passes the gunwales, he should turn onto his back and sit down into the boat. A kayaker can lean onto another decked boat, straddle

his own like a horse, and work his way to the cockpit. This can be pretty exciting in Class II rapids, so keep an eye out for trouble.

Efficient Boat Dumping

Some people have an awful time dumping swamped canoes and kayaks after a swim. The trick is to lift only the boat, not the water trapped inside. Use these techniques to minimize effort and avoid back injury:

• Kayaks and C-boats usually float upside down. Push one end onto shore, shoving the back end down at the last minute. This raises the front and lets some of the water out. Next, pull the front end farther onto dry land. Now, turn the boat slowly on its side so the water runs out of the cockpit. Lift the lower end very slowly so that more water pours out. If

Figure 7-8. A kayak-over-kayak rescue. The swimmer holds the paddles while the rescuer dumps the kayak. The ends of the kayak act like pontoons, making a rescuer's position quite stable.

Figure 7-9. A deepwater entry into a kayak. The rescuer leans onto the deck to hold it upright while the swimmer mounts it over the back end.

Figure 7-10. A deepwater entry into a canoe. The rescuer leans onto the canoe gunwales while the swimmer climbs in on the opposite side.

this is really hard, you're probably lifting too fast. When the water stops running out, lower this end to let more water drain out. Repeat as needed. To empty the last of the water, balance the hull on one knee just in front of, or behind, the cockpit. The water will collect in the shorter section of hull. Pushing down on the longer section provides leverage and rocks the boat from end to end. Raise and lower the boat like a see-saw until water stops draining out.

- Canoes respond better to a different technique. While parallel to shore, paddle the canoe to a beach or flat rock near the waterline. Get out and step on the near gunwale while simultaneously tipping the hull toward you. A short length of strap attached to the opposite gunwale works just like a raft flip line to make dumping easier. Let out the water slowly; a canoe can usually be emptied without ever being lifted off the ground.

Figure 7-11. By using a flip line attached to the off-side thigh strap anchor and standing on the near-side gunwales, even a small person can empty a swamped canoe.

Figure 7-12. Correct technique for dumping a swamped kayak.

When you're done, let it roll back into the river.

- Rafts are most efficiently dumped using a flip line, although some bailing may be required to reduce the load. This can be done in calm water or up against the shore.

Getting a Group Back Together

The aftermath of a long swim can be chaotic, with people and gear strewn on both sides of the river for hundreds of yards. Communication after one of these "yard sales" can be difficult.

Walking up and down the riverbank to get everything together takes a lot of time; in really rough country, hours can be wasted. Try to bring swimmers and their gear together at the same place. Bring the boat or paddle to the same side of the river as its owner; a throw line can be used to quickly pull an empty boat or paddle across the river. Swimmers should start walking downstream immediately to find their stuff. After a bad swim, someone should offer to help dump the boat or retrieve equipment while the swimmer recuperates.

Now that we've dealt with simple, routine problems, the next chapter takes up the less common but far deadlier problem of entrapment.

CHAPTER 8

In-Boat Entrapments, Body Pins, and Unconscious-Swimmer Rescues

Many seemingly innocuous rapids contain traps capable of capturing and holding unwary paddlers inside or outside their boats. It's never easy to rescue people who are held against an obstruction by the force of the river. These rescues quickly turn into life-or-death situations that demand cool thinking and decisive action. There's not always time for improvising strategy at the scene, so prior training and practice can make a vital difference.

In this chapter we consider three scenarios that present great danger to the victim and unusual difficulties to the rescuer: in-boat entrapments, body pins, and free-floating unconscious swimmers.

Entrapment inside the Boat

If a pinned boat collapses with a paddler still inside, entrapment results. In kayaks, the front deck can be forced downward, trapping the boater's legs. This may occur when the hull wraps around a rock, but there are other possible scenarios. For example, one end of the boat can be "pinched-pinned" between two rocks while the other is pushed downstream by the current. Pinch pins may occur horizontally, usually at an eddyline, or vertically at the base of a steep drop. A kayaker's feet can also slip in front of pedal-type footbraces after a head-on collision, forcing his body deeper into the boat and making a wet exit much more difficult.

The force of water, rather than a collapsing boat, may also prevent paddlers from bailing out. When running steep ledges, a kayak can hit bow-first, becoming stuck in a near-vertical position. In a *bow-first pin*, falling water rushes over a paddler's body and shoulders, making it difficult to climb out. In a center pin, the torso can be forced backward, against the rear deck, locking the paddler into his outfitting. This is called a *layback pin*. Escape is impossible unless he can regain a sitting position. In a *pinch pin,* the bow is caught between rocks, and the paddler is trapped as the boat collapses. Keyhole cockpits make wet exits easier but do not offer total protection.

Although entrapment occurs less frequently in open canoes, it is still a consideration. Canoeists paddle from a kneeling position, tucking their feet under a seat or thwart. As a canoe collapses, the seat may break loose, dropping onto the paddler's ankles. People wearing bulky boots or using seats set too low for safety may catch a foot even if the seat remains intact. In a small C-1, the low rear deck presents a similar hazard. In both boats, the danger can be reduced by installing pedestal-style seats. Another alarm-

Figure 8-1. A simulated center pin showing an entrapment in a kayak.

Figure 8-2. A stabilization line applied from upstream to support the trapped kayaker.

Figure 8-3. A vertical pin. The victim is being pushed down into the boat by the current.

Figure 8-5. A pinch pin. The bow of the kayak is caught between two rocks while entering an eddy. The stern is pushed around, collapsing the deck and trapping the boater.

Figure 8-4. A layback pin in a kayak. The victim cannot sit up and thus cannot release himself from the outfitting.

ing situation may result when the current pushes a canoeist's body backward, locking her legs into her thigh straps. She can't slip her legs back and out from under the thigh braces without first sitting up. Proper placement of the straps reduces the risk of a layback pin, but a pin may distort a boat's shape, allowing the straps to shift or tighten unexpectedly.

Rafts can also be involved in entrapment accidents. The usual cause is entanglement in foot loops or in lines attached to the boat. Occasionally, a raft will fold around someone

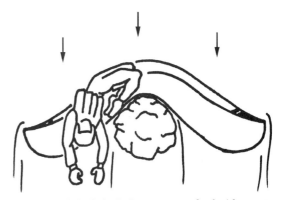

Figure 8-6. A leg-lock pin in a canoe outfitted with a seat or thwart. The victim's lower leg is pushed against the hull and the seat by water pressure.

during a pin. In the worst possible situation, a paddler may be shoved underneath the floor. In extreme cases, trapped people have been cut free with knives.

Body Pins

Water moves around solid obstructions, carrying swimmers with it. Although swimmers are less likely to be pinned than boats, they too can become wrapped around a rock, a tree, a bridge, or a bridge abutment in the same way as a boat. But some circumstances are more dangerous. Swimmers can be pushed against strainers: sieves of rocks, branches, or other debris. Powerful currents sweeping underneath large rocks may carry them into unavoidable, deadly traps. Paddlers or their gear can be hooked or snagged by protruding rocks or tree limbs. A swimmer can also get caught between a pinned boat and an obstruction. The force of the water is irresistible and unrelenting; it can push the strongest person underwater and hold him there indefinitely. In all but the mildest situations, self-rescue is utterly impossible.

Foot Entrapment

Foot and leg entrapments occur when a swimmer's feet are caught in cracks, crevices, or undercut ledges in the riverbed. This often results when paddlers try to stand up suddenly in deep, fast-moving water. As the current continues to push them downstream, they lose their balance and are pulled underwater. At this point, time is short and successful rescues are rare. Never risk standing up suddenly in fast-moving water without using the specialized wading techniques discussed in Chapter 3.

Unconscious or Helpless Swimmers

Swimming paddlers can be battered by the river until they're unable to protect themselves from the river or hold onto a throw line or grab loop. This is most often the result of a blow to the head, but it can also be caused by absorbing other impacts or unexpectedly inhaling small amounts of water. People released from serious entrapments may be unconscious or helpless, too. Even strong swimmers can become immobilized, and a life jacket may not be enough to prevent drowning.

Avoiding Trouble

The first defense against pinning and entrapment is to avoid potential trouble spots. Pinning accidents can happen even to the best paddlers. Some drops are notorious for these dangers, and using a sneak route or making a carry is wise. Certain drops are unusually hazardous to swimmers; and paddling skills, particularly the roll, must be quite reliable to minimize risk. A few rapids are so dangerous that small losses of boat control will lead to trouble; these should not be run by paddlers of ordinary ability. And swimmers must never, ever try to stand up suddenly in fast-moving water.

Flipped boaters can't see where they're going and may drift into pins during roll attempts. Here's how to evaluate the unseen risk while upside down: Scrapes and bangs, while unnerving, are not usually dangerous because the water is still moving the boat around the obstruction. But when the canoe, kayak, or raft comes to a complete stop against an obstacle, pinning is imminent. Water piles up onto all rocks in a rapid, creating a pillow. When a whitewater boat hits and sticks, the pillow shifts upstream, from the rock to the boat. This "transfer time" leaves the paddler a few seconds to escape before the full force of the river grabs hold. Don't be stubborn about bailing out; rolling a pinned boat is almost impossible. Once the "pillow transfer" is complete, the river truly grabs hold, and getting free is much more difficult.

Self-Rescue from Entrapment

In a layback pin (see Figure 8-4, page 101), a kayak is pinned at center and the paddler is pushed onto the rear deck by the water. This locks the paddler's legs into the outfitting and makes escape more difficult. Kayakers using boats with keyhole cockpits can simply release their knees and push them through the opening. This is not intuitive, however, and must be practiced. Those with smaller cockpits may find themselves trapped; they must fight their way back into a sitting position, then slide their rear end backward to allow their knees to clear the cockpit. Ropes offered by rescuers may facilitate this.

When canoeists are pushed backward, they must also sit upright in order to slip their knees out of the thigh straps. Straps set high in the crotch make escape even more difficult. Quick-release buckles can be helpful, but they should be placed at the gunwale end of the straps, where they can be easily reached in an emergency. A canoeist who can reach a quick-release installed on the bottom of the canoe probably won't need to use it.

Vertical pins are awkward and precarious. Water cascading over a victim's head and back pushes him down and forward. An air pocket can form, but it may disappear if the boat slips or shifts deeper into the drop. Even without the water pressure, it's not easy to climb up and out of a kayak cockpit. This is especially true on boats with the old-style smaller openings and pedal-style footbraces.

Kayakers should try this exercise: Secure a kayak to a steep (50°-plus) slope, then hop in and practice getting out. This is much harder than it looks! In a keyhole cockpit, kayakers can push one knee up through the opening and place one foot on the front of the coaming so their powerful leg muscles can lift them out. Bulkheads provide the best footing; trying to push off small, slippery, pedal-style footbraces can be tricky.

Climbing out of a vertical pin is risky for two reasons. First, bow pins are not always solid, and struggling may make the boat rotate or plunge deeper into the drop. Second, paddlers may fall over before both legs are out, at which point they'll be helpless, hanging upside down from the cockpit by their knees. These *leg-lock pins* (Figure 8-6, page 101) are uniformly fatal. The

Figure 8-7. The right way to climb out of a vertically pinned boat. Note the use of the stern painter for support.

person who is pinned must decide whether to risk an unassisted escape or wait for additional help.

Helping Trapped Paddlers

Helping pinned swimmers and entrapped boaters requires knowledge and speed. First, try to stabilize the victim in a heads-up position so he can breathe. If he's trapped underwater, rescuers have only a few minutes to act. If he can breathe, the group can take some time to develop a plan. Remember that a trapped person may not be secure; he may be struggling to avoid being pushed underwater, and his boat may shift position for the worst at any moment.

Don't be complacent, even in relatively straight-forward situations.

The victim's physical condition is a vital factor in your plan. Some people are strong, coherent, and able to describe exactly what assistance they need to work free. Others are so tired or scared that they can't help at all. Well-conditioned, experienced boaters generally fare the best; but pain, cold water, and a relentless current can wear anyone down. Even experts can quickly lose both strength and nerve.

If possible, talk to a trapped person. Is she in control or on the verge of panic? Does she seem strong, or is she hanging on by the slimmest of margins? Can she wait, or does she need immediate support? How much time do you have before the situation deteriorates? Does the victim have a plan, or do you need to take command? When possible, coordinate your actions with the trapped person. Try to let her know your plan and what you expect of her before you begin the extrication.

If a situation is desperate, call out to the victim, using her name if you know it. Let her know that people are coming to help. Several paddlers who were recovered from desperate situations reported having been disheartened when they couldn't see anything happening. Sometimes people on the shore just stared at them as the rescue was being organized out of their view. Conversely, victims reported a huge morale boost when told that help was on the way. When possible, have someone monitor the victim's condition, providing continuous encouragement. Sometimes this requires a calm, reassuring tone; in other cases, a more energetic and demanding approach is needed.

The best strategy is to move rescuers to the trapped victim. Whether they boat, wade, or swim doesn't matter, as long as the method is not too risky. Once on the spot, they can do what needs to be done. Sometimes they'll hold a trapped paddler's head above water, supporting him until more help arrives. At other times, they'll release the boat or give the victim the boost needed to work free.

Two or more paddlers working together on a small site can be effective as long as they don't get in each other's way. Crowding invites trouble because no one can get into a good position to pull or lift. Toes get stepped on; people fall in the river; nasty words are exchanged. The right number of rescuers is the minimum needed to do the job. Other people can be used as upstream lookouts or downstream backups. It often makes sense to evacuate uninjured paddlers first to give the rescuers more room to work, particularly with pinned rafts or tandem canoes.

Heads-Down Pinning

A heads-down pinning is a life-or-death matter. In this case the imminent risk of death justifies extreme measures, even though they will probably cause injury. It's reasonable to tie a rope to a victim's arm or leg while trying to pull him free. Try to pull a person out the way he went in, from upstream. Never pull with the current; this just draws the victim tighter into the obstruction.

In-Boat Entrapment Rescues

The first goal is to stabilize the victim. Hold the paddler's head above water until you can decide on a plan of action. Remember that a pinned boat may be precariously balanced; if it shifts position, the victim's head may be pulled underwater. It's important not to unbalance the boat until the trapped person can be supported or removed. Stabilize the boat if possible. In extreme cases, you may be forced to tie a rope around an unconscious victim's torso or arm.

Study the mechanism that holds the boat in place. Feeling around underwater helps; talking to the victim may also yield valuable clues. Don't rush unless you have to, and make sure there's enough help available to execute your plan.

Horizontal Pins

Center and end-to-end pins are not uncommon. Helping a trapped kayaker sit up may be all that's needed to work him free. With canoes, cutting through a collapsed seat or thigh brace may do

Sometimes You Just Get Lucky

The Big Sandy in northern West Virginia is one of my all-time favorite runs—hard enough to keep your attention, but not nasty enough to scare you. I'd taken out above Big Sandy Falls and set up my camera to photograph people running a steep chute just upstream. The left side of the chute is undercut, but no one had ever gotten in trouble there before. I photographed several people running the chute, then stopped to change lenses.

Looking up, I saw a boater heading into the chute. Her line was all wrong, and I smelled trouble ahead. By the time I put my camera down, she had flipped and slammed, head down, into the undercut left wall.

I reached over, grabbed an arm, and pulled. Her head was above water, but I couldn't lift the boat free. She was screaming for someone to get her out. I was scared to try to do it all myself because, if I dropped her, she'd be in big trouble. I yelled for help. Another guy ran up behind me. We tied a safety line to her boat in case we lost our grip, then lifted. Seconds later she was sitting on the ledge.

She felt better than I did. Reunited with her group, she ran the 15-foot falls below a few minutes later. I sat on a rock for 15 minutes before portaging. I never found out her name. But I do know that she was very lucky. Normally, the hardest thing in an entrapment rescue is getting to a trapped person, and in a heads-down pinning, you don't have much time. Fortunately, it happened right under my nose and there were others around to help.

—CW

the job. The broach loops attached to the front deck of many modern kayaks can be clipped into a haul line. You can then raise the deck, taking pressure off a trapped paddler's legs.

Sometimes a broached boat must be partly or completely unpinned to release the victim. Ideally, one person releases the craft while another supports and removes the trapped paddler. Remember: When the boat floats free, the victim may still be trapped. Don't let a canoe or kayak containing a helpless person be pushed downstream; plan ahead to keep the boat under control. Even with a safety line attached to the grab loop, you may need several people to control the craft.

Vertical Pins

Vertical pins are very awkward. While the boat usually remains intact, the paddler suddenly finds himself underwater, standing in a nearly upright position. He must battle the push of the oncoming water and the pull of gravity to climb out. In addition, the boat may be balanced precariously on its nose. A sudden shift of weight may make it rotate, slip lower, or flip. When this happens, the victim's air pocket often disappears. Sometimes a rescuer needs to extend a hand for stability and traction; at other times, a trapped paddler must be hauled out bodily.

Leg-Lock Pins

Sometimes a victim is pushed backward with a leg hooked over a kayak rim or canoe seat. The foot or lower leg is pressed against the hull and cannot swing free. These leg-lock pins (see Figure 8-6) are difficult to release without help. Broken bones are not uncommon. If the victim can't be helped into an upright position, the boat should be unpinned. Once this is done, the paddler almost invariably floats free.

Using Saws in Rescue Efforts

It may become necessary to cut into a boat to remove a trapped victim. River knives do not

Figure 8-8. A simulated vertical pin on the Upper Nantahala Narrows at low water. For the victim's safety, a line to the stern holds the boat in place.

work well; the best compact cutting tool available is a short, folding camp saw. These make quick work of fiberglass, Royalex, roto-molded hulls, wood canoe seats, and even aluminum. Cutting is an extreme measure, reserved for desperate situations. If it's not really necessary, the boatowner won't be pleased! When possible, ask the owner's permission.

Cutting into a pinned boat without injuring the victim requires care. In open canoes, you can usually see what's happening—but not always. Feel around underwater to figure out where the victim's legs are, and try to cut the outfitting as far away from the victim's body as possible. With broached kayaks, cutting into the front deck is chancy. If the wall has shifted or fallen over, the victim's legs may be encountered in unexpected places. Cold water numbs the body, and the victim may not feel the blade at first. Completely slicing off the back of a kayak is a safer way to unbalance the pin. This method also works with C-1s, but because the paddler's legs aren't under the deck, it's okay to cut on either end.

Rescuing Pinned Swimmers

When a person is pinned against an undercut rock, sieve, or strainer, rescuers should grab hold and *pull*! They must try to lift the victim's body out of the water quickly; once the hips are clear, the worst is over. Be careful when pulling on clothing, particularly the life vest. A PFD without a crotch strap can come completely off. Instead, reach down under the trapped paddler's arms and lock your hands across his chest or back. You can sometimes reach down and lock hands through the crotch. In extreme circumstances, you may have to let go of the victim, allowing her to pass under the obstruction. This is a dangerous, last-ditch undertaking, but it has worked in several situations.

Sometimes a paddler's leg, arm, or body will get caught between a boat and an obstruction. Support the victim first, then move the boat using the unpinning procedures discussed in Chapter 6. The aim is not to recover the craft, but to pull it back far enough to free the trapped person. Always roll the hull away from the trapped limb, not toward it, to avoid causing crush injuries. Pull the person free at the first opportunity and move him to safety before releasing the pinned boat.

Equipment Snagging

A paddler's gear may sometimes snag on branches or rocks. Rescuers can cut offending straps, ropes, and other gear with a knife. Be careful not to slice or stab the person you're trying to help, especially when working underwater. Use your free hand to feel ahead of the cutting edge, or lay your index finger along the back of the knife. You can place the dull side of a single-edged blade against a snagged person's body, then cut away from him. A seatbelt cutter is a safer, more controllable alternative.

Foot Entrapment

Foot entrapments are often deadly. Unless immediate support is provided, a victim will be pushed underwater after a few seconds' struggle. Rescue lines won't help, unless thrown from directly upstream. Trapped victims can often keep themselves upright with the help of flotation, such as an inner tube, boogie board, or the bow of an empty boat. If a victim is already underwater, wading rescues may work. A group of people moving together as a team can get into surprisingly deep water and pull a trapped person to the surface. The eddy created behind them provides a sheltered place to work. In a few cases, lowering a boat and sinking it above a narrow chute may divert enough water to enable rescuers to recover someone.

Stabilization Lines

A *stabilization line* is a rope stretched across a section of fast-moving water. In Chapter 5, we recommended this type of line to assist waders in fast current; it can also help trapped paddlers to maintain their balance. Rescuers can set up a stabilization line quickly to offer timely support to pinning and entrapment victims.

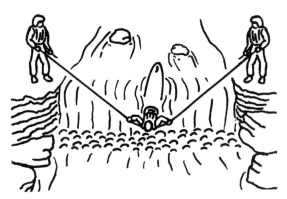

Figure 8-9. Using a stabilization line to support a paddler trapped in a vertical pin.

To do this, stretch a line across the river well downstream of the person you want to help, then belay it at both ends. Two or more throw lines can be linked together with carabiners for added length. Keep the line out of reach of the trapped person until the belayers are set; if the victim reaches the line and pulls on it unexpectedly, he can pull rescuers into the water. To make rope handling and communication easier, use midstream rocks or shallows to shorten the distance between belayers. If possible, hold the line out of the water so the current won't pull on it. Ideally, the two belayers should find secure stances well upstream of the victim while others serve as line handlers, managing the rope below. When help is limited, the belayers must lay the line in place before moving upstream into their stances.

Now, pull the line upstream to the trapped person. Haul it slowly until the victim can grab hold. Allow the line to sag into a deep "V," rather than keeping it tight, to reduce the strain on belayers. Move carefully as the rope comes within arm's reach of its target; you can injure someone by yanking or jerking too hard. Maintaining a steady, even pressure is more difficult than it sounds. Often, one side pulls harder than the other, the opposite side over-compensates, and the victim, who is trying to hold on to the line, is tossed to and fro. Try to place the line halfway up the torso of an entrapment victim, allowing him to drape his arms

over it. He can now remain upright with very little effort. Be careful how hard you pull back on the rope; you can cut someone in half if you aren't careful! Once the line is firmly in place, watch closely to see if the trapped person can work free.

Snag-Line Rescues

A line placed underneath a victim to provide lift and support is called a *snag line*. First developed by Nantahala Outdoor Center to release foot entrapments, it has been used successfully in the field. Snag lines can be set under the arms of trapped paddlers to support their torso and head, buying time for rescuers. In extreme cases, it can be used to pull someone free.

A snag line must often run below the surface of the water. Rescue bags stuffed with rocks were originally used to sink the line, but filling them is time-consuming and doesn't work that well anyway. When you guide the rope beneath a victim, the trick is to hold the line low. Sometimes the line handlers on both sides must hold

Figure 8-10. Using a stabilization line to rescue a victim in a simulated foot entrapment.

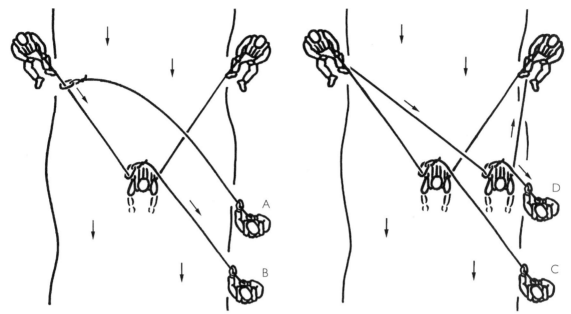

Figure 8-11. Grabbing hold of a victim on a snag line with a single tag line (A–B), then pulling the victim into shore (C–D).

the rope underwater. When the line is in place, pull it just tight enough to get the victim's head above water. Rescuers may be able to use this line to swim or wade out. Actually dragging the victim all the way out is possible but requires considerable force and carries a substantial risk of injury.

Foot-entrapment rescues using snag lines are difficult to execute successfully. Lives can be saved, but the difference between recovering a live paddler or a dead body is measured in minutes. The victim is often deep in the water, hard to see, and harder to reach. Getting the rope under the body is the hard part. Once the rope is in position, it will work its way down to the feet. To haul the victim's foot out the same way it went in, first let the line sag into a deep V, then pull hard upstream. Released victims will float free, so paddlers should be prepared downstream beforehand to pick them up and start resuscitation.

The V-angled ropes in a tag or snag line can be turned into a zip line when the ends are securely anchored. This will carry a rescuer directly to the victim (discussed in Chapter 5).

The biggest problem with this approach is that a zip line may stretch the line out from under the victim and compromise his support. This method can carry rescuers into dangerous places, so evaluate the risks carefully.

Cinch-Line Rescues

Even if a snag line is successful, a freed victim will be carried downstream by the river. A *cinch line* allows the victim to be securely held and retrieved by the rig. This advantage must be weighed against the increased complexity of the technique, which requires a skilled, practiced team to execute. Once the initial snag line is in place, a second rope is thrown across the river just upstream of the first line (see Figure 8-11). One end of the cinch line is attached to the snag line on the far shore with a carabiner and pulled down the line to the victim. When contact is made, the other end is moved slightly downstream of the tag line, creating a loop. The victim is now secured and can be pulled along the line to shore. Because the lines can be fouled and the victim pulled underwater, this is a potentially dangerous technique.

Figure 8-12. A snag line used in the same situation shown in Figure 8-10. The line slides under the victim's body and down to his feet, then pulls his feet free.

Other Techniques

If the victim is wearing a rescue life vest, rescuers can clip into his PFD. Alternatively, trapped paddlers may be able to clip themselves into a rescue line using a short tether. Paddle hooks have also been used to snag a life vest harness and pull someone free. Although these techniques have been used in extreme situations in Europe for some time, they are clearly dangerous.

Hard-boat paddlers can attempt a self-rescue by attaching a rescue bag to the broach loop of a kayak or the thwart of a canoe. The bag must be stored where you can reach it easily when seated in your boat. Once you toss the bag, the line can be picked up by rescuers downstream and used to pull you free. The backpack-style throw bags featured on some rescue life vests could be very useful here. In one case involving an open canoe in a desperate vertical pin, the victim tied his line to his center thwart and threw it out. His group then pulled the canoe end-over-end to freedom.

Unconscious-Swimmer Rescues

Imagine yourself watching a paddler run a difficult drop. Suddenly the boat flips, and the paddler bails out. He floats downstream passively, not trying to save himself. Sometimes the victim is not unconscious but merely stunned or out of breath. Either way, he's at the mercy of the current; no life jacket, however large or well-designed, will protect him from drowning. He must be rescued, but how?

Pushing an unconscious person to shore with the bow of your boat is extremely difficult in fast current. Shore-based throw lines aren't effective, either. A paddler must stay with the unconscious swimmer until the river calms down, making the rescue when water conditions permit. Hard boats and rafts can approach an unconscious swimmer safely. A strong kayaker or canoeist may be able to pull a small victim onto his front deck; in a C-2, one person can do this while the other paddles to shore. In a raft, one or two people can grab hold and pull someone in while the others maintain control and paddle to safety. If you are using a tow system, wrap the line around the victim's upper arm; this will allow him to be towed face-up. A webbing loop can be girth-hitched around the arm and used in the same way.

Often you must abandon your boat and swim an unconscious victim to shore. Think ahead carefully before trying this. You must be able to get to shore safely without being washed through dangerous drops. Backup can be provided with shore-based throw lines or a boat downstream, but often the rescuer must work alone. Be realistic about your limitations. And spectators, please don't try this without a life vest!

Sometimes you'll find an unconscious paddler trapped inside her boat. At other times the victim is conscious, but helpless. Tight-fitting boats and hard-to-release sprayskirts are the most usual cause of this problem; whether you should try to right the craft or release the sprayskirt and pull the victim out depends on the circumstances. In either case, you'll have to abandon your boat. In serious rapids, a snowplow or tow system can be used to push boat and victim into an eddy, where the rescuer can bail out and work the paddler free.

Strong-Swimmer Rescues

Swimming rescues are risky but may be the only effective help for an unconscious swimmer. The rescuer enters the water by bailing out of his boat or swimming aggressively from shore. In approaching a helpless swimmer, the safest direction is usually from upstream. The strong swimmer slides his legs underneath the victim's body, grabs hold, then pulls toward shore. Several types of holds are useful. Lifeguards are taught to grab a person under one arm, across the upper torso. This *cross-chest carry* requires an extra-long reach when performed on someone wearing a life jacket. Grabbing one or both shoulders of the victim's PFD is easier. It works best with tight-fitting "squirt-style" or "racer" life vests, but even then there's a risk of pulling off

Figure 8-13. A life vest carry leaves one hand free to catch a rope.

the device. The *life-vest carry*, developed by Rescue III, works with most conventional PFDs. On the side opposite the direction you plan to swim, shove your arm across and under the back of the life vest and grab the opposite shoulder. This is very secure, uses only one arm, and actually makes a victim's jacket fit more securely. The other arm is free to swim or catch a throw rope. In fast, deep water, getting to shore is a painfully slow process. Monitor your progress carefully and don't be afraid to let the victim go if the current is taking you into danger.

Helping Panicky Swimmers

Frightened or hysterical swimmers should be treated very cautiously. They can quickly capsize a kayak or canoe and really thrash a swimming rescuer. Rafts, being quite stable, can paddle right up and pull them in without capsizing. A person with the strength to scream or flail wildly in the water is not in immediate danger of drowning, so rescuers can stay well out of reach. Talk to them; let them know you're trying to help. Often, you can lead a panicky swimmer to safety by moving slowly to shore, always staying just out of reach. The panicked person will be drawn to follow.

Terrorized paddlers are not normally encountered on river trips, but if you're in the water and a victim actually attacks you, there are several possible responses. People who think they are drowning will want to get as high in the water as possible. They'll climb onto your head and shoulders if they can! Since they don't want to go underwater, diving down gets them off fast. You can also duck under them as they approach or, as a last resort, push them off with your feet. There are a number of holds and releases employed by lifeguards that a paddler would rarely use. They are best learned in a lifesaving course.

Tethered-Swimmer (Live-Bait) Rescues

A *tethered-swimmer rescue* involves tying a rescuer into a line via a quick-release harness, allowing her to swim into the river while on belay. This technique is used extensively in European slalom races and as safety backup for boaters attempting drops culminating in dangerous holes. The rescuer, in addition to being an able swimmer, must be familiar with the quick-release mechanism on her harness and comfortable swimming in current while tethered. The belayer, in addition to having good rope-handling skills, must be alert and ready to respond to unexpected problems.

Tethered swimmers need a spot where they can get into the water quickly. If the water near the shore is too shallow, wade out onto a rock or stand in the shallows near an eddyline. The belayer picks a good stance on shore; if a really strong pull is expected, a backup belay from a third person (described in Chapter 4) can keep them from being pulled into the water. If the belayer is wearing a rescue PFD, he can set up a self-belay, clipping in with a short tether (described in Chapter 5). Since both swimmer and victim will be swung in to shore after contact is made, be sure there's a safe spot downstream for them to climb out.

For tethered swimmers, timing is everything. There's a tendency for rescue swimmers to commit themselves too soon. Once in the water, the rescuer moves at the same speed as the victim, so it's not really necessary to "lead" the target. The rescuer should try to hit the water when the victim is as close as he will get.

Figure 8-14. A tethered swimmer prepares for a practice rescue of a helpless swimmer during a rescue class.

Figure 8-15. The rescuer makes contact, and the belayer pulls them both into shore.

Figure 8-16. Simulated rescue of a pinned paddler using a tethered wader.

The line handler gives the rescue swimmer enough line to move freely but not so much that it could get in the way. The swimmer must never forget the tether and should avoid wild stroking or rolling motions that can cause entanglement. The quick-release buckle on the harness is available if necessary. Techniques for approaching and grabbing hold of a victim are the same as in a nontethered rescue, but soon after contact is made, there will be a pull from the line, swinging both swimmer and victim into shore.

Body Recoveries

A difficult rescue may at some point turn into a body recovery. The realization comes slowly, but once the group recognizes that hope is lost, they must deal with powerful feelings. This is especially true when continuing the rescue is extremely risky. Breaking off a rescue and aban-doning a friend to the river will provoke feelings of guilt and anguish within the party, and feelings of intense anger among family and friends who are not yet ready to accept what has happened. Don't let your judgment become clouded by these emotions. Never risk your life to recover a corpse.

Paddlers should continue their efforts as long as possible without compromising their safety, sending for outside help in prolonged struggles. But cold temperatures, bad weather, exhaustion, or approaching darkness may force a group to call off the rescue and evacuate for their own safety. At other times, special equipment is needed to complete the extrication.

Once it is certain that the victim is dead, avoid any dangerous maneuvers. As group members become strung out and exhausted, they should be encouraged to stop. This is especially true when you are relieving another party that has been attempting a rescue for some time.

A failed rescue attempt, even when it involves professionals assisting an unknown person, takes a tremendous psychological toll. The death of a friend is even harder to handle. Often rescuers experience depression or anxiety for weeks afterward, never fully realizing the cause. Professional help should be sought as soon as possible so that healing can begin. The Critical Incident Stress Foundation (see Appendix C) or a local psychologist can be of invaluable assistance.

CHAPTER 9

First Aid

Whether an accident occurs on the James River in the middle of downtown Richmond or on an isolated western canyon days from help, medical problems must be treated correctly. A victim's injuries can often be handled quickly, allowing a trip to continue without delay. But extended on-site treatment and strenuous evacuations over difficult terrain may be required. An understanding of wilderness first aid is essential if paddlers are to make the right decisions.

Medical emergencies occur unexpectedly. In everyday life, we take sophisticated emergency response systems for granted. We often see outdoorspeople taking risks beyond their abilities, thinking that if they miscalculate, someone will dial "911" and summon rescue. This misperception has created what some have called a "generation of victims." Whitewater paddlers are wrong to rely entirely on local services and must plan for any emergency situation they could encounter. Reading this book is one form of preparation.

Paradoxically, many paddlers who learn how to unpin boats or help fellow boaters to shore neglect their first aid training. On a river, access to outside medical assistance is often limited, so knowledge and training are vital. Remember: A rescue is not really over until the victim has been checked and treated for injuries. Your actions can make the difference between an inconvenient accident and a tragic fatality.

First aid training has come a long way in the past decade. There are many levels of training available, from introductory first aid courses to

Wilderness EMT certification. Basic courses, given by groups such as the American Red Cross and the National Safety Council, provide a good foundation for more advanced programs concentrating on the treatment of serious injuries in isolated areas. The National Association for Search and Rescue has developed standard "protocols" for wilderness first aid, and organizations such as Wilderness Medical Associates teach excellent courses that focus on the needs of paddlers who are far from help in emergencies. Whatever course you take, periodic recertification is mandatory. Course content changes as new techniques are developed, and first aid skills require regular practice to keep them sharp. Just because you went through a program five years ago doesn't mean you are properly prepared today.

Entire books have been written on the subject of first aid. This chapter concentrates on specific problems that whitewater paddlers may encounter and is intended to supplement a basic first aid course. The key areas include *cold water near-drowning, shock, spinal and head injuries, heat- and cold-related emergencies, and shoulder dis-*

locations. Other injuries such as bleeding or broken bones may accompany these conditions, but they are covered thoroughly in regular first aid and emergency medical programs.

Protecting the Rescuer

Any medical emergency must be approached with an overriding concern for the safety of the rescuer. For example, a rescuer is often exposed to extremes of heat and cold. The clothing he wears offers minimal protection for daytime temperatures, and hypothermia may occur during an overnight bivouac. Day-trippers carry a limited food and water supply and are not prepared for extended evacuations or long waits for help to arrive. During hot weather, extreme physical exertion during an evacuation coupled with an inadequate supply of water can lead to heat exhaustion or heat stroke. In cold weather, a difficult rescue may burn calories that will be needed later to keep the rescuer's body warm.

On some rivers, these dangers are minimal. The key variable is how quickly and easily a group can gain access to standard medical care. When a patient can be transported to a medical facility quickly, the risk is low. This is often the case on roadside rivers, as well as on popular runs where radios carried by rangers or outfitters can quickly summon help via helicopter. But in isolated areas, help may be hours or days away. Wilderness protocols recognize the realities of these situations and, in many cases, change the rules accordingly. This helps to prevent rescuers from risking their lives when a victim can't be helped. (For more on rescue protocols, see "Deciding to Start CPR," page 120.)

Patient Evaluation

When evaluating an injured person on a river, paddlers should use the same principles taught in any standard first aid course. The American Red Cross program focuses on a simple plan of *check, call, and care.* In a river incident, the logical order of action remains the same. After decid-

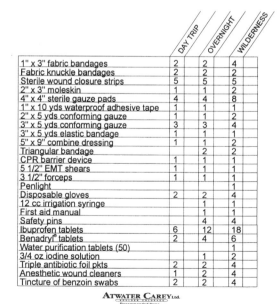

	DAY TRIP	OVERNIGHT	WILDERNESS	
1" x 3" fabric bandages	2	2	4	
Fabric knuckle bandages	2	2	2	
Sterile wound closure strips	5	5	5	
2" x 3" moleskin	1	1	2	
4" x 4" sterile gauze pads	4	4	8	
1" x 10 yds waterproof adhesive tape	1	1	1	
2" x 5 yds conforming gauze	1	1	2	
3" x 5 yds conforming gauze	3	3	4	
3" x 5 yds elastic bandage	1	1	1	
5" x 9" combine dressing	1	1	2	
Triangular bandage		2	2	
CPR barrier device	1	1	1	
5 1/2" EMT shears	1	1	1	
3 1/2" forceps	1	1	1	
Penlight			1	
Disposable gloves	2	2	4	
12 cc irrigation syringe		1	1	
First aid manual		1	1	
Safety pins		4	4	
Ibuprofen tablets	6	12	18	
Benadryl® tablets	2	4	6	
Water purification tablets (50)			1	
3/4 oz iodine solution		1	2	
Triple antibiotic foil pkts	2	2	4	
Anesthetic wound cleaners	1	2	4	
Tincture of benzoin swabs	2	2	4	

ATWATER CAREY Ltd.
Recommended Items

Figure 9-1. Recommended items for the whitewater paddler's first-aid kit.

ing the scene is safe, the rescuer first checks the victim for life-threatening injuries. If a life-threatening condition exists, he sends for help before patient care begins.

Caring for the patient generally follows a series of logical steps called the *ABCs* (*airway, breathing,* and *circulation*), which we have listed below. It is important to practice and perform your assessment in the same ABC, head-to-toe order each time in order to avoid missing valuable information. Although the ABCs cover the most life-threatening injuries, it is important to address spinal stabilization while the ABCs are being assessed (see "Spinal Cord Injuries" later in this chapter).

The list below is an outline of the ABCs; it is not intended to teach these techniques or to replace a basic first aid course.

Airway. Airway obstructions are caused more often by the tongue falling against the back of the throat than by any other type of airway obstruction. When the victim is unresponsive and does not appear to have a head or spinal injury, tilt the head back and lift the chin. If you suspect the patient has incurred spinal injuries, use a modified jaw thrust (a maneuver used to open the airway without tilting the head). Airway management doesn't end here but will be an ongoing responsibility through-out treatment and transport to medical help.

Breathing. Look, listen, and most important, feel, for breathing. Be alert for other problems that threaten the patient's ability to breathe, and then stabilize those conditions. If the patient is not breathing, steps must be taken to breathe for him. Like airway management, breathing assessment is an ongoing duty.

Circulation. Feel for a pulse at both the carotid artery in the neck and the radial artery on the thumb side of the wrist. If there is no pulse at the carotid artery, the patient requires immediate CPR. If you cannot detect a pulse at the wrist but you can find one at the neck, the patient's blood

pressure is low and he is probably in severe shock. Make every effort to maintain circulation by treating for severe bleeding and shock.

Disability. To determine a patient's level of consciousness, rescuers use the AVPU scale (alert, verbally responsive, responds to pain, totally unresponsive). Establish a base point from which progress or decline of the patient's condition can be monitored. This evaluation may also include assessment of movement, feeling, and pulse at the end of each extremity. Check all vital signs for both rate and character: Is there pulse and respiration? Are the pupils equally dilated and responsive? Check body temperature and the color and condition of the skin.

Expose and examine. Remove clothing and do a head-to-toe examination. Log-roll the victim to expose the back. Start at the top of the head and carefully examine each part of the body: head and shoulders, chest, abdomen and pelvis, each leg, each arm.

Feel, find, and fix. Feel the body to find tender spots and to check for deformity.

Get going. In cases of severe shock or injury, time is an important factor. Continue the ABCs but transport the victim to medical help as soon as possible.

Rescue Breathing and CPR

Life support is needed when a person stops breathing or when he has no pulse. These problems are interrelated but require different treatments. The difference between CPR and rescue breathing is sometimes misunderstood, and this misunderstanding can have serious consequences for the patient.

When a person can't breathe, the heart stops and the brain begins to die after as little as 4 to 6 minutes. A patient who is not breathing soon depletes the oxygen left in her lungs. The blood is therefore unable to pick up more oxygen, so the body begins to die. When a pulse is present, we need only force air into the lungs to provide life support. This is called *rescue breathing,* or *mouth-to-mouth resuscitation.* There are a number of documented cases in which a paddler miraculously breathed life into a member of his party.

When the heart stops, breathing also ceases. A pulseless victim cannot exchange oxygen in the lungs or transport it via blood circulation to the brain. *CPR,* or *cardiopulmonary resuscitation,* combines rescue breathing with a method of circulating the blood—chest compression. These skills are taught in American Red Cross, National Safety Council, and American Heart Association CPR classes and should be practiced at least once a year. It is in those classes, not in a book, that paddlers should learn these skills.

When administered to a victim with respiration too shallow or weak to be detected, rescue breathing does no harm. In some cases, such as hypothermia treatment, the warm, humidified air blown into the lungs aids in rewarming. But administering chest compressions to someone with a detectable pulse is very dangerous, and a weak heartbeat is always preferable to the minimal level of circulation provided by CPR. Improper hand positioning or overly vigorous chest compressions can break ribs, cause internal injuries, or even bruise the heart.

The Effectiveness of CPR

A person whose heart has stopped is in very grave danger. The chances of survival are directly related to the proximity of advanced medical care. A victim who receives CPR within 4 minutes of cardiac arrest, and advanced life support (ALS) within the following 8 minutes, has a 43-percent chance of survival. If that same victim does not receive ALS in under 16 minutes, the odds of survival drop to only 10 percent. A victim who receives CPR more than 8 minutes after cardiac arrest has only a 7-percent chance of survival if ALS is applied within 8 minutes, and almost no chance after 15 minutes.

These statistics were developed from a

OVERALL SURVIVAL RATES FOR CPR RECIPIENTS			
Elapsed Time To Basic Life Support (CPR)	Elapsed Time To Advanced Life Support		
	<8 Mins.	8-16 Mins.	>16 Mins.
<4 Mins.	43%	19%	10%
4-8 Mins.	27%	19%	6%
>8 Mins.	7%	0%	0%

Figure 9-2. CPR survival chart.

broad base of incidents in which CPR was used, and they probably include a high percentage of elderly people. The success rate for near-drowning victims on rivers, who are generally younger and in better physical shape, may be considerably higher.

CPR-trained whitewater paddlers have documented a few "saves," but there have been many failures. Two clear lessons remain: First, CPR must be initiated almost immediately. There is no time to look for someone with CPR training or to learn it from a quick reference card. Second, if advanced life support is not reached within 15 minutes, the patient's chances of survival diminish greatly.

Access and Evacuation

For paddlers, the chance of success with critical patients depends on evacuation and the availability of advanced life support. Rescuers must decide whether they are dealing with a wilderness situation or standard medical access. Ironically, some isolated roadside rivers may be hours away from help; on the other hand, a vast and rugged wilderness may have standard medical access through an outfitter or ranger with the ability to arrange evacuation by helicopter. A victim located close to a highway or suitable helicopter landing zone may have access to advanced life support equaling that in developed areas. Wilderness protocols are not appropriate here. But in areas with poor communication, long evacuations, and limited availability of emergency services, wilderness protocols should be followed.

Lengthy evacuations of cardiac arrest victims are seldom successful. Even short hauls over rough country require considerable effort. Any victim requiring CPR must be carried out and will require continued CPR during transport. Chest compressions are usually not efficient during a litter carry across difficult terrain, because the victim's chest must be compressed against a firm, unyielding backstop. Check the surface the victim is lying on before you begin, and move him from any irregular, soft, or springy surface to one that is hard and flat.

Age and Fitness

The odds of survival for patients requiring CPR vary considerably. Younger people in good physical condition have a better chance of survival than older or less fit people. This is recognized by most search and rescue organizations and is reflected in the protocols used by emergency medical services with wilderness responsibilities. But the circumstances of the drowning must also be considered, particularly water temperature.

The Life-Saving Effects of Cold Water

To estimate a drowning victim's survival time you must factor in the temperature and clarity of the water. A situation that would be hopeless during warm weather might prove survivable in the cold. Cold, clear water greatly increases the possibility that a victim will survive a prolonged immersion. Water temperatures below 70°F can be considered cold; the colder the water, the better the victim's chances. Under cold conditions, the acceptable time lapse between cardiac arrest and the successful application of CPR can be increased from the usual 4 to 8 minutes to a full hour.

Any cold-water near-drowning reduces pulse rate substantially. The patient's skin is blue-gray and feels cold and stiff; the person looks and feels dead. Finding a pulse under these conditions is extremely difficult. Normally, a rescuer checks for pulse and breathing for 5 to 10 seconds; but due to the unusually weak, slow pulse and respiration rates in a cold-water near-drowning, monitoring should be extended to 1 minute and should be performed with extreme care. As mentioned earlier, it does no harm to provide rescue breathing when a patient is breathing slowly on his own, but do not apply CPR if there is a pulse. Hypothermia patients are in an extremely delicate state; cardiac arrhythmias may be present, and any rough handling, such as unnecessary CPR, may send these patients into cardiac arrest.

Deciding to Start CPR

Unless you have a responsibility to provide care (e.g., river guide, ranger, or other EMS personnel), you are not legally required to begin CPR. But most of us will respond out of a sense of moral responsibility to the victim and his family. Base your decision to initiate CPR on careful observation so that you can make reasonable and logical decisions with regard to discontinuing it.

In the wilderness, the use of CPR falls under different rules than elsewhere. In most situations where hospital-level care is more than 2 hours away, additional thought should be given to the efficiency of CPR. Chest compressions are exhausting and can sap the strength of even the strongest rescuer, burning calories much needed for warmth and energy.

Present protocols for the use of CPR in the wilderness suggest it should not be initiated under the following circumstances, since it is likely to be ineffective and may endanger the rescuer:

- The victim has gone into cardiac arrest due to trauma.
- The victim is a cold-water drowning victim, with an immersion time of more than 1 hour.
- The victim is in cardiac arrest, and advanced life support is more than an hour away.
- The victim is in cardiac arrest, no one wit-

nessed the event, and the time of onset is unknown.

- Evacuation requires an extended cross-country carry on a litter.
- Giving CPR would expose the rescuer to danger.
- CPR should never be administered if a pulse can be detected.

Some authorities are now saying that the so-called "Golden Hour Rule," which recommends CPR for victims who have been immersed in cold water less than 1 hour, should be stretched to 2 hours. This has come about since successful resuscitations have been performed on victims well beyond the 1-hour limit.

The American Heart Association and other groups that deal with such protocols are now reviewing changes that may encourage broader use of CPR, with the caveat to discontinue after 30 minutes if the patient does not regain a pulse. Of course, even with a broader application, CPR still should not be started if there are obvious signs of fatal injury.

When hospital care is readily available, standard protocols are applied. Once CPR has begun, a rescuer has an obligation to continue. It is a generally accepted protocol that CPR should not be discontinued except under the following circumstances:

- Adequate spontaneous breathing and circulation has returned.
- Another rescuer has taken charge of the victim and continues CPR.
- A physician, EMT, or advanced life-support team has taken charge of the victim.
- The rescuer is physically unable to continue.
- An authorized person pronounces the victim dead.
- Continuing CPR would endanger the rescuer.

Legal Considerations

The guidelines listed above could cause problems in a wilderness situation. Although there is no legal requirement to begin CPR except in one or two states, a rescuer is legally obligated to continue CPR once he has started. Discontinu-ing CPR might lead to legal charges of "abandoning a victim." It is unlikely, however, that a lawsuit would follow. Any wilderness application lends itself to the exhausted- or endangered-rescuer defense. The victim was dead when CPR began, so, in order to award damages, a court would have to conclude that the pulseless victim could have survived.

Wilderness protocols currently under consideration will permit individuals in isolated areas to discontinue CPR after 30 minutes when outside help is not available; the hope is that these efforts will have restarted the heart. This approach has been recommended by many experts in wilderness medicine. Unfortunately, most state laws do not allow a rescuer trained only in CPR to make the decision to stop, nor do they distinguish between urban and wilderness settings. This has not yet caused problems for private individuals, but it is of concern to professionals such as park rangers, rescue squad personnel, instructors, outfitters, and guides. These people should consult local medical and legal experts and develop company or agency guidelines.

Coping with Failure

Most people have trouble dealing with the aftermath of an intense CPR effort. It's not uncommon for death to follow even after a pulse is restored. Attempting CPR for 30 minutes, even in hopeless cases, may help participants deal more easily with an unsuccessful rescue. They know they did everything they could, and this helps cope with the inevitable feelings of guilt. When a rescue is unsuccessful, it's important to remember the limitations of CPR: success, even under ideal conditions, is far from guaranteed. The psychological problems associated with failed rescues, known as *post-traumatic stress,* are very real. Anyone who has been involved with a fatal accident or an unsuccessful rescue is advised to seek professional counseling. The Critical Incident Stress Foundation (see Appendix C) has debriefing teams in most areas of the country. These teams can be mobilized within 48 hours to help individuals, groups, or organizations deal with the residual stress caused by both successful and failed rescues.

Near-Drowning Aftercare

When a near-drowning occurs and a person is revived, untrained rescuers may think that the victim is out of danger. This is definitely not the case. Even when a victim exhibits no apparent problems, hidden life-threatening complications may be present. Someone may appear okay, only to fall victim to complications hours after the incident. Lifeguards call these incidents *parking-lot drownings*. Anyone who has received rescue breathing or CPR must be kept under observation and examined by a doctor as soon as possible.

Drownings can be categorized as either wet or dry, depending on whether water is aspirated into the lungs. Only about 10 percent of all drowning victims die from true asphyxia, or *dry drowning*. The rest draw in water during a final attempt to get air, or water passes into their lungs while they are unconscious.

When water gets into the lungs, a waxy substance known as the *alveolar surfactant* can be washed away. This coating of the lung's inside surfaces maintains the elastic nature of the *alveoli* (air-filled sacs in the lungs), where oxygen is exchanged for carbon dioxide. Once this coating is washed away, the alveoli lose their ability to stretch, and the lungs are easily damaged. Leakage of body fluid, which can fill the lungs and drown the patient, follows over the course of several hours.

Another significant problem is the buildup of carbonic acid in the bloodstream during severe *hypoxia*, or oxygen deprivation to body tissue. If the victim has been submerged for a few minutes (long enough to lose consciousness), the oxygen in the bloodstream is depleted and replaced with carbon dioxide. Since blood is predominantly water, and since water and carbon dioxide react to form carbonic acid, a severe chemical imbalance called *acidosis* results. In a near-drowning, profound acidosis contributes to circulatory failure.

Another secondary process known as *osmo-sis* also occurs when water enters the lungs. The membranes lining the lungs allow water to pass through until the solutions on both sides are equal in concentration. Body fluids contain many elements in specific amounts that are vital to our life processes. In a freshwater wet drowning, water crosses the lung membrane and enters the blood. This dilutes the electrolytes in the bloodstream and causes red blood cells to rupture. In muddy water or in salt water, body fluid is drawn through the capillary walls and into the lungs. The lungs then fill with this fluid, making breathing impossible. The resulting decrease in blood volume can lead to shock.

Contaminants in the water such as bacteria or chemicals create additional problems. Bacteria may cause aspiration pneumonia, while chemicals in the water may cause additional damage.

Once these life-threatening processes have begun, they can continue to cause damage long after a victim has been revived and may not become evident for 24 hours or more. Any patient who has lost consciousness underwater, and even those who have drawn significant quantities of water into their lungs during a bad swim, should seek a doctor's advice as soon as possible.

Recognizing and Treating Shock

The human body functions best within narrow limits. Normally, it maintains its chemical balances, physical properties, and fluid levels automatically, making adjustments when disturbances occur. Shock occurs in the presence of conditions that alter the body's ability to maintain its internal balances. It can be triggered by physical trauma such as broken bones or severe bleeding, allergic reactions, dehydration, drug reactions, poisoning, infection, or sudden emotional stress.

Shock affects the respiratory and cardiovascular systems. When a person fails to maintain adequate blood pressure and circulation, oxygen and nutrients can't be delivered to the cells, and waste products can't be removed. The heart, brain, lungs, and kidneys are unable to regenerate the cells that die when the supply of oxygen is inadequate; a constant blood supply is required to avoid permanent damage. Other organs and tissues can be sustained with much less circulation.

The ability to distinguish between true shock and *psychogenic shock* (also called *acute stress reaction*) is key in determining how to treat the patient. Knowledge of how the injury occurred, a good secondary survey of the patient, and close monitoring of vital signs should tell you which variety of shock is present. Elevating the feet, loosening the clothing, and covering the person with a blanket are sufficient for psychogenic shock; but for shock caused by internal bleeding, leg fractures, or head trauma, intravenous fluids, oxygen, and immediate and swift transport to a medical facility are needed.

Patients suffering from an acute stress reaction will respond well to a little tender loving care. When the patient is suffering from injuries causing true shock, this treatment should also be applied, but serious efforts to transport the victim must begin.

Recognizing Shock

Shock must be recognized immediately. Its onset can be very rapid, threatening a patient's life before assistance is available. In other cases, it can sneak up on an injured person while those performing first aid are busy treating other patients. You should never assume that a stable patient is safe from shock.

The main symptoms of shock are:
- A restless or combative attitude
- Pale, clammy skin
- Rapid breathing
- Rapid pulse
- Thirst
- An increase in capillary-refill time (To check this, squeeze a fingernail until it turns white. Watch for the blood to refill and the bed of the nail to turn pink again.)
- Nausea, vomiting

- Dizziness, weakness, or a decline in the level of consciousness
- A decrease in blood pressure

It is important to recognize and treat shock in the early stages when the body is still able to respond. When shock first begins, the heart and respiration rates increase, blood is shunted away from the skin, and blood vessels constrict. When these responses fail, the blood pressure drops and the patient enters severe shock.

It is not necessary to know the actual blood pressure level but rather to be aware of any changes that might indicate a worsening or unstable condition. When shock worsens and blood pressure drops, one symptom may be the lack of a discernible pulse at the wrist, followed by the loss of a pulse at the brachial artery in the upper arm. A basic first aid course will teach you where this artery is located.

Treating Shock

Treatment for shock is a very high priority. Since the best management of shock is prevention, care of serious injuries should include immediate treatment for shock without waiting for symptoms. If a patient exhibits any sign of shock, treatment must begin without delay. This involves supporting the circulation of blood to the brain, heart, and lungs and includes the following steps:
- Control all obvious bleeding.
- Loosen constricting clothing. Handle the patient gently. If necessary, cut away clothing that can't be opened or loosened.
- Prevent loss of body heat, also taking care not to overheat the patient. Wrap him in a blanket or extra clothing and monitor body temperature and other vital signs.
- Position the patient to facilitate circulation. If there are no major injuries, a patient should lie flat on his back with his legs elevated. Don't elevate the legs if this could aggravate injuries to the spine, head, chest, or abdomen, or if there are fractures and dislocations in the legs or pelvis.
- The legs should be lowered if raising them restricts breathing by pushing the

abdominal organs against the diaphragm. Patients with lung or chest injuries may find that a semi-seated reclining position helps with labored breathing. If the pulse rate suddenly increases by 15 to 20 beats per minute when the patient is elevated from a flat to a seated position, he should be kept lying down.

- Note the patient's level of consciousness and watch for deterioration. This is the best indication of whether there is sufficient blood flow to the brain.
- Watch for vomiting and prevent aspiration of vomit. If vomiting occurs, roll the patient on his side and remove any remaining debris from his mouth before repositioning him on his back.
- Do not give food, drink, or ice to a patient in shock. This may cause vomiting.
- Monitor pulse, respiration, and blood pressure (if possible) every few minutes for changes in the patient's condition. Record this information when possible.

Assess and treat shock at the earliest possible moment. Watch for it during both rescue and treatment. If untreated, shock can turn an otherwise stable situation into a fatality.

Spinal Cord Injuries

As whitewater boats got tougher, paddlers got bolder. Running waterfalls and other drops with a significant vertical component exposes boaters to terrific forces. Bad landings or collisions with rocks can lead to spinal injuries. Proper care is vital; carelessness may cripple the victim permanently. The key to management of spinal injuries is early assessment: recognition, followed by appropriate care, may save the patient from suffering irreversible damage. Any traumatic injuries involving a fall, sudden impact, twisting, or bending have the potential for spinal damage.

An assessment includes:

- Examining the scene for clues as to how the injury occurred
- Interviewing the patient or bystanders to determine the mechanism of injury
- Performing a physical examination appropriate to your level of training

Most people quickly recognize situations that can cause neck injuries. But injuries to other areas of the spinal column can be less obvious. Any fall can injure the spine, including falls in which a person has landed in a standing position. Compression, twisting, and bending of the vertebrae can cause fractures. These injuries can occur when a boater impacts violently against a rock or if a boat strikes the bottom after coming over a steep drop. Boaters who are battered while hanging upside down under their boat may sustain impact injuries at any point along their spine. But it is especially important to suspect a *C-spine* (the *cervical spine,* or neck area) injury when there is evidence of an impact injury above the nipple line.

Interviewing the victim can help determine the extent of injuries and is a good way to determine if spinal management is needed. When using information supplied by the patient, it is important to be sure it's reliable. Patients with an altered level of consciousness due to intoxication, acute stress reaction, true shock, or the presence of a significant physical or emotional distraction may not be reliable. In a wilderness situation spinal injury can be ruled out, provided certain conditions exist:

- The patient did not lose consciousness, is alert, cooperative, sober, calm, and can provide information.
- The patient experienced no sharp pains along the spine when the injury occurred.
- The patient has feeling in all extremities, with no tingling or pins-and-needles sensations.
- There is no pain or tenderness along the spinal column.
- There is no weakness or paralysis.
- There is no deformity along the spinal column.
- The patient can exert equal force when asked to squeeze your hands or to push against your hands with his feet.

When the cause of injury suggests that spinal damage could have occurred and the conditions listed above are not met, the patient must be treated for spinal injury. It is estimated that in 20 to 30 percent of cases in which permanent paralysis occurs, improper handling significantly contributed to the paralysis. Until a spinal injury can be ruled out, it is extremely important to ensure that the spine is not moved more than is absolutely necessary. Immobilize the patient as soon as possible.

Immobilization may be difficult, and immediate life-threatening problems must take precedence. Bringing a victim to shore while protecting the spine in anything other than calm water is almost impossible without specialized equipment. Techniques for immobilizing the spine, head, and neck require the rescuer to use both hands, making swimming or paddling almost impossible.

Removing a patient with a spinal injury from the water is tricky at best. The life-threatening effects of hypothermia caused by cold water must be weighed against the risks of further injury. Whenever possible, the victim should be placed on a backboard (for details on backboards, see Chapter 10, page 142) before removal from the water. More often than not, a backboard is not readily available. If several people are available, the victim can be lifted in unison. One person stabilizes the head while three people approach on each side, sliding their hands under the shoulders, back, buttocks, and legs. The patient is slowly and gently lifted, taking care not to twist or bend the spine. If a group is not available to help, a *clothing drag* is a good option. The rescuer grasps the victim's shirt or jacket at the shoulders and drags the victim backward while cradling the victim's head and neck between his arms.

The first step in working with any patient is to take control of the head. Grasping the patient's head with both hands not only immobilizes it but also keeps the patient from sitting up or moving around. If the victim is wearing a helmet, inspect the head for injury and the shell for impact marks. If there are no life-threatening injuries

requiring removal of the helmet, leave it in place. Most helmets are just about the right thickness to elevate the victim's head to a comfortable and stable position on a backboard, and a helmet is easier to hold than the head itself.

Helmets should be kept in place except under the following circumstances:
- The helmet interferes with airway management or rescue breathing.
- There is evidence of underlying life-threatening injuries that must be treated.
- The helmet is too loose to properly secure the head for C-spine immobilization.
- The size of the helmet prevents the head from being immobilized in a neutral, in-line position.

If you do have to remove the helmet, do so carefully. First remove the chin strap while the head and helmet are stabilized by a second rescuer. Then, the first rescuer grasps across the lower jaw with one hand and carefully supports the neck and the base of the skull in the back with the other hand. The second rescuer, who is still stabilizing the helmet, can then slowly and cautiously spread and rotate the helmet as needed to clear the ears and slide it free of the head. The second rescuer then manually stabilizes the head in a neutral, in-line position by placing one hand on each side of the head until it has been fully blocked in on a backboard.

If there is no helmet in place or there is room underneath the helmet, a cervical collar or SAM splint should be placed around the victim's neck to stabilize the head. This is always appropriate, even when the suspected injury is in the lower back. To protect one part of the spine, it's best to immobilize the entire spinal column. The same effect can be obtained by padding the head on both sides with blanket rolls, life vests, or some other rigid padding.

Before blocking and securing the head to the backboard, be sure to secure the torso first. Should the victim need to be log-rolled onto his side due to vomiting, it would be difficult and awkward to control an unsecured body with the head strapped in. See Chapter 10 for further information on using backboards and litters.

Figure 9-3. Two methods of turning an unconscious swimmer with a suspected neck injury:
(1) The rescuer immobilizes the victim's head between his outstreched arms, then turns him over.

(2) The rescuer immobilizes the victim's head by bracing it between his hands, then turns the
body over by ducking underneath it. (series continues at top of page 127)

Note: Proper backboarding technique and methods for stabilizing the spine should be learned from qualified instructors as part of a wilderness first aid training program.

If you suspect that the patient may have a C-spine injury, monitor closely for breathing and shock. Injuries to the C-spine can compromise nerves that control the diaphragm, and thus stop respiration. Should this happen, initiate rescue breathing immediately. Other nerve damage can cause all of the blood vessels to dilate, sending the patient into shock. The onset of either of these problems can be sudden.

Head Injuries

Surprising as it may seem to nonpaddlers, kayakers and canoeists seldom hit their heads. But although serious impacts are rare, the potential for injury is always there. Failure to recognize the difference between a minor bump and a serious head injury can have life-threatening conse-

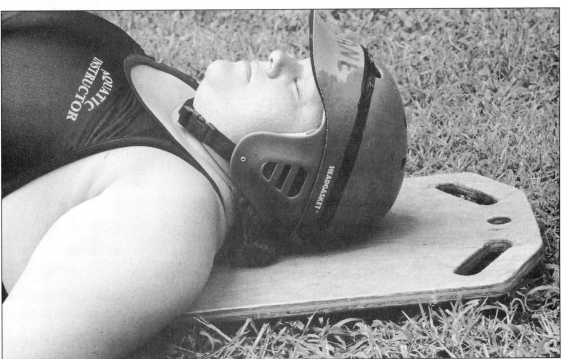

Figure 9-4. Proper head placement on a backboard for a person with a suspected spinal injury. The helmet supports the head in a natural position.

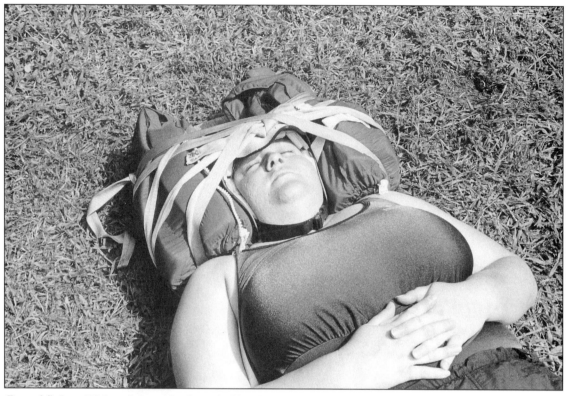

Figure 9-5. Immobilizing a helmeted head on a backboard with two life vests and a length of webbing.

quences. Swelling or bleeding within the limited confines of the skull can cause additional damage long after initial impact. When the incident points toward a possible head injury, the patient should be monitored for a number of prominent indicators. Early signs include:

- Severe, persistent headache or dizziness
- Persistent vomiting
- Altered levels of consciousness
- Difficulty in talking or slurred speech
- Drowsiness

Late symptoms include:

- Blood, possibly mixed with spinal fluid, coming from around the eyes, the ears, or the nose
- Pupils unequally dilated or unresponsive to light, or fixed and dilated
- Loss of consciousness
- Seizures

While the symptoms in the first group may indicate the possibility of a serious head injury, there are also other possible causes. Most could be the result of shock. If the mechanism of injury suggests a possible head injury and one or more symptoms are present, the patient should be closely monitored, immediately evacuated, and examined by a doctor without delay.

When a head injury head has been sustained, it is critical to avoid reinjury. The brain remains quite sensitive and prone to swelling for days or weeks after the initial injury. Reinjury during that time—even minor events—can cause the brain to swell, with dangerous results.

One misconception is that a patient with a head injury must be kept awake. Sleep is nature's way of controlling damage. It's perfectly appropriate to allow the patient to sleep, as long as he is awakened occasionally (once an hour) and restored to his previous level of consciousness. Monitoring levels of consciousness allows the caregiver to become aware of a deteriorating condition, which warrants desperate measures to evacuate the patient quickly.

Hypothermia

The human body functions only within a narrow temperature range. Warmth must be maintained to support the chemical and metabolic functions sustaining life. When the body cools below acceptable levels *(hypothermia),* there is a significant loss of strength, coordination, and alertness. Patients suffering from hypothermia may become unable to paddle effectively or to assist in their own rescue.

Paddlers must often contend with water that is dangerously cold. The effects are felt with surprising speed. Just like the effects of windchill, those of moving water produce an enhanced cooling effect that multiplies the impact of cold water. But hypothermia does not always occur in cold weather. Unexpected summer storms can soak an unprepared boater, or the wind can steal heat from his body. An unprotected boater who takes a long swim on a cool, overcast day may find it hard to rewarm. An injured victim may experience hypothermia as shock sets in.

Levels of Hypothermia

The human body has three layers: an outer, superficial layer; an intermediate layer; and the inner core. The superficial layer consists of the skin and subcutaneous tissue; the intermediate layer is made up of the extremities, skeletal and muscular tissues, and some lesser organs; the inner core contains the most critical organs: the heart, lungs, and brain. When hypothermia sets in, the body prioritizes heat distribution. It works to keep the vital core warm, hoarding the additional calories required to heat parts of the body that are not necessary for survival.

As the body begins to chill, the first signs of hypothermia come in the form of muscle tension and goose bumps. This nonshivering heat generation can double the metabolic rate. As the core temperature continues to drop, shiver-

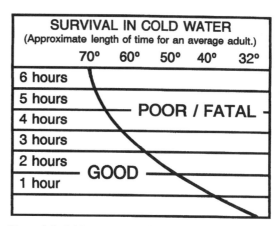

Figure 9-6. *Cold-water survival rates.*

ing begins. These uncontrolled contractions can increase the metabolism to five times the normal rate. Now the body is burning roughly 400 calories per hour. That's approximately the number of calories in two Snickers candy bars. Under the right conditions, the body can still rewarm itself.

At some point, the body starts to realize it is beginning to lose its battle to heat all its layers and decides it can survive without the superficial one. By shunting the blood flow away from the skin and outer tissues, it reduces the flow by about 1 to 2 percent. Strenuous activity could increase heat output, but the body has limited stores of fuel. Heating the entire body might burn what reserves are left and leave the victim to cool even more quickly.

When core body temperature falls below 95°F, shivering diminishes. The patient may become confused; reasoning becomes clouded. With continued heat loss, the body decides to sacrifice parts of itself so that the brain can survive. By reducing the area being heated, life is prolonged. First, the body decides it doesn't need the extremities, and carbon dioxide and lactic acid build up in these areas. Then it begins to shut down blood flow to unnecessary organs. And finally, it will limit flow to the three organs that sustain life itself.

As the body continues to cool, the victim begins to lose touch with reality. In some cases, they experience atypical mood swings and may become argumentative or combative when assistance is offered. Once the core body temperature drops to 90°F, shivering is replaced by muscle rigidity, and mental facilities are severely impaired. The victim is semiconscious, progressing toward unconsciousness. As the core temperature continues to drop, the metabolic rate diminishes, oxygen consumption drops, and respiration slows. Cardiac output also slows and weakens, resulting in further reduction in blood flow.

As lung and cardiac function diminish, cardiac arrhythmias develop, and ventricular fibrillation, a spasm of the heart muscle, eventually leads to cardiac arrest. A review of hypothermia symptoms follows:

- Temperature above 95°F. Conscious and alert. Vigorous uncontrollable shivering, pain or numbness in extremities, loss of manual dexterity, slurring of speech.
- 90° to 95°F. Conscious. Mildly impaired mental facilities. Diminished shivering is replaced by muscle rigidity.
- 86° to 90°F. Semi- or fully unconscious. Severely impaired mental abilities; may appear intoxicated. Rigid muscles, cardiac arrhythmias.
- 80° to 86°F. Unresponsive, unconscious. Rigid muscles, dilated pupils barely responsive to light, diminishing or nonexistent pulse and respiration, blue-gray skin color.
- 80°F. Ventricular fibrillation, cardiac arrest. Pupils fixed and dilated. Death.

Loss of body heat occurs in a number of ways that may affect a paddler simultaneously:

- *Radiation:* Heat is given off to a cooler environment directly. The amount lost to cold water is many times that of cold air.
- *Conduction:* Heat passes out of the body directly into a cooler object, such as the ground an injured person is lying on.
- *Convection:* Heat rises away from the body into the air. Clothing helps prevent this.
- *Evaporation:* Heat is removed from the body as water or perspiration evaporates and the skin dries. This is why wet clothing should be removed from hypothermia victims.
- *Respiration:* Heat is continually lost as cold air is drawn into the lungs, warmed, and then exhaled.

Treating Hypothermia

Different levels of hypothermia require different treatments. First, observe the symptoms, then diagnose the severity of the victim's condition and apply appropriate treatment.

Before treating hypothermia, it is important to determine whether the situation calls for wilderness protocols. If a medical facility can be reached within two hours, it is best to stabilize the moderately or severely hypothermic victim and transport him rather than risk medical complications that cannot be treated in the field.

A hypothermia victim with a body temperature of more than 95°F is conscious and alert. Remove wet clothing and replace it with dry, warm garments. Often a change of clothes and on-shore physical activity is sufficient. An open fire, heat packs, and warm, sweet liquids can speed rewarming. Remember: The caloric value of the sugar in a sweet liquid is more important than the warmth; these calories provide fuel for the body to rewarm itself. Avoid alcohol and caffeine; both dilate surface blood vessels and make rewarming more difficult. Heat packs should be applied under the arms, around the head and neck, and in the crotch area if possible.

Moderately hypothermic victims have a core temperature of 90° to 95°F. These patients are becoming impaired; shivering diminishes and mental confusion begins. They will not rewarm spontaneously and require the application of outside heat to survive. Their behavior is sometimes irrational, and they cannot be counted on to help themselves. Because the body can't rewarm itself, external heat is always necessary for recovery. In more severe cases, the rescuer must consider the possibility that cardiac arrhythmias may be present, making the victim extremely vulnerable to rough handling.

Rewarming a moderately hypothermic patient must be done slowly. Cold blood is trapped in the extremities and, with body functions interrupted or slowed, it is not only cold but also acidic. If this blood is reintroduced into the system too quickly, two things can happen, neither of them good. First, the core temperature drops rapidly. Second, the acidity may cause cardiac arrest. While physical activity is usually a good way to generate heat, a moderately hypothermic patient cannot afford to waste the calories or encourage the circulation of cold blood from the surface back into the core.

Since it may cause further rapid drops in temperature and even cardiac arrest if a moderately hypothermic victim physically exerts himself, it is important to take this into consideration not only at the treatment stage, but also when choosing a method of rescue.

In the field, a person can be placed near a fire or "sandwiched" between two people in a sleeping bag, but this method seldom works except in mild hypothermia situations. Other rewarming options are preferable. Rafters can place one boat upside down on top of another, creating an enclosed space. If several people go inside, that space will heat up quickly. This is a great place to rewarm someone. A tub of warm (110°F) water, if available, is excellent for rewarming. The water should be warm, not hot. Place the victim's torso in the water, leaving the arms and legs outside. This helps to rewarm the core first and minimizes the danger of aftershock. Remember that the patient may be in worse condition than was initially thought. Watch carefully for signs of diminished consciousness, which indicates a deepening hypothermic state.

Severe hypothermia occurs when the victim's body temperature is below 90°F. The situation may seem hopeless, but the patient has entered a "metabolic icebox" from which she may be revived in a hospital setting. Stabilize the patient, minimizing further heat loss, and transport quickly to a medical facility.

Both cold-water near-drowning victims and severe hypothermia victims have a diminished pulse and respiration. Vital signs may be slow and weak enough to require longer monitoring time than usually taught in CPR classes. Check the pulse for a full minute; it is unacceptable to provide CPR before heart function stops. On the other hand, rescue breathing forces prewarmed air into the core, and this may help stabilize the victim.

Cardiac arrhythmias are to be expected, and if cardiac arrest occurs, the half-hour period required by wilderness protocols does not begin until the patient has been rewarmed. Remember, the patient isn't dead until he is "warm and dead."

As with many other medical treatments, the use of CPR in severe hypothermia cases is controversial. Some physicians believe that once a discernible pulse can no longer be found, CPR should begin. The problem is, *to administer CPR while cardiac function is still present is the worst thing you can do.* And there is a possibility, according to some experts, that the heart may still be beating but at such a reduced rate that no pulse can be felt.

On the other hand, some experts in the field of wilderness prehospital care feel that CPR should not be started on a severely hypothermic victim. Regardless of the controversy, do not begin CPR on a severely hypothermic patient in the field if any of the following symptoms or conditions are present:

- A discernible pulse or breathing.
- Signs of severe trauma.
- Severe blood loss.
- A frozen chest.
- Rapid transport to a medical facility is not possible.
- Providing CPR will pose a risk to the rescuer.

Hypothermia always affects a rescuer's strategy. A victim who is close to hypothermia should not be further exposed to cold water. The physical ability of a victim experiencing hypothermia may be so diminished that he can't take care of himself. In severe cases, a victim must not exert himself because of possible complications.

Hyperthermia

Hyperthermia (overheating) occurs when a patient's body temperature rises out of control. Although paddlers are less likely to experience hyperthermia than hypothermia, they are often exposed to cold water and warm air simultaneously. Dressing for the cold water and exerting themselves on dry land often leads to overheating. Tropical and desert runs often are hot enough to cause heat-stress injuries on their own. Hyperthermia can exhibit itself in two ways, *heat exhaustion* and *heat stroke*. Another related problem, *dehydration*, can also have a negative effect on individual performance and, in later stages, can lead to hyperthermia.

Dehydration

The human body needs a constant supply of water not only for good health, but to metabolize food. Boaters wearing cold-weather gear often consciously limit their fluid intake in an effort to avoid the need to urinate during the day. While this may seem to control the inconvenience of getting out of a boat and removing layers of clothing, it can yield unexpected and unfavorable results. At other times, a paddler simply doesn't drink enough water to replace fluid loss in a hot, dry climate. A loss of as little as 10 percent can be fatal. With as little as a 4-percent loss, physical performance is seriously impaired; even being as little as "2 quarts down" noticeably reduces capabilities. Fluid loss, when combined with heavy physical exertion, can cause the body to lose control of its ability to regulate its internal temperature. This can lead to heat exhaustion or stroke.

The best treatment for dehydration is prevention. It can happen at any time of the year and does not require strong sunlight or extreme heat to occur. In fact, a mild breeze on a cold day can remove remarkable amounts of water from a small area of skin, such as the face and neck. A dry climate, even when cool, often causes considerable water loss without your knowing it. Most people eventually become thirsty, but by then the body is already dehydrated and recovery takes time. After you've had a drink of water, your body will need at least 30 minutes to regain its strength and efficiency.

Recent studies show that bulking up on fluids prior to physical activity helps prevent dehydration, while the adverse affects are minimal. With any water loss, the body will also lose electrolytes. This can present problems ranging from mild muscle cramps to cardiac arrhythmias. Electrolytes are easily replaced but, like rehydration, this may take 30 minutes or more. There are a number of sports drinks on the market that make excellent substitutes for plain water.

One of the most easily recognized signs of dehydration is the color and odor of your urine. The accuracy and convenience of a visual self-examination, while you are otherwise taking care of business, is undeniable. When the urine becomes a dark yellow, is cloudy, or has a strong odor, dilution is weak; the body is retaining fluids due to dehydration. If the urine is clear and has a relatively mild odor, this usually indicates a sufficient level of hydration. One minor problem, however, occurs when you consume coffee, tea, or other products containing caffeine. Caffeine is a diuretic and causes the kidneys to work overtime to produce urine. This can lead to a faulty indication of hydration when checking the urine and may itself contribute to further water loss.

With the new dehydrated fibrous snack bars, recognizing dehydration has become even more important. Mistaking a weak feeling or loss of physical ability for a lack of calories or a need for food can lead to problems if you are in fact experiencing mild dehydration. Water is necessary to metabolize food. In the case of high-fiber foods, this is even more of a problem, since fibrous foods absorb and lock up even more of the fluids that the body lacks. In short, eating high-fiber foods while dehydrated can lead to an even higher level of dehydration.

Heat Exhaustion

Heat exhaustion is actually a form of shock caused by the loss of fluid. A person who is hot and wearing layers of clothing does not benefit from the evaporation of perspiration that is produced by the body to cool itself. If this normal cooling doesn't occur, the body compensates by producing even more sweat. This cycle soon depletes the volume of water and electrolytes in the body, and the person begins to experience a mild form of *hypovolemic shock*, or a loss of blood volume.

Signs of heat exhaustion are dizziness, weakness, and nausea accompanied by cool, clammy, gray skin and profuse sweat. Headache may also occur. The pulse is often rapid, and body temperature may be slightly, but not severely, elevated. Treatment for heat exhaustion includes removing the patient from the hot environment, loosening or removing clothing to aid in cooling, and rehydration with a liter of water or a balanced sports drink diluted with 50 percent water. It will usually take at least half an hour for the patient to absorb the fluids and electrolytes necessary to reverse his symptoms. Monitor the patient closely through recovery.

Heat Stroke

While not as common as other heat- and hydration-related problems, heat stroke is probably the most dangerous. Heat stroke occurs when the body's natural cooling system is overwhelmed by the environment or activities in which the patient is engaged. Its onset can be quite rapid; the patient's temperature rises suddenly to a level that can destroy tissue. Symptoms of heat exhaustion may sometimes precede heat stroke, but not always. Heat stroke can also be caused by overdressing a person during an evacuation. The clothing worn for cold-water protection must be adjusted to prevent overheating in a shock victim or an unconscious victim. Failure to do so may have serious consequences. One paddler suffered irreversible brain damage because he was carried out wearing a drysuit.

As the victim's heat regulation mechanism shuts down, symptoms appear. These include hot, dry, or flushed skin; dizziness; confusion; weakness; and a feverish feeling. The victim's body temperature may rise as high as 106°F—high enough to do considerable damage. The first sign of heat stroke is often unresponsiveness and a strong, rapid pulse that becomes increasingly weak as blood pressure drops.

Heat stroke is a life-threatening condition; prompt and aggressive action must be taken to reduce the patient's temperature. This problem deserves a "whatever-it-takes" attitude, including cooling with wet towels or, better yet, immersion in cold water. Any patient who has suffered heat stroke requires immediate medical attention.

Shoulder Dislocations

Shoulder dislocations are one of the more common injuries experienced by paddlers. They occur when the current pulls or pushes the upper arm out of the shoulder socket. Many different treatments have been suggested over the years, ranging from stabilization and evacuation to the use of traction or leverage to relocate the joint. The problem with either approach is that any movement in a dislocated shoulder causes excruciating pain. It is imperative to stabilize the joint before moving the patient. Always monitor the patient closely for signs of shock until he reaches a medical facility.

Stabilizing the Injury

Stabilization, followed by rapid evacuation to a medical facility, is the most conservative approach. An orthopedic surgeon, working with X-ray equipment and drugs in a hospital setting, is more likely to reduce the dislocation without injury to the joint or arm. Before transport, the affected arm is placed in a sling. Take time to find the most comfortable position possible. An additional strap is placed across the upper arm, around the chest, and tied under the uninjured armpit. This minimizes the pain. Often the victim can walk out under his own power, but he should be accompanied by others to assist him if needed.

Joint Reduction

Reducing a dislocated joint means simply relocating the bones to their proper orientation. In a wilderness situation in which a medical facility cannot be reached within a reasonable amount of time, a dislocation should be reduced. There are a number of good techniques, but each falls into one of two categories. *Passive methods* require the patient to move the affected arm through a range of motion, allowing the joint to relocate on its own; *aggressive methods* use traction to reposition the affected limb. Since aggressive methods risk additional damage to the joint, passive approaches should always be tried first. Both passive and aggressive methods can easily be learned from competent instructors.

Every paddler has experienced stiffness in a joint after an injury. Shoulder dislocations are no different. This stiffness is actually *muscle-splinting*, or the body's way of stabilizing the injured joint. Unfortunately, in a shoulder dislocation, the muscle spasms that cause stiffness also interfere with relocating the joint. A shoulder dislocation should be reduced as soon as possible. The more time that elapses, the more stiffness will occur. The sooner you start, the better.

Passive Relocation. Paddlers will most commonly experience anterior dislocations, where the head of the humerus (upper arm bone) is forced forward and out of the joint. The passive technique described below is remarkably safe and reliable for reducing this type of injury. Often the first aid provider does little more than coach the patient through the procedure, allowing treatment to begin as soon as the victim is out of the water.

- The patient can be treated from a supine or sitting position. One person should stand behind the patient, keeping the patient's shoulders horizontal. A second person will support the elbow of the affected arm as the patient raises it to a horizontal position.
- The patient then rotates the forearm externally to a position behind the ear, as viewed from the side.
- The arm is then lowered while maintaining the externally rotated position. After being lowered, the arm is rotated internally to a position where a sling may be applied.

It is important to allow the patient to proceed at his own speed. A slow, gentle, careful motion is preferred to one that causes pain. The dislocation will sometimes reduce during the external rotation, but more often this will occur while the arm is being lowered or internally rotated. In studies done in 1982, this technique was successful in reducing 83 percent of the first-time anterior shoulder dislocations, and 86 percent of the recurrent dislocations treated. In the unsuccessful attempts to use this method, one of two conditions pertained. Either the patient was very muscular, or more than 30 minutes had elapsed since the dislocation had occurred.

Aggressive Relocation. When passive methods fail, traction is needed to compensate for the stiffness associated with the muscles splinting the joint. In a method similar to the passive method described above, approximately 10 pounds of traction are applied to the joint as the relocation is accomplished. This is best done by

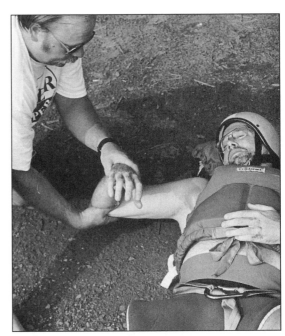

Figure 9-7. Aggressive joint reduction: (1) Place the patient on his back. Holding the elbow, gently help the patient to raise his arm. This action may be very slow, requiring up to 15 minutes.

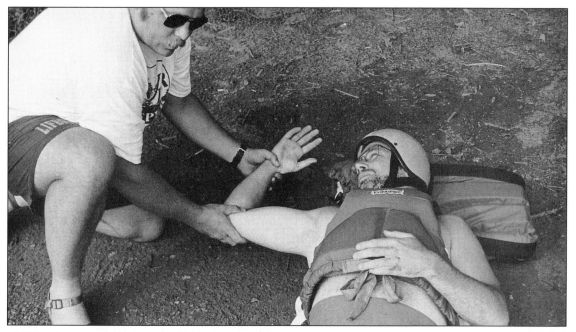

(2) When the arm reaches the "baseball" or "hitchhiker" position, with the thumb pointing toward the ear, apply gentle traction by pulling back at the elbow and wait for relocation to occur.

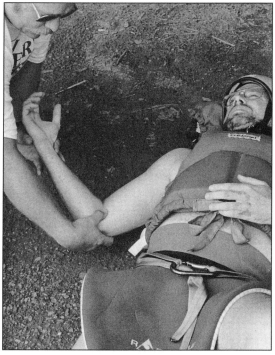

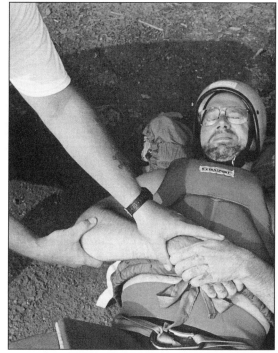

(3 and 4) Gently return the arm to the patient's body. The passive method is similar, but uses no traction.

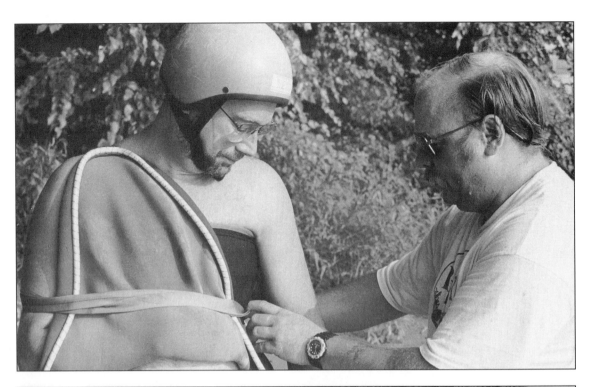

Figure 9-8. The Glen Carlson method of immobilizing a dislocated shoulder, using a sprayskirt and a webbing loop. Note that the arm is held securely across the chest and against the body.

those trained in wilderness medicine, or left to a physician.

Rehabilitation

Shoulder dislocations almost always cause damage to surrounding ligaments and may damage circulation and nerve function. These injuries often do not heal well and have prematurely ended many paddling careers. It's vital to recognize the need for medical care even in those cases when the joint has been relocated. Many aspects of this injury lead to chronic pain and further dislocations in later years. An examination by an orthopedist, followed by aggressive rehabilitation in a sports-medicine facility, is essential. Do not rush to get back on the water; a steady, patient approach to recovery is always best. Exercises prescribed by a physical therapist must be performed regularly, with the healing process stretching out over several years.

Emergency medical care is a rich and constantly evolving field. Regular training is a must for any paddler. Like a seat belt, it's nice never to have to use it, but it's good to know it's there.

Once the patient has been treated, the next step is to bring him safely back to civilization. Evacuation is discussed in the next chapter.

CHAPTER 10

Evacuation and Transport

Transporting a badly injured person through wild country and back to civilization can be exhausting for rescuers and their patients. Evacuating by river requires great caution, excellent judgment, and the support and cooperation of the entire group. Waiting for help, while often the safest option, leaves the victim and his caretakers exposed to the elements for hours or even days. Walking out requires stamina and good wilderness navigation skills; a litter carry, even for a short distance, is time-consuming and extremely strenuous. Many otherwise competent rescuers make bad choices during the evacuation phase. Groups must always take the quickest and least strenuous approach to carrying out a rescue while making sure that they have the personnel, skill, and time to carry out their plan.

Deciding whether to paddle out, transport over land, or wait for help requires careful thought. The surrounding terrain, especially the distances involved and the location of roads and trails, limits your options. The nature of the injury and the strength of the party must also be evaluated. When a carry is being considered, factors such as the availability of materials for building a litter, the improvisational skills of the party, the terrain to be traversed, and the personnel available are all important. When sending for help, the strength of the local emergency medical care system and its probable response time must be weighed against the gravity of the injury and the expected weather conditions at the site. Let's review each option individually.

Sending for Help

Sending for help is frequently the most reasonable approach. Some people remain with the victim while others hike out or paddle downstream to find help. The advantage is that severely injured paddlers, especially those with spinal injuries, are not moved until the proper equipment and skills are available. The disadvantage is that this takes time, perhaps a lot of time. On a readily accessible roadside river, this is not an issue; in an isolated wilderness, it is your primary consideration. As the group attempts to find help, both victim and caregivers are exposed to the elements. An unexpected overnight bivouac is at best uncomfortable; at worst, life-threatening. Some injuries (such as severe head trauma, heart attack, or profound shock) are true medical emergencies that require the extra effort to get the victim to medical help as fast as possible. You must decide whether the severity of the injury justifies the risk.

Paddling Out

Paddling out is often the fastest and least strenuous option. An injured person can float flat water and easy riffles and be helped around more significant drops. This requires considerable patience and support from the group. Members of the party must assist by traveling slowly, helping the injured person as needed. Never take foolish risks, particularly on runs beyond an injured paddler's skills. Miscalculation can lead to a swim, and thus a risk of further injury, hypothermia, and shock.

Floating Out

Floating out is usually quicker and far less strenuous than a carry up and out of a steep gorge. Rafts are often available, particularly on popular runs. With severely injured persons, a short float to a road-end or a helicopter landing site can

Figure 10-1. A canoe catamaran ready for use. (Jane C. Sundmacher photo)

save everyone a lot of time and trouble. Never tie an injured paddler onto a raft or other watercraft. This poses a real threat of drowning should the craft become unstable. Sneak routes are usually chosen through most rapids. If a rapid presents particularly difficult problems, the patient may be walked or carried around.

A raft is usually the best choice for evacuating a patient, but open canoes can be used too. If the patient is not badly injured, he or she can be transported in a tandem boat, in a sitting position. Two open canoes can also be lashed together, forming a makeshift catamaran for added stability. To do this, tie a couple of stout sticks across the thwarts of both boats. In building a catamaran, take care when using today's shorter, high-rocker solo craft. To minimize control problems, you should try to use two canoes of similar size and design.

The victim's boat must either be left on the

A State of Confusion

Rivers pass through some pretty rugged country. You can't know just *how* rugged until you're faced with the challenge of transporting someone who can't paddle. I was leading a first-timer's trip on the Cheat River in 1992. We'd seen the group ahead of us take an unconventional route down High Falls, where one of their folks had flipped and swum. After the run, we paddled over to them.

The swimmer was banged up, cold, and scared. There were nasty bruises on one cheekbone, and her right hand was cut and swollen. She couldn't hold a paddle. The options were not good. It was late and getting cold. Three big rapids separated her from the takeout. Looking downstream at the Maze, I saw that the shores were steep and the portage options weren't appealing. The group couldn't decide what to do; I talked to them a bit, but really couldn't offer much help, as I was responsible for the 12 inexperienced people following me.

Fortunately, Chris Koll and his wife, Caron, showed up. Chris is one of the strongest kayakers I know, and he was paddling a high-volume creek boat. I asked him if he could help the woman, and then continued down with my group.

Impatient with the group's indecision, Chris instructed the woman to lie on his back deck and lock her hands around his waist.

Thus loaded, he paddled the "dog-water" (anything under Class IV). At the big drops he landed, walked the injured paddler around, then came back and ran his boat through. At his urging, the group took the empty kayak, attached the sprayskirt, and tied the waistband shut. This allowed them to herd it downstream to the takeout with little effort.

The injured paddler's group was using a shuttle service with several dozen other people on board. The others didn't want to wait, so we agreed to shuttle everyone else out. Some of the paddlers in our party gathered towels and dry clothes as I sat on the bridge and waited nervously. Chris and Caron appeared first; we helped the injured paddler get dry and clothed, then one of our vehicles took her to a hospital in Morgantown, where she was treated and released. The rest of the two groups piled into the remaining cars for a crowded ride back to the put-in.

In retrospect, things worked out well. River evacuations, when possible, are the fastest and easiest alternatives. Had they sent for help, it almost certainly would not have arrived before dusk. A night out would have been uncomfortable—perhaps worse. A walk-out would have taken several hours and would probably not have been finished before dark.

—*CW*

river or shepherded downstream. Tandem canoeing teams or rafting crews may be broken up to handle the extra boat. With a kayak or C-1, put the sprayskirt back on the boat and tie the opening closed; decked boats rigged this way have run miles of Class V water unassisted.

Walking Out

Patients who are able to walk out on their own should be encouraged to do so, taking a route suited to their ability. Remember that an injured paddler may have difficulty traversing steep riverbanks and trails. Shock may set in unexpectedly, rendering him helpless. To minimize risks, first carefully assess a victim's condition, including his stamina and fitness to cover the terrain ahead. An injured paddler should be accompanied by two people whenever possible; if problems are encountered, one person can care for the victim while the other goes for help.

Carries

If the injury is serious enough, the group must consider carrying the injured person. Carries are much more time-consuming and strenuous than the rescues discussed previously. Movement for its own sake is foolish; the goal is not merely to remove the patient from the accident site but also to ensure safe transport to a medical facility. A long carry over unfamiliar terrain can create additional problems and can cause the patient significant pain. In planning your route, consider the terrain ahead. Hauling an injured person up even a moderately steep and rocky slope is slow, dangerous work. Appropriate safeguards must be taken to avoid falls. For this reason, it's usually best to go around steep slopes whenever possible. Ingenuity is vital, and the more people there are to share the load, the better. Plan for a relief crew; the litter team may need to rest after less than a half mile of carrying.

One- and Two-Person Carries

If the victim is only slightly injured, and when distance is short and over easy terrain, you may consider carrying the victim. This is far more difficult than most people imagine. Single-person carries are seldom practical for moving anyone larger than a child or small adult. Even two-person carries are practical only over short distances on even terrain.

Litters

Any evacuation of a seriously injured paddler requires a litter for several reasons:

- Pain can lead to shock and must therefore be minimized. A litter allows a patient to be held securely by a number of people, ensuring a smoother ride.
- It is easier to lift and carry a litter than the injured person alone.
- The litter can be attached to belay and haul

Figure 10-2. The fireman's carry is good only for very short distances.

Figure 10-3. This two-person carry requires a wide path to work effectively.

lines for greater safety on steep slopes.
- The litter itself will protect the victim from rocks and debris.
- Teams of rescuers can most easily "spell" each other when a litter is used, making it possible to cover long distances with reasonable efficiency.

Injured paddlers should be placed on the litter carefully; the right position minimizes discomfort and helps to keep their condition stable. Patients usually are most comfortable on their back. When carrying a victim uphill, keep the head at the high end of the litter. If a spinal injury is suspected, secure the body so that the spine will not move. Get a backboard before evacuating the patient even if this requires a substantial wait.

Backboards are readily available on many commercially run rivers and when properly rigged provide a secure litter. If local emergency units get involved, a *basket,* or *Stokes, litter* may be available. The methods of securing a victim to a litter or backboard are much the same: a set of straps holds the victim securely while preventing movement of the injured portion of the body. If there are slopes or embankments to traverse, the patient must be secured against sliding up or down. Be careful not to place straps across injured parts! Under ideal circumstances, the victim is attached at the chest, pelvis, and feet. Padding is included around the head and knees for comfort. If the patient is unconscious or unable to protect himself, his arms should be gently tied down. This reduces the chance of an arm becoming caught between the litter and a tree or rock. If the arms are not restrained, the patient should be instructed to hold them on top of his body.

Moving the Patient

Techniques for placing the patient on a litter vary according to the position in which the victim is found. When a C-spine injury is suspected, tight-fitting helmets should be left in place and stabilized (see Figures 9-4 and 9-5, pages 127–128; see also page 125 for conditions under which you *would* remove a helmet). The key to moving a victim with a suspected spinal injury is to lift the entire body as a unit. At least four people are needed to control the head, body, and legs, and in some techniques a fifth person is needed to slide the board underneath the victim. Two techniques are shown in Figures 10-5 and 10-6 (page 144–145). Handling spinal injuries requires specialized training; if you lack the skills and gear, keep the person comfortable and send for skilled medical help.

Improvising Litters

If a backboard or Stokes litter is not handy when trouble strikes, it may be practical to construct an improvised litter in the field. This is not a good idea if the patient has a suspected spinal injury! Before constructing a litter, consider the terrain ahead, and whether it will be possible to

Figure 10-4. "Packaging" a victim for a steep-slope evacuation involves tying securely at the shoulders, hips, and feet. If the person is unconscious, the arms and hands should be tied gently across the body to avoid crush injuries. (Greg Kobol photo.)

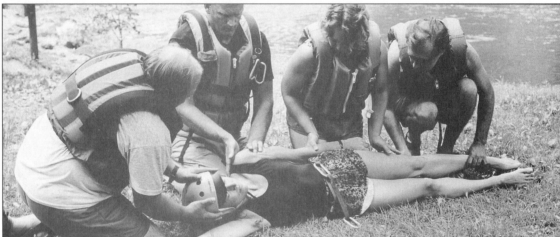

Figure 10-5. Rolling a person with a suspected spinal injury onto her back or onto a backboard prior to transport requires several people working together: one each for the head, shoulders, hips, and legs. (Greg Kobol photos.)

Figure 10-6. One method of placing an injured person on a backboard: the rescuers lift in unison (top) and slide the board underneath (bottom). (Greg Kobol photos.)

adequately stabilize and protect the victim. Sometimes sending for help is faster and safer.

To construct an improvised litter, run two poles through the arms and bodies of three or four paddle jackets or PFDs (Figure 10-7). Alternatively, wrap two poles with a blanket or sleeping bag (Figure 10-8). Both methods work well on even ground. Unfortunately, stabilizing the victim on such a litter is difficult. There is nothing worse than having an injured patient slide off a litter!

Canoes and kayaks with their internal outfitting removed can serve as litters, but there is no easy way to tie the victim in securely. Removing the outfitting is time-consuming, and there are few good handholds for the litter bearers.

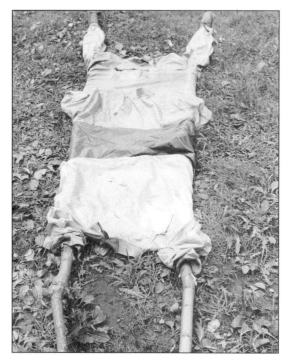

Figure 10-7. A litter constructed from two poles and three paddle jackets. *(Greg Kobol photo.)*

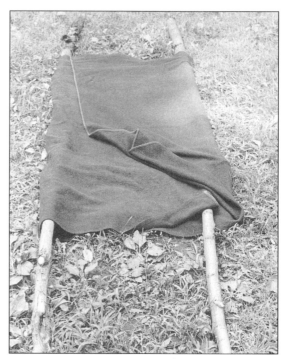

Figure 10-8. A blanket litter works because the friction between the layers holds the litter together. *(Greg Kobol photo.)*

The boat itself is surprisingly heavy and may have to be dragged, producing an uncomfortable bumpy ride for the patient. If you're lucky enough to be near railroad tracks, you can place the boat sideways on the tracks and push it to civilization.

If a sleeping bag or similar padding is available, a very effective litter can be fashioned from rope (see Figure 10-9, steps 1–4). Add a few saplings for rigidity, and you have a workable litter that encapsulates the patient's body and is stable in any position. It will hold the patent securely in rough terrain and has many points available for lifting or connecting a belay line. Remember that in warm weather the padding could cause the patient to overheat. Monitor the patient's temperature, and provide sufficient ventilation for comfort.

Carrying a Litter

Carrying a litter is exhausting. The standard military canvas stretcher that most people are famil-

Figure 10-9. Steps in constructing an emergency litter with a blanket and rope: (1) Lay out two stout poles and a length of rope. *(Greg Kobol photos.)*

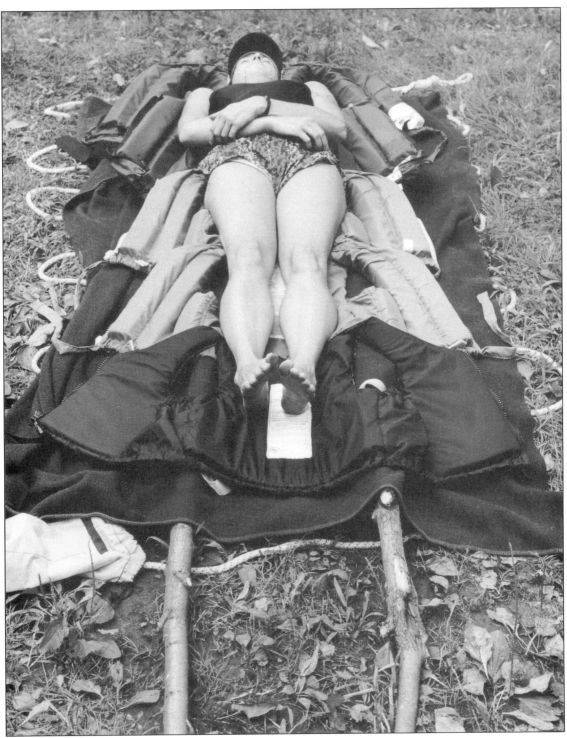

(2) Spread out a blanket and pad the litter with life jackets.

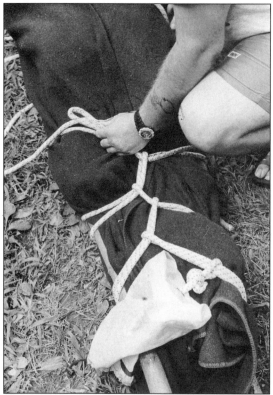

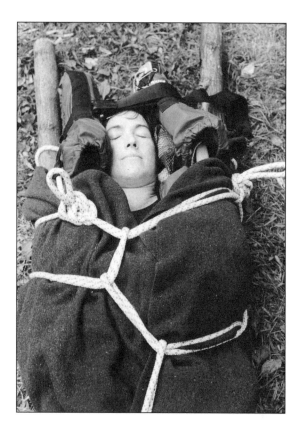

(3 and 4) Secure the victim.

(5) Transport.

iar with has two handles at each end. A common misconception is that each pair of handles is meant for one person to lift. On a short carry, such as would be found in an army M.A.S.H. unit, this might be true; in the field it takes one person at each of these handles to get the job done. To even the load on the litter bearer, attach a web strap to the litter handle next to the hand grasping the rail, then run it over the shoulders and down to the opposite hand. This allows litter bearers to transfer some of the weight to their shoulders. This strap can also be used when carrying either a backboard or improvised litter.

An effective litter carry over long distances requires lots of help. Most people cannot carry a litter more than half a mile without relief. While the primary objective is to get the patient to medical help, ongoing care must also be provided. This can be easily forgotten when the terrain is

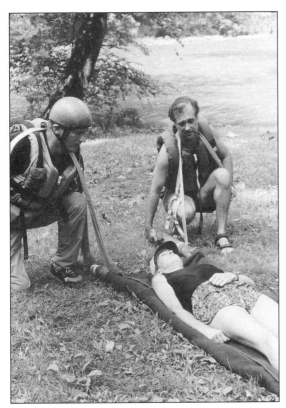

Figure 10-10. Lifting the litter using a webbing loop distributes the weight across the rescuer's shoulders. (Greg Kobol photo.)

rough, but care is critical to the welfare of an injured person. One member of the team should be appointed to monitor the patient's condition. Another team member should be appointed to lead the group and coordinate its movement in rough terrain. Any member of the team has the option to call for a "stop" as needed.

Additional help becomes especially useful in rough country. Rather than lifting a litter over an obstacle, the group can pass it from person to person across the barrier. This is less strenuous and eliminates the unsteadiness encountered when a team is climbing in places with poor footing.

Steep-Slope Evacuations

Steep slopes are deceptively dangerous. The only real difference between falling down a

steep, 30-foot, 60° slope and falling off a 30-foot-high cliff is the number of times you'll hit the ground! Hillside evacuations are risky for all concerned; if the rescuers should fall, the danger to the patient is clear. Time-consuming steps must be taken to belay the litter and keep it under control. The steeper the slope, the more sense it makes to go around rather than up.

A steep slope is any angled terrain on which a slip can cause the litter team to fall or slide uncontrollably. This can be as little as 30° or as much as 45°, depending on the footing. As the angle increases, so does the difficulty of transport. Slick rocks, mud, or ice will add to the danger.

Belay Lines and Haul Lines

When a steep embankment cannot be avoided, it's best to use a backboard or commercially constructed litter. This permits a belay line to be attached. Tethers are also secured to each of the litter tenders. These prevent the whole "package" from sliding down the slope if it is dropped. When footing becomes extremely difficult and uphill progress begins to suffer, a haul system should be added. Unlike a belay line, which serves as protection when a fall occurs, a haul line assists the litter tenders by actually lifting the load up the slope.

When a belay or haul line is attached, litter tenders are tethered to the litter with a web harness. This prevents them from falling or slipping and helps them keep their footing in difficult terrain by giving them a third point of support in addition to their legs. The litter tenders lean back into the line for support as the haul line provides the uphill force to move the team forward.

To tether the tender to a litter with an adjustable connection, a prusik loop can be tied back on itself with a prusik knot. This is accomplished by tying a prusik knot (see Appendix A) onto two fingers, then removing the fingers and sliding the other end of the loop through in their place (Figure 10-11, page 150). The loop formed by the prusik knot is then carabinered to the harness, and the other end of the prusik

Figure 10-11. A prusik knot is used to create an adjustable connection for litter bearers in a vertical rescue.

loop is carabinered to the litter. Fixed tethers made from rope or webbing can also be used.

Without teamwork the safety of the victim and the litter team can be jeopardized. One person acts as leader of the litter team and a second person manages the raising system. Idle chatter should be kept to a minimum so the members of the group can give full attention to the commands of their team leader. The two leaders communicate with each other during the raising or lowering to keep it running smoothly.

Using Mechanical Advantage

Steep slopes may require mechanical assistance to move the litter uphill. A 1:1 system with a prusik brake or *Muenter hitch* (see Figure 10-12) serves as a simple belay, and easily flows into more technical systems if needed. The belay line is kept taut and the brake prusik or Muenter hitch is advanced as required. It's not necessary

Figure 10-12. The Muenter hitch is used for belaying and controlled lowering. Note the locking pear-shaped carabiner.

2:1 Raising System

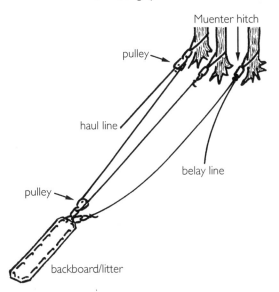

Figure 10-13. This low-angle raising system uses a 2:1 mechanical advantage. Note the separate belay line.

Figure 10-14. A counterweight system used in conjunction with a 2:1 mechanical advantage is extremely effective for steep-slope evacuations. Two people, tied into the haul line and leaning back (above), use their weight to provide all the power needed to raise the litter. Note the separate belay line below the haul system. As shown in Figure 10-13, there is a pulley at the top of the litter. By leaning back into their harnesses (below) the attendants are able to "float" the backboard, eliminating the need for constant heavy lifting. (Greg Kobol photos.)

to apply tension to negotiate the hill.

Several hauling systems can be used to pull the litter and team up a steeper slope. A rescuer tied to the other end of the 1:1 belay line can walk downhill as the litter rises, creating a 1:1 counterweighted haul system. With steeper slopes and

heavier loads a mechanical advantage is needed and can be added by means of a 2:1 (or greater) haul system (Figure 6-13, page 81).

Going Downhill. If the litter must be lowered down a steep slope, the same principles apply. The litter is backed down the slope with the victim's head and the litter team facing uphill. A Muenter hitch can be used as a belay device, and for added safety a prusik brake can be set on the line immediately below it. Should the litter team lose control, the tended brake prusik is released as the tension is applied against the Muenter hitch, locking the belay line.

Vertical Rescue

As the ground steepens, rescuers cross the line from a low-angle to a high-angle rescue. It is important to understand the difference between the two. In a low-angle environment, the litter bearers support their own weight and the weight of the litter, while the belay or haul line aids progress up the slope. In high-angle rescues the rope supports the weight of both the litter and the team. This is best left to those with the training and equipment needed to do it safely. Unprepared rescuers should "back off" as these boundaries are approached.

Helicopter Rescue

Helicopters are a remarkable resource, but their limitations must be understood. Too often a ground crew has little or no experience working with them. Being expensive to buy and run, "choppers" are usually owned by government agencies or the military. Unless you are in an area with preplanned helicopter support, you can expect significant delays in obtaining one while appropriate clearances are obtained. The expense and delays usually limit helicopter transport service to people with severe injuries. Because of these disadvantages, other options should be fully explored prior to requesting this type of assistance.

Helicopters are very agile but cannot land on all types of terrain. While there are a few daring pilots (mostly Vietnam veterans) who will do almost anything, most will not risk themselves or their machines by attempting marginal landings. While waiting for a chopper to arrive, move the patient to a suitable landing zone. Choose an area that is flat and clear to ground level, at least 60 to 100 feet in every direction from where the helicopter is expected to land. When possible, select an area where the pilot can take off and land at an angle, rather than force a straight vertical landing. Clear away loose debris that could be swept into the rotor or engine intakes. Mark the landing-zone perimeter. As the craft approaches, you can provide useful information about wind direction by using smoke; throwing up handfuls of dirt, pine needles, or leaves; or allowing a strip of cloth to blow in the breeze. Only one person should face the helicopter and provide directions; all other personnel should turn away to avoid confusion.

Stay clear of the landing zone during landing and take-off. The downdraft from the rotors can shoot dirt, stones, and other debris into unprotected eyes, and has a significant cooling effect as well. Look away and shield the patient

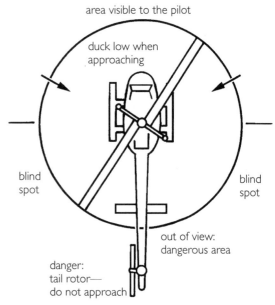

Figure 10-15. *Approaching a helicopter. The pilot has best visibility in the front of the aircraft, and has a blind spot in back.*

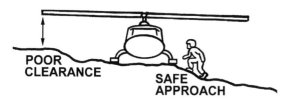

Figure 10-16. Never approach a helicopter from the uphill side.

from the downdraft. Do not approach the helicopter; allow the crew to come to you. The main rotor on some aircraft may dip as low as 4 feet from the ground directly in front of the craft. The safest approach is as directed by a crewmember. When instructed, crouch low to the ground and approach on the downhill side from the 2 o'clock or the 10 o'clock position. These warnings are particularly important with rear-loading helicopters; the tail rotor and lack of visibility from the pilot's position present potential hazards. The rear of the helicopter is the pilot's blind spot. In the absence of the crew, wait for a signal from the pilot before approaching the machine.

If a helicopter arrives after dark, do not shine flashlights at the oncoming aircraft. This can blind the pilot and slow the operation. Mark the perimeter of the landing zone with low-intensity lights, such as flashlights aimed toward the ground, or chemical light sticks. Avoid using flares or fires that are too bright or could be blown by the rotors into nearby combustible material.

Be prepared to give the flight medics a full report of the patient's condition, including the cause of injury. This information is not only crucial for continued care, but may also advise the medics of injuries that can be adversely affected by drastic changes in altitude.

Psychological Considerations

Whatever means of moving the patient are employed, pay attention to the patient's mental state. Make every effort to reassure the victim that you are doing all you can to ensure a quick and safe evacuation. Keep the patient's morale as high as possible. Speak to the patient directly. If you don't know his or her name, find out what it is and use it.

Try to be supportive in what you say. Careless statements about how awful someone looks or how poor the chances of recovery are can actually send an injured person into shock! Lying to someone whose injuries are clearly severe can destroy your credibility; focus on the efforts being made to get help and on the competence of providing first aid. Although the presence of friends can be a tremendous morale booster, those in contact with the victim should keep a positive attitude. Those who cannot control their emotions should be helped to settle down and kept away until they do.

Always make patients aware of what you are doing, and what you expect of them. This eliminates some of the feelings of helplessness that often occur as the rescue progresses. Give patients as much control as possible; let them say when they are ready to go, especially if a proposed treatment or movement is difficult or painful. Giving them something to do to help the rescue, such as holding a rope, blanket, or dressing in place, may help their spirits.

CHAPTER 11

Advanced River Rescue Skills

Almost all river accidents can be handled using the methods described in previous chapters, but other situations require specialized skills. These techniques are more complex than those discussed previously and often require considerable equipment and time to set up. We'll discuss several of them because they're well worth knowing. The skills in this chapter are advanced; most are not taught in basic river rescue courses.

Boat-Lowering Systems

A floating platform sitting just upstream of an accident can be extremely helpful, especially if wading and swimming approaches are too dangerous or if unsurvivable rapids lie downstream. Boat-lowers require the right gear, good rigging skills, and an appreciation of the loads on each component of the system. Since they take a good deal of time to set up, they're better suited for recovering bodies or equipment than live victims.

Rafts, stable and unsinkable, are ideal for use in boat-lowering systems. Self-bailers handle best; they float high in the water, creating minimal drag and strain on the set-up. Individual open canoes are too tippy to be lowered successfully, but two canoes can be joined by lashing two stout branches across the thwarts amidships to create a remarkably stable catamaran. These "cats" take some time to rig successfully. The two canoes should be of similar design; many short solo boats will be difficult to control because of their high rocker. They are typically used more conservatively than rafts because of the increased risk of swamping.

Ferrying Lines

Often the most difficult part of setting up a lowering system is getting lines from one side of the river to the other. Each control line must reach diagonally all the way across the river to allow a full range of adjustment. This isn't a problem on narrow streams, but it's almost impossible on wide rivers. Tying lines together creates problems because the knots can't pass smoothly through a pulley or a carabiner.

Ferrying a rope across the river, much like paddling itself, depends on working with, rather than against, the current. Often a rope can be paddled over fairly easily. The end can be attached to a tow system, 'binered to a webbing loop slung over the shoulder, or hand-held (Figure 11-1, page 156). To reduce entanglement risk, hold or hang the webbing loop on the side of the body that the rope is coming from. This way, if the rope hangs up, the person ferrying it can let go before it pulls her over.

The surface area of a ⅜-inch rope extending 50 feet across the current is about 1.6 square feet. Even a strong paddler will have trouble pulling it upstream against a fast-moving river. What can be done to reduce the pull? One technique involves carrying a long length of light line. Parachute cord presents minimal drag and can then be used to retrieve the rope. Another method is called the *reverse pendulum* (Figure 11-2, page 157). By moving well upstream of the final objective before ferrying across, the line travels downstream with the boat, minimizing drag.

Other solutions are trickier and not always successful. Lifting the rope out of the water to prevent drag may help, but the weight of the rope itself tends to pull a boater backward. When a long ferry makes it difficult to keep the rope off the water, "skipping" the line back upstream momentarily takes pressure off the paddler. This technique works much like using a jump rope: the rope is briefly pulled tighter, then lifted out of the water and flipped back upstream. It now floats with the flow as the ferry continues. If possible, have someone stand on the opposite shore, ready to receive the line.

Many otherwise successful ferries fail when a paddler isn't able to get out of his boat and onto shore before being pulled back into the current.

Securing a Lowered Boat

Once you have selected the boat to be lowered, the bow must be secured to the lowering rig. Swamping increases the strain on a rope system enormously; the boat quickly becomes uncontrollable and the rigging is often torn apart. To make swamping less likely, attach the rope low on the bow of the boat being lowered, close to the water's surface. This tends to lift the bow up and out of the current, keeping the inside dry. To spread the load, use multi-point anchors when affixing the harness. You don't want the rescue craft to suddenly come loose in the middle of an operation. A good harness is shown in Figure 6-12.

Telfer-Lower Setup

A *telfer lower* involves suspending a boat from a static line stretched across the river. A system of lines and pulleys is used to control its position. Telfers put tremendous strain on static lines even under ideal conditions; the rushing water creates an enormously powerful vector pull that exceeds the breaking strength of many ropes. If the oncoming water washes over the bow of the craft being lowered, even a heavy-duty ½-inch static water rescue line with a breaking strength of 4,500 pounds may fail! This has been captured in amusing detail in videos of clinics, but the consequences could be far from humorous. An experienced team of paddlers with the right gear needs between 30 to 45 minutes to set up a telfer, which rules it out for many rescue situations.

As the name suggests, a "static" rope is designed to minimize stretch. Because of the huge load this line must carry, use the strongest rope available. It's definitely not a good idea to use a standard ⅜-inch rescue bag rope; even if it were long enough, the stretch would make the lower difficult to manage.

Don't overtension a static line. Stress can be reduced by adding 10 feet of downstream slack

Figure 11-1. Ferrying a line. Hooking a webbing loop over the shoulder opposite the source of the line you're ferrying feels more secure, but if the line snags, the boater will be pulled over.
(Jane C. Sundmacher photo.)

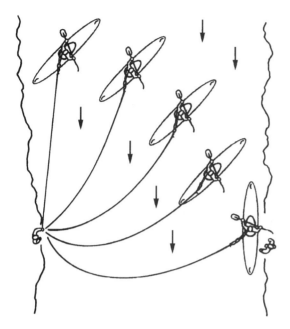

Figure 11-2. In a reverse pendulum ferry, the rope travels with the current—minimizing drag—as the paddler moves across the river.

(under load) for every 100 feet of river width. This concept, known as the *rule of ten*, reduces the mechanical advantage on a vector pull to 2.5:1. Stretch varies considerably among different lines, and the load changes with the speed of the current, making it hard to guess exactly how much to tension a static line. One way to prevent overtensioning is to tighten the rope (using a 3:1 Z-rig) by pulling on it with only one or two people, but even this is only approximate. Slack can be added to a system under load if the rigger plans to do so ahead of time, but it's risky. Taking excess rope in is far less practical.

Once the static line has been tensioned, tie off the end. To create a built-in "safety valve," leave a small amount of slack behind the brake prusik in the Z-rig. As the pull from the lowered boat approaches 900 pounds, the prusik will begin to slip. This releases extra rope, making the vector pull less extreme, thereby reducing strain on the static line and—we hope—preventing a catastrophic failure. A slipping prusik also serves as a clear warning to the res-

Figure 11-3. A harness system for rafts that works on a telfer lower. Note the low attachment point to raise the bow and the three-point anchor system to distribute the weight between several D-rings.

Figure 11-4. A telfer lower in action. (Jane C. Sundmacher photo.)

cue team that they are entering dangerous territory. If the prusik fails, the tied-off rope should catch the load.

After tensioning the static line, prepare the control system. The simplest type of telfer system uses only two control lines. One pulls the suspended craft toward one bank or lets out rope to allow movement toward the opposite bank. The second line, set on the opposite shore, controls the upstream/downstream movement of the suspended craft. There are a number of variations to this system that work equally well.

The raft is handled through a movable control point that allows rescuers to adjust the position of the suspended craft. A pulley is placed on the main static line, which is then connected by a carabiner to a small prusik or web loop. (Figure-eight descenders are not strong enough for this use. Rescue professionals use a steel

ring.) The loop serves as a common connection point for all other components. The upstream/downstream control line is connected to the bow of the craft being lowered. It then passes through a second pulley connected to the loop by a carabiner. Lastly, a right/left control line from the opposite bank is clipped into the loop. The system is now ready to use.

You can pull the raft into the current using the right/left control line coming from the far shore. Let out the upstream/downstream line at an equal pace or the craft will start to move upriver. Similarly, when pulling the raft toward the opposite side of the river, pull in the upstream/downstream control line at the same speed that you let out the right/left line to keep the raft from slipping downstream.

On-board rescuers should stay in the back of their boat to avoid weighting the bow, which would cause the boat to take on water. They can

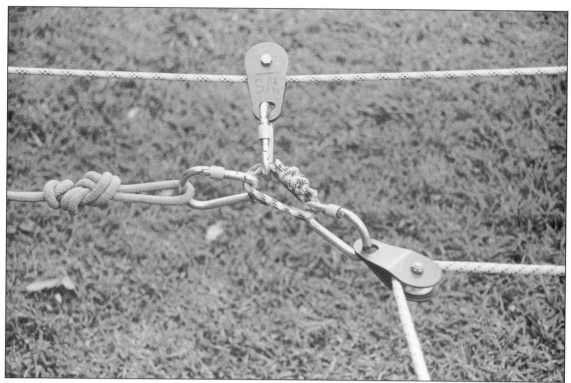

Figure 11-5. A close-up of a telfer-lower control system.

use their paddles to keep the craft straight. Shore teams must be especially alert when lowering through large waves or holes; the boat may begin to surf, then break suddenly to one side. Avoiding these spots is smart but not always possible. To avoid flipping or swamping, the rescue team can lean back and pull the boat downstream with draw strokes. Final positioning may require a number of small adjustments; have patience and give the raft time to settle in. Right and left tethers are sometimes attached to the stern to improve control.

Once the victim has been reached, bring the team to shore by working the raft sideways when possible. Pulling the boat back upstream is very difficult, even with mechanical advantage.

Quick Lowers

Quick lowers are a cross between a telfer lower and the life jacket tethers described in Chapter 5. They can be set up more quickly than a full-

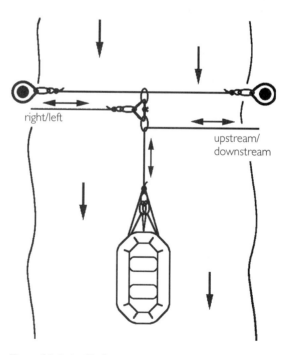

right/left

upstream/
downstream

Figure 11-6. A telfer lower.

rigged telfer and, because they place less strain on the ropes, are better suited to the equipment paddlers typically carry. In experienced hands, they can be as effective as a telfer, but rescuers accustomed to other systems may need to be conservative in setting goals.

Two-Point Quick Lower. A two-point lowering system provides a fast and simple way to deploy a raft or canoe catamaran to any given spot in the river, while maintaining control from shore. Two ropes, one from each bank, run from the bow of the rescue boat to a secure anchor on shore, where a Muenter hitch (see Figure 10-12, page 150)—used with a large pear-shaped carabiner—provides a secure, easily adjustable connection. To minimize the pull, allow the boat to drift downstream of these anchors until the angle of the control lines to the current approaches 45°. The team can maneuver a craft into any position by adjusting the length of the lines.

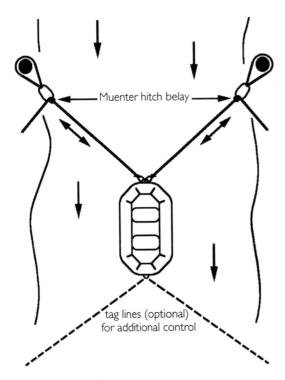

Figure 11-7. A two-point boat lower. Stern tag lines can be added to create a four-point lower.

Four-Point Lower. Occasionally, a two-point lower fails to place the raft exactly where it's needed. This is often the result of currents that kick the raft to one side at the wrong moment. In this case, adding control lines from both shores to the back of the raft will hold it securely in any position. These lines should run diagonally downstream from the boat to the shore.

Communication

Rescuers on shore often cannot communicate verbally with rescuers in a tethered craft due to the noise of the water, so hand signals must be used. These should be discussed before the boat is launched. It's important to make large gestures when signaling; for example, move your whole arm and hand when pointing, rather than just a finger. When the leader faces the river, upstream and downstream signals are often shown by pointing to the right or left. Lateral movement across the current is often indicated by motioning toward or away from the leader, but this can be difficult to distinguish accurately from a distance. To avoid confusion, you can agree in advance that motion overhead will indicate that the leader wants the craft to move away from the leader and that a motion downward, at waist level, indicates movement toward the leader. Signals can be passed from the boat to the leader in the same way.

Other useful signals include clenched fists overhead to indicate "STOP," a palms-down motion to indicate "SLOW," and a crossed-arms or hugging posture to indicate that the victim has been retrieved.

High-Angle Rescue

Paddlers stranded in steep gorges and boats pinned on bridge abutments are difficult to reach. Often the only approach is from above. This is dangerous for paddlers who lack training in technical climbing. Reading a book is not sufficient preparation for this type of rescue. Basic rock-climbing instruction is highly recommended; aside from being challenging and fun, it gives paddlers a new appreciation for the skills and dangers involved in crossing vertical terrain. This section is included here only as a basic introduction to these techniques.

Safety Factors

Bridge lowers and rappels are very risky with the marginal ropes normally carried by paddlers. Rock climbers and rescue squads use ropes 5 to 10 times stronger than those usually found in a rescue bag. Vertical rescue demands strict attention to rope strength. If a climbing rope fails, serious injury or death results.

The ratio of the expected pull on the line to the breaking strength is called the *safety factor;* climbers and rescue professionals normally seek a factor of 15:1. While this may seem excessive, it was developed to take into account many elements that reduce the strength of a rope, such as deterioration due to age, exposure to water or heat, hidden damage caused by shock loading when catching falls, and weaknesses created by knots and tight bends. A 170-pound rescuer needs to use a rope rated at 2,550 pounds breaking strength; if the rescuer and the victim are pulled up simultaneously, the rope should be rated at twice that. A nylon-sheathed, polypropylene water rescue rope is one possible choice: The breaking strength of a ⅜-inch line made this way is roughly 3,600 pounds, and the nylon sheath increases strength and heat resistance.

Since lowering systems use friction to slow the descent, heat buildup can be a problem. Polypropylene rope loses 50 percent of its strength when heated to 150°F, roughly the temperature of a car hood on a sunny day. The Spectra line found in some high-strength throw bags is stronger but is also heat sensitive. Nylon climbing ropes have much more heat resistance but can also melt in extreme circumstances. Rescuers may increase their safety margins by using doubled ropes, lowering the lightest person on their team, and moving very, very slowly to minimize heat build-up. Wetting the rope causes some loss of strength but offers some pro-tection against heat build-up due to friction. Specialized climbing ropes are safest.

When working with ropes as lifelines, watch out for sharp edges and rough rock. These can destroy a rope in seconds. Any time the line crosses a rock edge, it must be padded. Special pads are sold for this purpose; but a shirt, smooth piece of wood, or other item can be used.

Rappelling

Rappelling down cliffs and overhangs is a job for people with specialized equipment and training. But on a steep riverbank, ropes can be used more for control than to support the full weight of the rescuer. On steep embankments, a low-angle rappel may be the easiest, fastest, and safest access. Once while we were teaching a class at Zoar Rapid on the Deerfield River, an aluminum canoe pinned and wrapped. The riverbank was lined by a steep, 40-foot-high embankment of rough, irregular rock. The fastest and safest way to move downstream was to climb up to the road, run to a spot just above the accident, and use a low-angle rappel to descend to the river's edge. For a low-angle rappel, you can use a *dulfer wrap* (described below) or construct a harness and use a carabiner and Muenter hitch. Either method requires practice to use effectively, and special care to avoid rope burns.

A dulfer wrap requires no additional equipment and is quick to set up. The rope is first connected to a secure anchor. The person rappelling faces the anchor and straddles the rope, which passes behind the right leg, crosses the front of the body, and passes over the left shoulder. The rappeller then grasps the rope behind him in his right hand, which controls the rate of descent. Doubled ropes make it possible to place the line around an anchor rather than tying into it. This enables the rope to be pulled free from below. This also makes the rappel more comfortable by increasing the surface area of the supporting rope. Move slowly; considerable heat is generated. Gloves are recommended to avoid rope burns.

Figure 11-8. A dulfer wrap rappel in use on a steep slope.

Figure 11-9. An arm wrap rappel on a steep slope.

A modified *diaper harness* is self-adjusting and can be constructed with 10 to 15 feet of webbing. First, tie the webbing into a large loop using a water knot (see Appendix A), then hold it behind you with both hands. There is now a loop of webbing on either side of your body. Pull these two loops around in front of your body and place your hands and forearms through them. Then reach between your legs with both hands and grasp the section of webbing hanging below your buttocks. Pull it through your legs, then pull it through the loops at each side. Adjust the webbing as you pull until the two small loops from between your legs pass through the loops of webbing on each side. "Lock off" the harness so it won't loosen up by tying the two loops together, then clip into both loops with a carabiner.

Systems for Lowering and Raising a Rescuer

Rappelling, while dramatic and fun, is a dangerous way to descend. A lowering system is safer if you use a reversed Z-rig or piggyback rig to eliminate the heat buildup associated with friction devices. It can also be used to pull a rescuer back up without changing the setup. A second belay line is always tied around the rescuer's harness to support his or her weight if the main line should fail. This rope is kept as snug as possible without actually supporting the rescuer's weight. It can be belayed with a prusik knot or run through a Muenter hitch.

If a person's hair or clothing should become caught in a lowering system or rappel device while a rescuer is on the rope, cutting the hair or

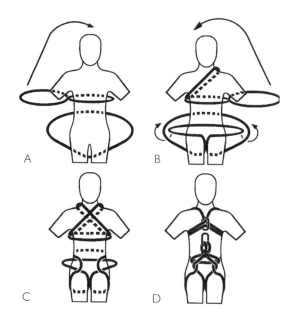

Figure 11-10. A chest and modified diaper harness used in vertical rescues.

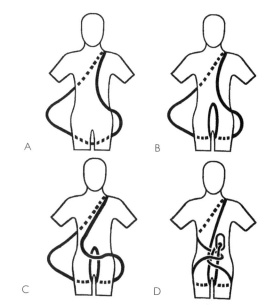

Figure 11-11. The Hansen harness.

clothing with a knife is a dangerous option. One slip of a sharp blade against a loaded rope could cause a tragedy. It's better to pull the rope back in the opposite direction, releasing the jam.

Good communication is a must when operating a lowering system. If there is a misunderstanding, someone could be dropped! The

lowering team and the rescuer must always know exactly what is happening. Signals should be discussed beforehand. Avoid using words like *whoa, ho,* and *go;* instead, use unmistakable terms like *up, down, slow,* and *fast.* The "STOP" command must always be obeyed instantly. Acknowledge commands by repeating them.

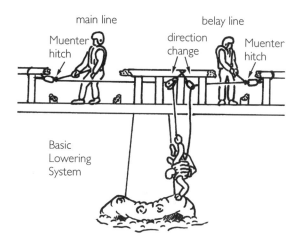

Figure 11-12. A bridge lower rigged to show separate belay and haul lines, using a Muenter hitch to control the descent.

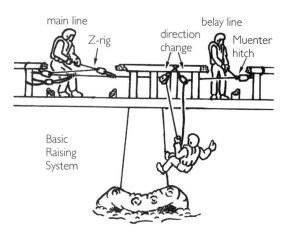

Figure 11-13. A bridge raising. Note the Z-rig attached to the haul lines to increase pulling power.

Figure 11-14. *Dropping over the edge and moving into position to help. Note the use of a double line.*

A typical sequence sounds something like this:

Rescuer: "Belay on?" (Is the belayer ready?)

Belay tender: "On belay!" (Yes, the belay is set.)

Rescuer: "Lower!" (The rescuer is ready to be lowered.)

Lowering team: "Lowering!" (Lowering the rescuer.)

Rescuer: "Stop!" (STOP!)

Lowering team: "Stopping!" (Stop acknowledged.)

Rescuer: "Belay off!" (The belay is no longer needed.)

Belay tender: "Off belay!" (The belay is no longer on; slack is available.)

Rescuer: "Off rope!" (The rescuer is disconnected from the rope.)

Keep the lowering or raising system simple. The 3:1 Z-rig used to free boats provides plenty of power. As the mechanical advantage increases, more and more rope must be pulled through to raise an object a given distance. This increases equipment requirements and slows the operation.

The simplest raising system uses a 1:1 change of direction and a counterbalance. This is ideal for hauling a litter up a steep embankment. Set the change of direction at the top of a slope; the counterweight is created by having one or two members of the team walk downhill. Their weight supports the litter and lifts the load.

If more power is needed, a piggyback rig can be added to the line. The piggyback can be set up with a second rope rather than being limited to whatever length is left over. When a distance to be covered is greater than the length of rope, any knots joining lines must be passed through the system. It's relatively easy to do this.

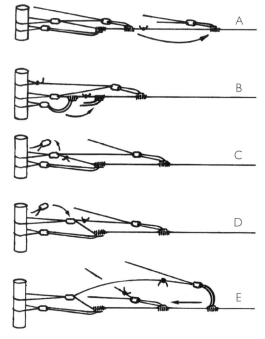

Figure 11-15. Passing a knot through a Z-rig hauling system: (A) While the brake prusik holds the load, the traveling prusik is removed and placed on the other side of the knot. (B) With the end of the haul line secured and holding the load, the brake prusik is removed and placed on the other side of the knot. (C) With the brake prusik holding the load, the change of direction is removed and . . . (D) . . . placed on the other side of the knot after the anchor has been extended. (E) As the knot approaches the traveling pulley, the traveling prusik is moved down the rope until the knot clears.

First, tie off the haul line. Next, remove the prusik on the piggyback rig. Last, reattach the rig on the other side of the knot and continue the lift. Any weight on the system must be belayed separately so that both victim and rescuer are protected. At no time should the knot joining the two lines be disconnected. (See Figure 11-15 for passing a knot through a Z-rig.)

Changes of direction can often be used to your advantage. On a narrow bridge, for example, a change of direction can turn the system parallel to a road to make hauling easier. If anchor points are not available, as is the case with some modern concrete bridges, vehicles can be used. Pad any sharp edges being used as anchors and avoid putting the rope in contact with grease and gasoline. Do not use bumpers as anchor points; some new designs are not strong enough. The frame, the axles, the post between doors, openings through wheels, and leaf springs make good connection points. To prevent accidental movement, set the emergency brake and remove the keys from any vehicle being used as an anchor.

The Carlson Cinch

If an entrapment victim can't be reached directly, it may be necessary to tie a rope to him and pull upstream. But cinching a line around a trapped person who is well out of reach can be almost impossible. Glen Carlson, a well-known rescue instructor, has developed numerous variations on a technique that accomplishes this task. One variation of his *Carlson cinch* is shown in Figure 11-16 (page 166). Reserved for life-threatening situations, this innovative technique has accounted for several documented saves.

Let's use foot entrapment as an example. A stabilization line is first set up to keep the trapped person's head above water. This may allow the victim to work free. If not, a second snag line can be run across the river and worked up under the victim's legs. If pulling the line upstream won't free the foot, a cinch system might.

A second line, which will be used as a tag line, is clipped to one end of the snag line that

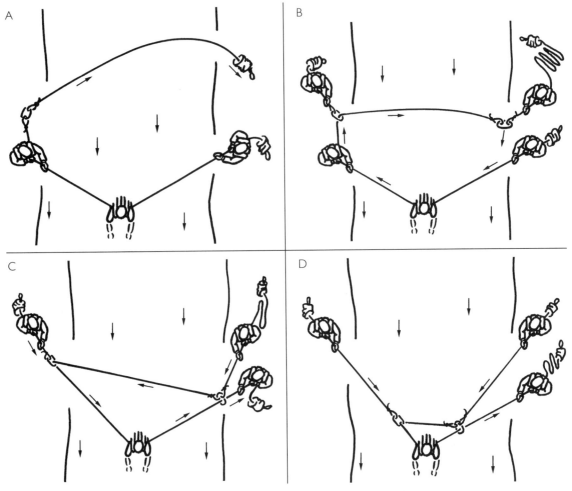

Figure 11-16. The Carlson cinch: (A) The snag line and river right tag lines are clipped together. (B) The river right tag line is attached to a second tag line from river left, then . . . (C) . . . clipped into the first on the river right side. (D) The snag line is pulled in while the two tag lines are used for control, gradually tightening the loop around the victim.

is already up under the victim's legs. The tag line is then thrown back to the opposite side, above the victim (Figure 11-16A). A third tag line is clipped into the snag line as the second tag line pulls the end of the snag line back with it to the other side (11-16B). Once the carabiner connecting the end of the snag line to the first tag line reaches the opposite side, it is clipped back across the snag line, forming a loop (11-16C). Pulling in on the snag line reduces the size of the loop, while the tag lines maintain control (11-16D).

When using a cinch line, everyone involved must know what they are doing. The wrong actions can injure or kill the person you're trying to help. For example, if the victim is being pulled into one shore, and the line handlers on the opposite side fail to give slack, the victim may be held underwater. The pressure from the cinch can also cause injury to the person you're trying to help. The cinch is best used to grab an ankle or leg. Avoid tightening the loop tightly around a victim's waist, as this may cause severe internal damage. The two tag lines control the size of the loop as it is tightened: keep it from closing down so tight that it hurts the victim. This system takes considerable practice and teamwork.

A Carlson cinch also takes time to set up. Often, the victim must be stabilized during this period. When all you need is moderate control to prevent a victim from floating free, the simple stabilization and snag lines described in Chapter 8 are sufficient.

Low-Head Dam Rescues

Dams claim the lives of both novice and experienced paddlers every year. Some dams can be run at favorable water levels by skilled boaters, but a surprising number of people who should know better get lured into danger. Dam rescue can be extraordinarily difficult. The best advice for whitewater paddlers is to exercise great caution around these structures, allowing more than the usual margin for error. Portaging is a nuisance but is often sensible.

When water passes over a ledge or the face of a dam, it draws the falling water down and under; this leaves a void, and water flows upstream to fill it. This action in turn creates a recirculating current, or *hydraulic,* that traps floating debris and whitewater boats. A hydraulic is capable of drowning a person wearing a life jacket.

Dams have been described as "drowning machines" because, unlike natural formations, they are perfectly regular. There are no breaks

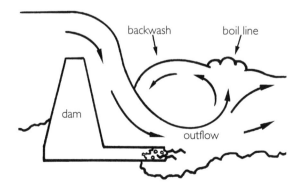

Figure 11-17. A hydraulic, or recirculating current, that forms by low-head dams.

in the recirculating current that could allow a trapped victim to float free. The regularity of the face and concrete walls at either end prevent objects from being worked out at the edges. This leaves only two routes for escape: down and under the recirculating current or over the top of it.

Self-Rescue

Self-rescue from a hydraulic requires that a victim swim into the water coming over the face of the dam, ball up, and travel to the bottom with the main flow. Once she reaches the main current, she must swim underwater as long as possible. If she surfaces too early, she can be pulled back into the recirculating flow. At the base of most dams is a lip that extends under the hydraulic and keeps the dam from being undermined by the current, but the lip may be broken or contain exposed rebar and debris. The danger in allowing oneself to be forced underwater is that the rebar and debris can trap or injure a swimmer.

The current in a hydraulic is violent. Victims have been impaled on tree limbs, beaten up by debris, and had clothing and PFDs pulled from their bodies. It's not unusual to be recirculated underwater without coming to the surface; one of the authors came within 6 inches of the surface during three cycles before fully surfacing on the fourth, only to be pulled back in for more. Knowledge, a cool head, and plenty of good luck helped him survive.

When you dive down, your life vest has surprisingly little negative effect. Hydraulics are highly aerated—the water may be as much as 60 percent air—and life vest flotation is seriously diminished by aeration; so, a lot of buoyancy is necessary to bring you to the surface. It is not necessary to remove your PFD to escape; on the contrary, a tired victim will need this flotation to survive after escaping the hydraulic.

Unmanned Kayak Rescues

When victims are out of reach of shore-based throw lines, an *unmanned kayak rescue* is the quickest way to reach them. As the name implies, a tethered kayak is launched into the hydraulic without a paddler in the boat. This technique works best in strong, unbroken hydraulics and may not work at every dam. As with any rescue technique, practice is essential.

Start by connecting a rescue rope to the bow of a kayak. The air bags can be left in place, or removed if they provide too much flotation. Launch the kayak stern-first into the hydraulic. If possible, start from above so that the boat can be pushed partway out before going into the boil. The bow will partly fill with water, so it sits lower and downstream of the stern, which has more flotation. Pulling on the tether sets a ferry angle. The kayak moves across the river, pulling the rope behind it. Maintain control by tugging on the rope; in strong hydraulics, a great deal of strength is required to keep the craft from moving forward.

Take the "kick" of the hydraulic into consideration. If the current pushes from one side to the other, this force should be put to work. For example, when the dam is built at an angle to the current, launch from the upstream end. A quick look should tell an experienced paddler which side will allow him or her to make best use of the water.

When the kayak reaches the victim, he can grab on, using it for flotation. He can then be hauled across the face of the dam to shore or pulled downstream, over the boil, to safety. Choosing the right strategy depends on the circumstances. Avoid pulling a swimmer through debris caught in the hydraulic. If the victim will be pulled free at the center of the river, backup rescuers should be waiting downstream in their boats to help.

There are a few limitations to this technique. Debris in the boil may cause the kayak to hang up. If there are spots where the main flow breaks through the hydraulic, the kayak may be pushed out, and controlling the kayak will feel something like flying a kite. But even these spots, where the current breaks through the backwash, can sometimes be crossed.

Boat-Based Dam Rescues

If the river is too wide for lines to be used, rescues can be mounted from directly below. Low-head dams often have extensive recirculation patterns that pose a danger to downstream paddlers. The area that separates the downstream from the upstream flow is called the *boil line*. The boil line must not be crossed while performing a rescue. Any craft working nearby should be tethered by a safety line, either to the shore or, on very wide rivers, to a boat directly downstream. If the rescue boat is pulled into the boil, it can be pulled out immediately.

If the tether runs to the riverbank, it should be set at an angle of more than 45° to the face of the dam on the downstream side. The more perpendicular the lines, the easier it is to retrieve someone in trouble. Lines can be connected from both sides of the river for added safety. On very wide rivers, the tether can be attached to a downstream boat. In an emergency, that craft can be swamped, creating a sea anchor to pull the rescue boat back out.

Once the tethered boat is in position, a rope can be thrown to the victim. Rafts are stable enough for most people to stand on and throw. Canoes and kayaks are not, and sitting or kneeling throws lose much of their power and accuracy. Throw the rope overhand, in line with the length of the boat. A sideways throw has a destabilizing effect that leads to capsizing. A tandem canoe has the advantage of allowing the rear paddler to stabilize the one in front. If you hit your target, hold on to the rope and keep your weight low. Those manning the tether will pull you free.

Tag-Line Rescues

A tag line allows rescuers to assist a trapped paddler from the safety of shore. It requires enough rope to reach across the river with plenty to spare. The line can be ferried upstream or downstream of the dam, depending on where the current poses the fewest problems. The downstream side is safer, since the rescuer cannot be washed over the drop by accident.

Flotation attached at the midpoint of the tag line gives a trapped victim something to hold on to. This can be a life vest or a kayak with air bags. Once the victim has received the line,

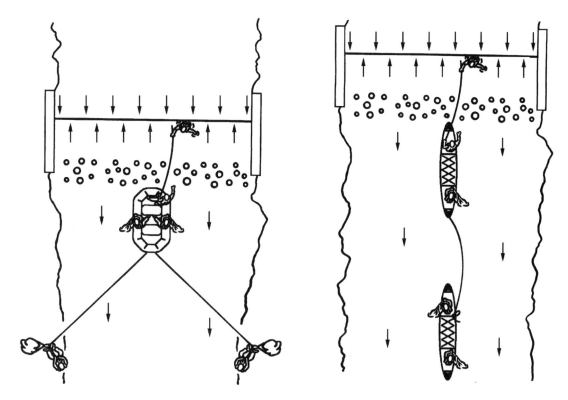

Figure 11-18. Two variations on a tethered-boat rescue. The rescue boat can be belayed from shore (left) or from a second boat positioned well behind the boil line (right).

there are two options. He can be pulled to one side across the dam face, or the rescuers can move the lines downstream and pull him out over the boil. As with the unmanned kayak rescue, consider what will happen during the recovery. Recirculating debris can be a problem when pulling someone out lengthwise, but freeing someone in midriver without backup can leave the victim floating helplessly downstream. Both risks must be considered.

This book covers a wide range of techniques and skills. No two rescues are alike, and no one technique will work well in every situation. The chances of recovering a victim improve when rescuers have many different techniques to work with. But knowing these skills is not enough; you must be able to deploy them successfully. Knowing when to use each method requires good judgment, which comes only with training

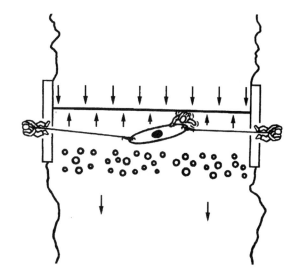

Figure 11-19. A tag-line dam rescue using a kayak as flotation.

and practice. There is no substitute for working with a qualified instructor, followed by regular practice with your own group.

Reading this book is only the beginning, since new techniques are constantly being developed. The knowledge gained from your reading and training, combined with an open mind, may lead you to better ways of handling difficult river rescues. Your experience, judgment, and training may make the difference to someone in trouble. And that makes the effort worthwhile.

Discovering a New Rescue Technique

Rescue methods are often developed in a somewhat random way, but from modest beginnings come useful ideas. They start with a serious situation and are followed by experimentation born of necessity. This is true of the unmanned-kayak dam rescue technique.

In my younger, more reckless days, I found myself side-surfing my kayak in a hole known for being sticky and unforgiving. I was drawn farther in, toward the middle of the hydraulic, where the water plunged steeply over a ledge. I flipped and came out of my boat.

Swimming in this hydraulic was not at all like body-surfing in my favorite play hole. In fact, it was very frightening. I distinctly remember surfacing twice to within 6 inches of the surface, only to be dragged back down for another cycle. When I finally reached air on my third time around, I really wanted to get out of there.

But attempting to swim out was futile. I couldn't get past the boil line, and the backwash was overpowering me and dragging me back again. Looking back into the hole, I saw my kayak bouncing and surfing, but still on the surface. This looked like a good place to go. Working with the current, I reached my boat and grabbed one end. I wrapped one arm around the end of the boat and held onto the cockpit with the opposite hand.

What happened next was unexpected good luck. The kayak began to sit with my end submerged. The bow lifted and pointed upstream—like a squirt boat blasting a hole—and the boat set a ferry angle against the onrushing water. The current quickly ferried me back out the way I'd come in! Afterward I filed the experience away in my mind and thought no more of it.

A couple of years later, while taking a professional rescue course in Ohio, I saw how an inflated fire hose could be fed into a hydraulic and carried across the current to a victim. What a neat idea! But could a paddler accomplish the same thing without carrying a fire hose? Suddenly I realized that if a kayak weighted at one end could blast across the face of the dam with a rope attached, I might be able to reach a victim lying out of throw-line range. Kayak air bags are smaller in the bow than in the stern; when swamped in a hole, water collects in the bow. Maybe this would create the weight differential I needed.

With that idea in mind I began to experiment. Early results were encouraging. One cold December day Charlie and I, accompanied by our wives, drove all over the Schulkill and Lehigh River Basins, guidebooks in hand, throwing kayaks into every "dam" hydraulic we could find. It worked, and a new rescue technique was born. If your mind is receptive, you will find and exploit similar opportunities, and develop new ideas that really work.

—WAS

APPENDIX A

Knots

Stoppers

Figure-Eight Stopper

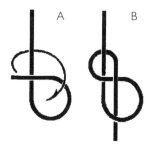

Figure A-1. The figure-eight stopper is used to hold something in place on a rope, such as the foam block in the bottom of a throw bag.

Knots That Form a Loop

Figure Eight on a Bight

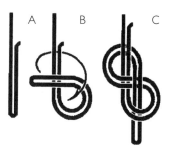

Figure A-2. A figure eight on a bight creates a strong, reliable loop in the end of a rope. It is now used in place of the bowline knot because it is easier to tie, easier to untie after being loaded, and much stronger.

In-Line Figure Eight

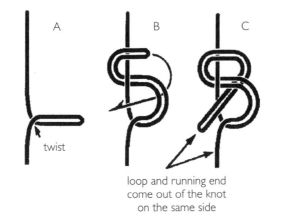

Figure A-3. An in-line figure eight creates a loop at mid-line made to be pulled in the line with the rope.

Butterfly Knot

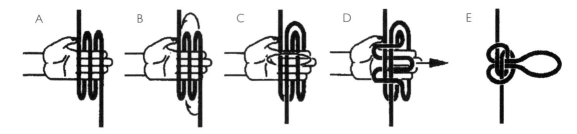

Figure A-4. The butterfly knot creates a loop at mid-line that pulls perpendicular to the rope.

Double-Eyed Figure 8

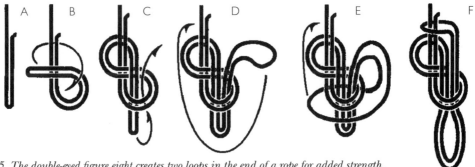

Figure A-5. The double-eyed figure eight creates two loops in the end of a rope for added strength.

Knots That Connect Two Ends

Figure-Eight Tracer

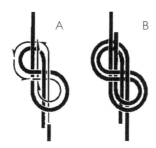

Figure A-6. Two lines can be joined by running the end of one line back through a figure-eight stopper tied in the other line. Best used for ropes of equal diameter, this knot is easily untied. The figure-eight tracer can also be used to tie a loop around an object.

Double Fisherman's Knot

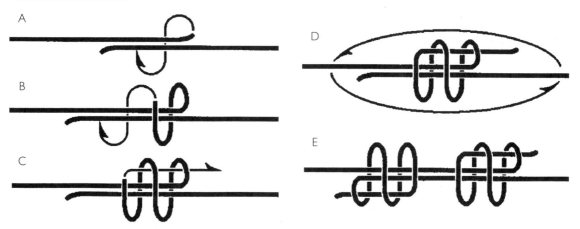

Figure A-7. To join two ends of a rope together securely, a double fisherman's knot is ideal. After loading, this knot is difficult—if not impossible—to untie. Small differences in rope diameter can be accommodated.

Water Knot

Figure A-8. The water knot is used to join two ends of webbing. This knot is actually another tracer knot, built upon a simple overhand knot.

Square Knot

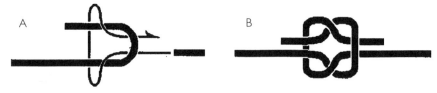

Figure A-9. The square knot is easy to untie and is suited to situations where high loads are not expected.

Sheet Bend

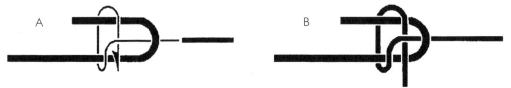

Figure A-10. A sheet bend is used to join two ropes of significantly different diameters. This is particularly useful when tying a line to the end of the painter from a pinned canoe.

Knots That Adjust

Prusik

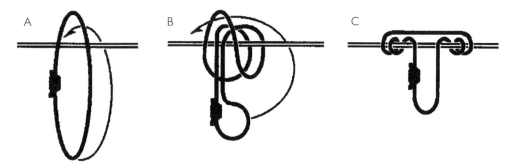

Figure A-11. The prusik knot creates a movable connection point on a haul line. Note that the double fisherman's knot is located away from the prusik knot where it won't rub against a carabiner clipped into the loop.

Two Half Hitches

Figure A-12. Two half hitches are easy to tie and can easily hold a light load.

Taut-Line Hitch

Figure A-13. Similar to two half hitches, a taut-line hitch combines a good grip and easy adjustment. It should only be used where light loads will be applied.

Knots for Tying Off

Clove Hitch

Figure A-14. A secure way to tie off a boat to shore.

Clove Hitch with Release

pull to release

Figure A-15. With a quick-release option for added safety, the clove hitch is useful when towing boats.

Slip Knot with Release

pull to release

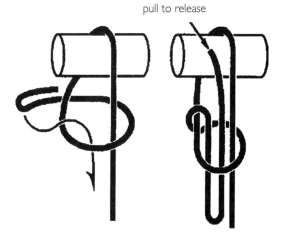

Figure A-16. A releasable slip knot for towing boats.

Safety Code of the American Whitewater Affiliation

Adopted 1959–Revised 1987

CHARLIE WALBRIDGE
Revision Chairman

PETE SKINNER
Production Coordinator

This code has been prepared using the best available information and has been reviewed by a broad cross section of whitewater experts. The code, however, is only a collection of guidelines; attempts to minimize risks should be flexible, not constrained by a rigid set of rules. Varying conditions and group goals may combine with unpredictable circumstances to require alternate procedures.

I. PERSONAL PREPAREDNESS AND RESPONSIBILITY

1. **Be a competent swimmer,** with the ability to handle yourself underwater.

2. **Wear a lifejacket.** A snugly-fitting vest-type life preserver offers back and shoulder protection as well as the flotation needed to swim safely in whitewater.

3. **Wear a solid, correctly-fitted helmet** when upsets are likely. This is essential in kayaks or covered canoes, and recommended for open canoeists using thigh straps and rafters running steep drops.

4. **Do not boat out of control.** Your skills should be sufficient to stop or reach shore before reaching danger. Do not enter a rapid unless you are reasonably sure that you can run it safely or swim it without injury.

5. **Whitewater rivers contain many hazards which are not always easily recognized. The following are the most frequent killers:**

   A. **HIGH WATER.** The river's speed and power increase tremendously as the flow increases, raising the difficulty of most rapids. Rescue becomes progressively harder as the water rises, adding to the danger. Floating debris and strainers make even an easy rapid quite hazardous. It is often misleading to judge the river level at the put in, since a small rise in a wide, shallow place will be multiplied many times where the river narrows. Use reliable gauge information whenever possible, and be aware that sun on snowpack, hard rain, and upstream dam releases may greatly increase the flow.

   B. **COLD.** Cold drains your strength, and robs you of the ability to make sound decisions on matters affecting your survival. Cold water immersion, because of the initial shock and the rapid heat loss which follows, is especially dangerous. Dress appropriately for bad weather or sudden immersion in the water. When the water temperature is less than 50°F, a wetsuit or drysuit is essential for protection if you swim. Next best is wool or pile clothing under a waterproof shell. In this case, you should also carry waterproof matches and a change of clothing in a waterproof bag. If, after prolonged exposure, a person experiences uncontrollable shaking, loss of coordination, or difficulty speaking, he or she is hypothermic and needs your assistance.

   C. **STRAINERS.** Brush, fallen trees, bridge pilings, undercut rocks or anything else which allows river current to sweep through can pin boats and boaters against the obstacle. Water pressure on anything trapped this way can be overwhelming. Rescue is often extremely difficult. Pinning may occur in fast current, with little or no whitewater to warn of the danger.

   D. **DAMS, WEIRS, LEDGES, REVERSALS, HOLES, AND HYDRAULICS.** When water drops over an obstacle, it curls back on itself, forming a strong upstream current which may be capable of holding a boat or a swimmer. Some holes make for excellent sport; others are proven killers. Paddlers who cannot recognize the differences should avoid all but the smallest holes. Hydraulics around man-made dams must be treated with utmost respect regardless of their height or the level of the river. Despite their seemingly benign appearance, they can create an almost escape proof trap. The swimmer's only exit from the "drowning machine" is to dive below the surface when the downstream current is flowing beneath the reversal.

   E. **BROACHING.** When a boat is pushed sideways against a rock by strong current, it may collapse and wrap. This is especially dangerous to kayak and decked canoe paddlers; these boats will collapse and the combination of indestructible hulls and tight outfitting may create a deadly trap. Even without entrapment, releasing pinned boats can be extremely time-consuming and dangerous. To avoid pinning, throw your weight downstream towards the rock. This allows the current to slide harmlessly underneath the hull.

6. **Boating alone** is discouraged. The minimum

party is three people or two craft.

7. **Have a frank knowledge of your boating ability,** and don't attempt rivers or rapids which lie beyond that ability.
   A. Develop the paddling skills and teamwork required to match the river you plan to boat. Most good paddlers develop skills gradually, and attempts to advance too quickly will compromise your safety and enjoyment.
   B. Be in good physical and mental condition, consistent with the difficulties which may be expected. Make adjustments for loss of skills due to age, health, or fitness. Any health limitations must be explained to your fellow paddlers prior to starting the trip.

8. **Be practiced in self-rescue,** including escape from an overturned craft. The Eskimo Roll is strongly recommended for decked boaters who run rapids of Class IV or greater, or who paddle in cold environmental conditions.

9. **Be trained in rescue skills,** CPR, and first aid with special emphasis on recognizing and treating hypothermia. It may save your friend's life.

10. **Carry equipment needed for unexpected emergencies,** including footwear which will protect your feet when walking out, a throw rope, knife, whistle and waterproof matches. If you wear eyeglasses, tie them on and carry a spare pair on long trips. Bring cloth repair tape on short runs, and a full repair kit on isolated rivers. Do not wear bulky jackets, ponchos, heavy boots, or anything else which could reduce your ability to survive a swim.

11. **Despite the mutually supportive group structure described in this code, individual paddlers are ultimately responsible for their own safety, and must assume sole responsibility for the following decisions:**
    A. The decision to participate on any trip. This includes an evaluation of the expected difficulty of the rapids under the conditions existing at the time of the put in.
    B. The selection of appropriate equipment, including a boat design suited to their skills and the appropriate rescue and survival gear.
    C. The decision to scout any rapid, and to run or portage according to their best judgment. Other members of the group may offer advice, but paddlers should resist pressure from anyone to paddle beyond their skills. It is also their responsibility to decide whether to pass up any walk out or take out opportunity.
    D. All trip participants should constantly evaluate their own and their group's safety, voicing their concerns when appropriate and following what they believe to be the best course of action. Paddlers are encouraged to speak with anyone whose actions on the water are dangerous, whether they are a part of your group or not.

II. BOAT AND EQUIPMENT PREPAREDNESS

1. **Test new and different equipment** under familiar conditions before relying on it for difficult runs. This is especially true when adopting a new boat design or outfitting system. Low volume craft may present additional hazards to inexperienced or poorly conditioned paddlers.

2. **Be sure your boat and gear** are in good repair before starting a trip. The more isolated and difficult the run, the more rigorous this inspection should be.

3. **Install flotation bags** in non-inflatable craft, securely fixed in each end, designed to displace as much water as possible. Inflatable boats should have multiple air chambers and be test inflated before launching.

4. **Have strong, properly sized paddles or oars** for controlling your craft. Carry sufficient spares for the length and difficulty of the trip.

5. **Outfit your boat safely.** The ability to exit your boat quickly is an essential component of safety in rapids. It is your responsibility to

see that there is absolutely nothing to cause entrapment when coming free of an upset craft. This includes:

A. Spray covers which won't release reliably or which release prematurely.

B. Boat outfitting too tight to allow a fast exit, especially in low volume kayaks or decked canoes. This includes low hung thwarts in canoes lacking adequate clearance for your feet and kayak footbraces which fail or allow your feet to become wedged under them.

C. Inadequately supported decks which collapse on a paddler's legs when a decked boat is pinned by water pressure. Inadequate clearance with the deck because of your size or build.

D. Loose ropes which cause entanglement. Beware of any length of loose line attached to a whitewater boat. All items must be tied tightly and excess line eliminated; painters, throw lines, and safety rope systems must be completely and effectively stored. Do not knot the end of a rope, as it can get caught in cracks between rocks.

6. Provide ropes which permit you to hold on to your craft so that it may be rescued. The following methods are recommended.

A. Kayaks and covered canoes should have grab loops of ¼" + rope or equivalent webbing sized to admit a normal sized hand. Stern painters are permissible if properly secured.

B. Open canoes should have securely anchored bow and stern painters consisting of 8-10 feet of ¼" + line. These must be secured in such a way that they are readily accessible, but cannot come loose accidentally. Grab loops are acceptable, but are more difficult to reach after an upset.

C. Rafts and dories may have taut perimeter lines threaded through the loops provided. Footholds should be designed so that a paddler's feet cannot be forced through them, causing entrapment. Flip lines should be carefully and reliably stowed.

7. Know your craft's carrying capacity, and how added loads affect boat handling in whitewater. Most rafts have a minimum crew size which can be added to on day trips or in easy rapids. Carrying more than two paddlers in an open canoe when running rapids is not recommended.

8. Car top racks must be strong and attach positively to the vehicle. Lash your boat to each crossbar, then tie the ends of the boat directly to the bumpers for added security. This arrangement should survive all but the most violent vehicle accident.

III. GROUP PREPAREDNESS AND RESPONSIBILITY

1. Organization. River trips should be regarded as common adventures by all participants, except on specially designated instructional or guided trips. The group is collectively responsible for the conduct of the trip, and participants are individually responsible for judging their own capabilities and for their own safety as the trip progresses.

2. River Conditions. The group should have a reasonable knowledge of the difficulty of the run. Participants should evaluate this information and adjust their plans accordingly. If the run is exploratory or no one is familiar with the river, maps and guidebooks, if available, should be examined. The group should secure accurate flow information; the more difficult the run, the more important this will be. Be aware of possible changes in river level and how this will affect the difficulty of the run. If the trip involves tidal stretches, secure appropriate information on tides.

3. Group equipment should be suited to the difficulty of the river. The group should always have a throw line available, and one line per boat is recommended on difficult runs. The list may include: carabiners, prusik loops, first aid kit, flashlight, folding saw, fire starter, guidebooks, maps, food, extra clothing, and any other rescue or survival items suggested by conditions. Each item is not required on every run, and this list is not meant to be a substitute for good judgment.

4. **Keep the group compact,** but maintain sufficient spacing to avoid collisions. If the group is large, consider dividing into smaller groups or using the "Buddy System" as an additional safeguard. Space yourselves closely enough to permit good communication, but not so close as to interfere with one another in rapids.

   A. **The lead paddler** sets the pace. When in front, do not get in over your head. Never run drops when you cannot see a clear route to the bottom or, for advanced paddlers, a sure route to the next eddy. When in doubt, stop and scout.

   B. **Keep track** of all group members. Each boat keeps the one behind it in sight, stopping if necessary. Know how many people are in your group and take head counts regularly. No one should paddle ahead or walk out without first informing the group. Weak paddlers should stay at the center of a group, and not allow themselves to lag behind. If the group is large and contains a wide range of abilities, a designated "Sweep Boat" should bring up the rear.

   C. **Courtesy.** On heavily used rivers, do not cut in front of a boater running a drop. Always look upstream before leaving eddies to run or play. Never enter a crowded drop or eddy when no room for you exists. Passing other groups in a rapid may be hazardous: it's often safer to wait upstream until the group ahead has passed.

5. **Float plan.** If the trip is into a wilderness area or for an extended period, plans should be filed with a responsible person who will contact the authorities if you are overdue. It may be wise to establish checkpoints along the way where civilization could be contacted if necessary. Knowing the location of possible help and preplanning escape routes can speed rescue.

6. **Drugs.** The use of alcohol or mind altering drugs before or during river trips is not recommended. It dulls reflexes, reduces decision making ability, and may interfere with important survival reflexes.

7. **Instruction or guided trips.** In this format, a person assumes the responsibilities of a trip leader. He or she may pass judgment on a participant's qualifications, check equipment, and assume responsibilities for the conduct of the trip normally taken by the group as a whole.

   A. These trips must be clearly designated as such in advance, as they could expose the leader to legal liability. Trip or personal liability insurance should be considered.

   B. Even on trips with a designated leader, participants must recognize that whitewater rivers have inherent hazards, that each person is still responsible for their decision to participate and their safety on the water.

IV. GUIDELINES FOR RIVER RESCUE

1. **Recover from an upset with an Eskimo roll** whenever possible. Evacuate your boat immediately if there is imminent danger of being trapped against rocks, brush, or any other kind of strainer.

2. **If you swim, hold on to your boat.** It has much flotation and is easy for rescuers to spot. Get to the upstream end so that you cannot be crushed between a rock and your boat by the force of the current. Persons with good balance may be able to climb on top of a swamped kayak or flipped raft and paddle to shore.

3. **Release your craft if this will improve your chances,** especially if the water is cold or dangerous rapids lie ahead. Actively attempt self-rescue whenever possible by swimming

for safety. Be prepared to assist others who may come to your aid.

  A. **When swimming in shallow or obstructed rapids,** lie on your back **with feet held high** and pointed downstream. Do not attempt to stand in fast moving water; if your foot wedges on the bottom, fast water will push you under and keep you there. Get to slow or very shallow water before attempting to stand or walk. Look ahead! Avoid possible pinning situations including undercut rocks, strainers, downed trees, holes, and other dangers by swimming away from them.

  B. **If the rapids are deep and powerful,** roll over onto your stomach and swim aggressively for shore. Watch for eddies and slackwater and use them to get out of the current. Strong swimmers can effect a powerful upstream ferry and get to shore fast. If the shores are obstructed with strainers or undercut rocks, however, it is safer to "ride the rapid out" until a safer escape can be found.

4. **If others spill and swim,** go after the boaters first. Rescue boats and equipment only if this can be done safely. While participants usually assist one another to the best of their ability, they should do so only if they can, in their judgment, do so safely. The first duty of a rescuer is not to compound the problem by becoming another victim.

5. **The use of rescue lines requires training;** uninformed use may cause injury. Never tie yourself into either end of a line without a reliable quick-release system. Have a knife handy to deal with unexpected entanglement. Learn to place set lines effectively, to throw accurately, to belay effectively, and to properly handle a rope thrown to you.

6. **When reviving a drowning victim,** be aware that cold water may greatly extend survival time underwater. Victims of hypothermia may have depressed vital signs so they look and feel dead. Don't give up; continue CPR for as long as possible without compromising safety.

V. UNIVERSAL RIVER SIGNALS

STOP: Potential hazard ahead. Wait for "all clear" signal before proceeding, or scout ahead. Form a horizontal bar with your outstretched arms. Those seeing the signal should pass it back to others in the party.

HELP/EMERGENCY: Assist the signaler as quickly as possible. Give three long blasts on a police whistle while waving a paddle, helmet or life vest over your head. If a whistle is not available, use the visual signal alone. A whistle is best carried on a lanyard attached to your life vest.

ALL CLEAR: Come ahead (in the absence of other directions proceed down the center). Form a vertical bar with your paddle or one arm held high above your head. Paddle blade should be turned flat for maximum visibility. To signal direction or a preferred course through a rapid around obstruction, lower the previously vertical "all clear" by 45 degrees toward the side of the river with the preferred route. Never point toward the obstacle you wish to avoid.

VI. INTERNATIONAL SCALE OF RIVER DIFFICULTY

This is the American version of a rating system used to compare river difficulty throughout the world. This system is not exact; rivers do not always fit easily into one category, and regional or individual interpretations may cause misunderstandings. It is no substitute for a guidebook or accurate first-hand descriptions of a run.

Paddlers attempting difficult runs in an unfamiliar area should act cautiously until they get a feel for the way the scale is interpreted locally. River difficulty may change each year due to fluctuations in water level, downed trees, geological disturbances, or bad weather. Stay alert for unexpected problems!

As river difficulty increases, the danger to swimming paddlers becomes more severe. As rapids become longer and more continuous, the challenge increases. There is a difference between running an occasional Class IV rapid and dealing with an entire river of this category. Allow an extra margin of safety between skills and river ratings when the water is cold or if the river itself is remote and inaccessible.

The Six Difficulty Classes

Class I: Easy. Fast moving water with riffles and small waves. Few obstructions, all obvious and easily missed with little training. Risk to swimmers is slight; self-rescue is easy.

Class II: Novice. Straightforward rapids with wide, clear channels which are evident without scouting. Occasional maneuvering may be required, but rocks and medium sized waves are easily missed by trained paddlers. Swimmers are seldom injured and group assistance, while helpful, is seldom needed.

Class III: Intermediate. Rapids with moderate, irregular waves which may be difficult to avoid and which can swamp an open canoe. Complex maneuvers in fast current and good boat control in tight passages or around ledges are often required; large waves or strainers may be present but are easily avoided. Strong eddies and powerful current effects can be found, particularly on large-volume rivers. Scouting is advisable for inexperienced parties. Injuries while swimming are rare; self-rescue is usually easy but group assistance may be required to avoid long swims.

Class IV: Advanced. Intense, powerful but predictable rapids requiring precise boat handling in turbulent water. Depending on the character of the river, it may feature large, unavoidable waves and holes or constricted passages demanding fast maneuvers under pressure. A fast, reliable eddy turn may be needed to initiate maneuvers, scout rapids, or rest. Rapids may require "must" moves above dangerous hazards. Scouting is necessary the first time down. Risk of injury to swimmers is moderate to high, and water conditions may make self-rescue difficult. Group assistance for rescue is often essential but requires practiced skills. A strong Eskimo roll is highly recommended.

Class V: Expert. Extremely long, obstructed, or very violent rapids which expose a paddler to above average endangerment. Drops may contain large, unavoidable waves and holes or steep, congested chutes with complex, demanding routes. Rapids may continue for long distances between pools, demanding a high level of fitness. What eddies exist may be small, turbulent, or difficult to reach. At the high end of the scale, several of these factors may be combined. Scouting is mandatory but often difficult. Swims are dangerous, and rescue is difficult even for experts. A very reliable Eskimo roll, proper equipment, extensive experience, and practiced rescue skills are essential for survival.

Class VI: Extreme. One grade more difficult than Class V. These runs often exemplify the extremes of difficulty, unpredictability and danger. The consequences of errors are very severe and rescue may be impossible. For teams of experts only, at favorable water levels, after close personal inspection and taking all precautions. This class does **not** represent drops thought to be unrunnable, but may include rapids which are only occasionally run.

APPENDIX C

Resources

Most of the books and videos listed below can be purchased from Alpenbooks, 3616 South Road, #C-3, Mulkiteo, WA 98275. The American Canoe Association sells all its publications directly. Books, films, and videos marked with an asterisk (*) are available through the National Association for Search and Rescue. (For addresses and telephone numbers of these two organizations, see "National Organizations" at the end of this appendix.)

Books

Rescue and Safety

Best of the River Safety Task Force Newsletter by Charles Walbridge. American Canoe Association: 1983.

*CMC Rope Rescue Manual by Frank and Smith. CMC Rescue, Inc.: 1992.

*Critical Incident Stress Debriefing by Jeffrey Mitchell and George Everly. Chevron Publishing: 1990.

Emergency Care and Transportation of the Sick and Injured, 5th ed., James D. Heckman, MD, ed. American Academy of Orthopedic Surgeons: 1991.

*High Angle Rescue Techniques, 2d Ed., by the NASR Staff. Kendall-Hunt: 1992.

Hypothermia by William Forgey. ICS Books: 1985.

Hypothermia, Frostbite, and Other Cold Injuries. James A. Wilkerson, ed. The Mountaineers: 1986.

Knots for Paddlers by Charles Walbridge. Menasha Ridge Press: 1995.

Medicine for Mountaineering and Other Wilderness Activities, 4th Ed. James A. Wilkerson, ed. The Mountaineers: 1992.

*Medicine for the Outdoors: A Guide to Emergency Medical Procedures and First Aid, Rev. Ed., by Paul S. Auerbach. Little, Brown: 1991.

*On Rope by Allan Padgett and Bruce Smith. National Speleological Society: 1989.

Outdoor Emergency Care: Comprehensive First Aid for Nonurban Settings, 2d Ed., by Warren D. Bowman, MD. National Ski Patrol: 1993.

*Personnel Safety in Helicopter Operations: Helirescue Manual by Patrick LaValla and Robert Stoffel. Emergency Response Institute: 1988.

River Rescue by the Ohio Department of Natural Resources. Ohio State University: 1980.

*River Rescue, 2d Ed., by Les Bechdel and Slim Ray. AMC Books: 1989.

River Safety Report 1989–1991 by Charles Walbridge. American Canoe Association: 1992.

River Safety Report 1986–1988 by Charles Walbridge. American Canoe Association: 1989.

River Safety Report 1982–1985 by Charles Walbridge. American Canoe Association: 1986.

Standard First Aid and Emergency Care, by the American Red Cross Staff. Mosby Year Book: 1993.

Swiftwater Rescue by Slim Ray. (This book is targeted at rescue squads and other rescue professionals. Expected publication date: October 1995. Order from the author: 68 Finalee Street, Asheville, NC 28803.)

*Water Rescue: Basic Skills for Emergency Responders by David S. and Sarah J. Smith. Mosby Year Book: 1994.

Wilderness Medicine, 3rd Ed., by William Forgey. ICS Books: 1994.

*Wilderness Search and Rescue by Tim Setnika. AMC Books: 1980.

Paddling Techniques

Canoe Handbook by Slim Ray. Stackpole Books: 1992.

The Complete Inflatable Kayaker by Jeff Bennett. Ragged Mountain Press: 1995.

Kayak by William Neally. Menasha Ridge Press: 1993

The Complete Whitewater Rafter by Jeff Bennett. Ragged Mountain Press: 1996.

Whitewater Handbook for Canoe and Kayak by Bruce Lessels. AMC Books: 1993.

Films and Videos

The American Canoe Association (ACA) Film Library rents most of the films and videos listed below. Write the ACA for a full list of titles or call the film library at 800-826-0132. (For other pertinent addresses and telephone numbers, see "National Organizations," which follows.)

*"Cold, Wet, and Alive." An excellent video presentation of how hypothermia develops. From Nichols Productions, distributed by the ACA.

*"Critical Incident Stress." This video from Chevron Publishing investigates the symptoms of post-traumatic stress and ways to deal with it. Available through the National Association for Search and Rescue.

*"Drowning Machine." This film covers the dangers of low-head dams and some basic rescue techniques. From Film Space Productions, 615 Clay Street, State College, PA 16801.

*"Heads Up! River Rescue for River Runners." A video survey of recent trends in river rescue for whitewater paddlers. From Russ Nichols/Walkabout Productions, distributed by the ACA.

"River Rescue" by Anne Ford and Les Bechdel. Good coverage of many of the skills discussed in Bechdel and Ray's book. From Gravity Sports Films, 100 Broadway, Jersey City, NJ 07306; 800-346-4884.

*"Swept Away—A Guide to Water Rescue Operations." This expensive video from Alan Madison Productions covers rescue in flat and moving water. Available through the National Association for Search and Rescue.

The following three films by Russ Nichols are excellent. They were produced for the American Red Cross but are difficult to obtain since the Red Cross discontinued its small-craft training courses.

"Margin for Error." Discusses decision-making and rescue skills.
"Uncalculated Risk." Discusses the dangers of river paddling.
"Whitewater Primer." Presents the basics of water reading and boat handling.

Training Resources

Canyonlands Field Institute, Box 68, Moab, Utah 84532; 801-259-7750. Gives an excellent big-water rescue course for Western river outfitters.

Nantahala Outdoor Center, 13077 U.S. 19 W, Bryson City, NC 28713; 704-488-2175. Was the first to develop river rescue courses for paddlers, and now teaches the Rescue III and American Canoe Association programs. Call for a course listing.

Ohio Department of Natural Resources, Division of Watercraft, Building A, 4435 Fountain Square Drive, Columbus, OH 43224; 614-265-6504. Has developed an excellent river rescue course covering boat handling, dam rescue, and flood rescue for firefighters, rescue squads, police, and other professionals. Call for information.

PRI Rescue Training Specialists, 17 Terrill Avenue, Mercerville, NJ 08619; 609-586-8366. Teaches both the ACA and Rescue III courses. Owner Wayne Sundmacher is co-author of this book.

Rescue III, P.O. 519, Elk Grove, CA 95759; 800-457-3728. Has an excellent river rescue program with the aggressive, in-water approach needed by paddlers. The Swiftwater Rescue Technician (SRT 1) course is taught more than 300 times each year and is widely recognized by rescue professionals and river outfitters. Rescue III also runs the Swiftwater Rescue 2 program and flood rescue seminars. Call for a course listing.

Solo, Inc., RR 1, Box 163, Conway, NH 03818; 603-447-6711. Offers a variety of courses, including Wilderness First Responder, Wilderness EMT, Vertical Rope Rescue, Vehicle Extrication, Wilderness Trauma, and a number of other skills and leadership programs. Call for information.

Charlie Walbridge, 230 Penllyn Pike, Penllyn, PA 19422; 215-646-0157. Co-author of this book and teacher of the ACA River Rescue Program.

Wilderness Medical Associates, RFD 2, Box 890, Bryant Pond, ME 04219; 207-665-2707. Offers Wilderness First Responder and Wilderness EMT courses, which teach the skills needed to treat severe injuries when professional help may be hours or days away.

Wilderness Medical Society, P.O. Box 2463, Indianapolis, IN 46206; 317-631-1745. A national organization that studies the problems of backcountry medical care and develops course materials and standards.

National Organizations

American Canoe Association (ACA), 7432 Alban Station Blvd., Springfield, VA 22150; 703-451-0141. Sells and rents videos, produces safety-education materials for paddlers, teaches canoeing and kayaking of all kinds, certifies instructors in each discipline, and has developed an excellent two-day river rescue course for paddlers roughly equivalent to the SRT 1 program. Call for information.

American Red Cross, 17th and D Street, Washington, DC 20006; 202-728-6400. At one time a major source of small-craft safety instruction, it still controls many useful books and videos covering this subject. Its Basic First Aid and CPR programs present sound introductions to emergency care that every paddler should have. For course information, contact your local Red Cross chapter.

American Whitewater Affiliation (AWA), P.O. Box 85, Phonecia, NY 12646; 914-688-5569. Developed the AWA Safety Code, promotes river safety nationwide, and works on conservation and access issues.

Critical Incident Stress Foundation International, 5018 Dorsey Hall Drive, Ellicott City, MD 21042; 410-730-4311; 24-hour Hotline, 410-313-2473. Can direct you to a Critical Incident Stress Debriefing Team in your area; has developed a two- to three-hour, seven-step debriefing process that is almost completely successful in preventing post-traumatic stress disorder. It's staffed by volunteers, so there's no fee.

National Association for Search and Rescue (NASAR), P.O. Box 3709, Fairfax, VA 22038; 703-352-1349. Its Basic Water Rescue Preparedness curriculum introduces nonboater rescuers to water safety. There's a good introductory moving-water skills segment, quite similar to Day 1 of the ACA or SRT 1 program.

National Organization for River Sports, Box 6847, Colorado Springs, CO 80904; 719-579-8759. Represents private whitewater boaters on access and safety issues.

INDEX

See also river hazards; swimming self-rescue techniques

whitewater rescue. *See* rescue skills/training

Wilderness EMT/EMS certification, 117, 185
   responsibility, 121

wilderness first aid protocols, 117
   for CPR, 119, 120–21

for hypothermia, 130, 131

Wilderness Medical Associates: courses, 117, 185

Wilderness Medical Society, 185

wraps
   dulfer, 161–62
   inside (and outside) loop (anchor system), 73–74
   around rocks, 74, **76**

tensionless (no-knot), 71–72
wrapping (boat) for rotation, 69–70

zip lines, 59–60, 109
Z-rig (Z-drag), 80–83, 157, 162, 163–65